D0734788

The Last Nixon Watch

The Last Nixon Watch

BY

JOHN OSBORNE

Cartoons by PAUL SZEP

THE NEW REPUBLIC BOOK COMPANY, INC.
Washington, D.C.

Published in the United States of America in 1975
by The New Republic Book Company, Inc.
1826 Jefferson Place, N.W., Washington, D.C. 20036

This book consists in part of articles that appeared in *The
New Republic* between January 1974 and September
1974. The title is derived from "The Nixon Watch," the
standing head under which John Osborne reported the
Presidency for that magazine. Apart from some changes
of tense for present clarity, the correction of typographi-
cal and similar errors, and the addition of updating
addenda at the end of a few chapters, the originals have
not been altered for this publication. All articles are
reprinted by permission of the publisher.

Library of Congress Cataloging in Publication Data

Osborne, John, 1907-
    The last Nixon watch.

    "Consists in part of articles that appeared in the
New republic between January 1974 and September
1974."
    1. United States—Politics and government—1969-
1974—Addresses, essays, lectures. 2. Nixon,
Richard Milhous, 1913-   —Addresses, essays,
lectures. I. Title.
E855.086   973.924'092'4   74-34340
ISBN 0-915220-00-8

Printed in the United States of America

To Gilbert A. Harrison, who as editor-in-chief of The New Republic *gave me the opportunity and the freedom to write about Richard Nixon as I wanted to, this book is gratefully dedicated.*

CONTENTS

The Last Nixon Watch

The Nixon Time
An Overview

This addition to the last of my columns in *The New Republic* on the Nixon presidency is a modest undertaking. It is not intended to be a review of Mr. Nixon's presidency, nor of how the tragedy to which he brought himself and the country came about. It is intended only to be in part a recollection of how it was to be a reporter at the White House in the Nixon time; in part a dredging from memory and from old notes of some points about some of the people who served and misserved Mr. Nixon; and in part a set of impressions, mine and others', of this saddening and extraordinary man in the best and in the last, worst days of his presidency.

Richard Nixon and the Nixon presidency were wonderful subjects. The reporters who covered him and his presidency on a regular basis, at and from the White House, were lucky people. They were especially so if the assignment was, as it was for me, their first of the kind. I'd been in and out of the White House on intermittent newspaper and magazine assignments since the early years of President Franklin D. Roosevelt and on a very few occasions I'd even been in its office wings and in adjoining offices as a lowly employee of the Roosevelt administration. But Richard Nixon in 1968 and President Nixon in 1969 and afterward were the first candidate for the presidency and the first incumbent President to whom I had been regularly assigned. This happened late in a long, up-and-down-and-up career in journalism, mostly for magazines that shared my natural respect for The Establishment, and I was ripe and ready for the Nixon peak of what Arthur M. Schlesinger, Jr., correctly termed The Imperial Presidency. Perhaps the concept of my column and the title that I eventually put on it — "The Nixon Watch" — concentrating as it did upon the man in the presidency with a controlling respect for the presidency as an institution that generally exceeded respect for the man, contributed in a small way to the imperial notion. The concept and the title certainly reflected the notion.

Nixon was a wonderful subject partly and precisely because of characteristics that the members of the attending press corps endlessly discussed and reported. There was "the Private Nixon." What a boon he was! When he was invisible and inaudible to us, hidden behind the screen of assistants who either refused to talk about him at all or did it in such manifestly serving ways that they were imperfectly believed and sparsely quoted, the remoteness of this President and the care taken to shield him from public eye and understanding made innumerable stories. When he appeared, and he actually did so more often during the first couple of years than we who were employed to observe his every detectable move realized or admitted to ourselves and our audiences, the tiniest details of his manner, dress, expression, demeanor were grist for us. His restless hands, those usually unmanaged and seemingly unmanageable hands, and his mouth, that mean and twitching mouth and the frozen smile that could appear in an instant and vanish in the next instant, were of special interest and frequent note for me. Not that this sort of thing was all plus for the journalists and minus for him. One of the first kindly things that I wrote about after his inauguration, and one of the first of quite a few kindly remarks that enraged my *New Republic* constituency and inculcated an impression that I somehow was a Nixon spy implanted at that journal, was the effect of his smile.

It was seen to remain on the mouth for a discernible time, and remaining, to seem warm and genuine for the first time in my observation of it. The suggestion was that even Nixon might grow in the office.

There were the Nixon dogs, at the beginning two small dogs belonging to Mr. Nixon's daughters. On two occasions that I happened to observe and record, the dogs were hustled through the West Wing lobby (where journalists then hung out) by the White House electrician. The first time one of the ushers, a Mr. Hallman, ordered the electrician to get them out of there before they soiled the floor. The parading of the dogs was a ploy to catch the attention of lounging photographers; it eventually succeeded in producing some front-page pictures, and my printed notation of it as an indication that people who cherished little dogs couldn't be all bad indicated to some of the new President's assistants that maybe I wasn't, either.

And there was Mrs. Nixon. During the 1968 campaign and during the first months of the first term, she added to the interest in her husband in a way that I brought myself to mention only a couple of times. She was said to hate campaigning. She looked it, and Mr. Nixon publicly gave her reason to hate it on occasion in my view. On a platform near Los Angeles, in a fashion so crass that it could not be missed, he ignored her presence and with that horrible treacly grin of his beckoned her to join the line of guests after a local politician reminded him of her existence. At Saginaw, Mich., mingling with a troop of deaf-and-dumb children, she didn't hear him when he called her back to a makeshift platform and jumped as if she had been flicked with a whip when he roared, "*Pat!*" At Williamsburg, giving an outdoor interview to a television crew, she looked so ghastly that I, another reporter and a Nixon assistant who were passing by agreed that she must be ill. Mr. Nixon was standing nearby in the yard, laughing with some friends. In the East Room at the White House, on the first public occasion of the Nixon presidency, she visibly winced again, though not as shockingly as she had been seen to do at Saginaw, when the President broke in upon and corrected her greeting to Nixon campaign workers.

Gradually, after the first months at the White House, Mrs. Nixon was seen to bloom. Without checking back through all of the columns in the Nixon years, I have an uneasy feeling that I never reported the change in Patricia Nixon as clearly and emphatically as I should

have. It is also a fact, though not an excusing fact, that the change and
the bloom became most apparent when ruin was closing in upon
President Nixon and there was much else than his wife's appearance
to report. Still and all, let it be noted that I never traveled with her
press party on the trips that she took without her husband and that I
never invaded the press briefings that her press secretaries gave,
mostly to female reporters, in the East Wing at the White House. We
males and the females, when they were not occupied to the eastward,
frequented the West Wing. It was hinted to me, mostly by some of the
female reporters, that the occasional presence of a male reporter —
any male reporter — would have been welcomed at Mrs. Nixon's
briefings. Disgracefully, I chickened.

Mr. Nixon and his presidency were wonderful for another reason
that only a toughened old bird like me would freely confess to. The
man took his press company to marvelous places. There appear to be
some in the successor press party who welcome Gerald Ford's affinity
for Vail, Colo., and its wintry ski slopes. Not I. Mr. Nixon's
preference for warm places, notably Key Biscayne in Florida and San
Clemente in southern California, was mine, too, and I'll be forever
grateful to him for enabling me to charge to my employer the expense
of so many stays in or near those places. Mr. Ford appears at this
writing in December 1974 to be as bent as Mr. Nixon was upon
journeying about the world. But there's something about the early
Ford White House, or rather a combination of somethings ranging
from a marked decline in the professional level of the White House
press corps to a pervasive deadening note in the White House as such,
that arouses doubt that traveling with the Ford press party will be as
much fun and be as rewarding journalistically as traveling about the
globe with Richard Nixon's press party was. This is partly and could
be entirely because of a difference in the two men that time and
propinquity are not likely to erase. Mr. Nixon in person was an
interesting, puzzling, intriguing, baffling man for the reporter to
watch. Mr. Ford, and this is said with total respect, is not an
interesting man to watch. Watching him may be compared with
perpetual attendance at a Kiwanis luncheon. And that brings us to
the nub of the point, I think. The media keep a death watch on all
presidents, reporters who go wherever the President goes on the
chance that somebody will try to kill him. A related but somewhat
different watch was kept on Richard Nixon. Even in the first years of

The Nixon Time—An Overview

his presidency, before it gradually became clear in and after mid-1
that some definitely irrational things had been done for him if not \
him, reporters who followed and observed him as closely as I tried to
did so in part because, way down and in some instances not so far
down in their consciousnesses, there was a feeling that he might go
bats in front of them at any time. Nobody felt that about Gerald Ford
in December 1974. I'll never quite forgive myself for not being in
Denver, Colo., when President Nixon declared a murderer then on
trial in Los Angeles guilty as charged and at New Orleans in August
1973 when the President successively turned in a demonic fury upon
his press secretary, Ronald Ziegler, and behaved so oddly during an
address that followed that even a tape of the speech does not convey
adequate intimation of the worse that was to come. Mr. Nixon's
observed behavior, physical and mental, during his last presidential
trips abroad, to the Middle East in June and to Russia in July of 1974,
gave me stories that I'll never cease to be proud of. There were
touches on Gerald Ford's trip to the Far East and Vladivostok in
November 1974 that added to accounts of that journey, but they for
the most part had to do with what he said and permitted to be said,
not with how he looked and behaved. One of Mr. Ford's topmost
assistants assumed when he read my report that I'd learned of the
touches in question without being on the trip. No Nixon assistant
would have thought that possible.

The old notes that were mentioned at the start of this screed take us
back to 1968, in midcampaign, when Nixon's people confidently
expected the victory that he was about to win and spoke of their man
and of some of the people who went to the White House with him —
many of the latter, indeed, are sources of the notes — with a
perception, a prescience and a lack of prescience that are worth
evoking now.

Here is Tom Evans, a partner in the sometime Nixon-Mudge law
firm in New York, the firm where John Mitchell and Leonard
Garment met up with Nixon and joined fortunes with him, talking at
breakfast in the Somerset Hotel in Boston about many of the crowd
that soon would be running the White House and the country. I hear
that Garment, whom I have yet to meet, is "a liberal Jewish
Democrat" and "a bona fide, card-carrying genius." Tom's big point
about John Mitchell, a point that all of the Nixon men were making
about him and that Mitchell made for himself, was that to dismiss

him as "a municipal bond lawyer," as the media generally did, was to overlook the wide acquaintance with politicians and officials, state and local, that municipal bonding expertise provided. There's much about others — Bob Haldeman among them, sure to be Nixon's administrative chief at the White House and, along with Mitchell, in 1968 very much in charge of candidate Nixon's campaign timing. There is much favorable mention of the policy men who deal with the candidate's speech ideas and texts — Jim Keogh, Ray Price, Pat Buchanan, Martin Anderson — all men who figured at the Nixon White House, some of them to and beyond the very end, and, to hear Evans tell it, good men all. They were indeed "good" men. Richard Nixon, it was assumed, would have no others about him. One is reminded in these notes and from memory of the years to come that in general, in a sense and not always a limited sense, that was very true. Mr. Nixon's men were competent, at evil when that was what they were called upon to be competent at. The outstanding memory of Tom Evans is not in these Boston notes and it has to do with someone whom he didn't mention in Boston. Evans for a time was national director of the 1968 Citizens for Nixon, a relatively innocent precursor of the 1972 Committee for the Reelection of the President, and it was in that capacity in Washington that he first told me about Richard Nixon's developing affection for Gov. Spiro T. Agnew of Maryland. Nixon cultivated Agnew before the latter broke with Nelson Rockefeller and Evans often dropped little references to what was to him, Evans, a rather puzzling friendship. In the lobby of the Miami Beach hotel where Nixon was staying, hours before his nomination and before he was to choose his candidate for the vice presidency, I happened to meet Evans at the door and naturally asked, who was it going to be? He grinned at me and said as he whirled through the swinging door, "Remember that Maryland fellow I kept telling you about?" I remembered, right enough. I didn't believe it, I couldn't, and I was caught flat-assed the next morning when candidate Nixon introduced candidate Agnew.

Here is Bryce Harlow, also in Boston in 1968 at the Somerset, lunching and talking. Harlow was from Oklahoma; he'd worked for an Oklahoma congressman and for Dwight Eisenhower at the White House and in 1968 he was on leave from Procter and Gamble to work for Nixon. Harlow is respected to the point of reverence in political Washington. Without quoting him precisely or directly, here is

Harlow on Richard Nixon in 1968: He is a *professional.* His professionalism as a politician, a candidate, an officeholder accounts for the quality in him that seems artificial, false, contrived to so many people and especially to journalists. After 20 years of walking through the minefields, he knows where the mines are and where he'll get a leg blown off if he missteps. So he's careful, defensive. But it's not the evasion, duplicity, superficiality that are so commonly charged to him. It's professionalism. The subject of the foregoing remarks is the Nixon who put in those tapes and kept them in. He is the Nixon who promoted Harlow at the White House, brought him back for a second stint when the trouble began to rain in, and through much of that time lied to Harlow and persuaded Harlow to tell in President Nixon's behalf lies that Harlow believed to be truths. With all of this recalled in December 1974, the following words of Harlow on Nixon in direct quotation marks leap at me from the fading page of typed notes: "I think he is going to make an extremely able and effective President of the United States. If he makes any mistakes as President, they will be made on purpose."

Two fragments from two other notes of that early time, in 1968 and 1969, must suffice to call back something of the confidence, the belief, the hope, the ambition and the calculation that conditioned the beginnings of the Nixon presidency and have gone down with Richard Nixon.

At an interview with John Mitchell at his campaign office in New York on October 27, 1968, I told him that by grace of a South Carolina friend I was illegally present at a caucus of the South Carolina Republican delegation in Miami Beach when Mitchell promised that Mr. Nixon would consult Senator Strom Thurmond about the choice of a candidate for Vice President. This was meant to mean, was understood to mean and was applauded for meaning that no candidate who was unacceptable to Thurmond and in favor of aggressive desegregation of Southern schools would be selected by Mr. Nixon and submitted to the convention. Mitchell looked at me with unforgettable calm and said that he had said and meant no such thing. He also said to me, as he was saying to all reporters who asked him about it, that he had no intention and no prospect of joining the Nixon administration. My notes conclude: "He implied — I don't recall the exact words, it was partly manner — that nothing less than a cabinet or major agency directorship would suit him anyhow. I had a feeling that he could imagine himself Nixon's Attorney General, nothing less, but it was all impression. His major thrust was, he expected to return to the law firm." I think he did, poor fellow. At his trial in the court of federal Judge John Sirica, on the afternoon of December 11, 1974, he seemed to me still to have the look of impenetrable certainty that he had when he lied to me, knowing that I knew he was lying, about the South Carolina delegation and his promise to it. Perhaps one of the troubles of our time was and is that I didn't particularly object to his lying on that occasion and still consider that in some respects he was a better-than-average Attorney General.

The last of my early notes jumps us to December 16, 1969, in the so-called White House "theater" that had been built for Lyndon Johnson's television appearances, a form of self-satisfaction that he considered it his right to demand at any hour of day or night. Nixon never suffered from *that* malaise to that extent. Anyhow, here at the podium and in some fragmentary notes of mine are Bryce Harlow (already sufficiently quoted), John D. Ehrlichman and Daniel Patrick Moynihan. The purpose of their staged appearance and remarks, attributable by fiat of Press Secretary Ronald Ziegler only to "White House sources" and to hell with that now, is to convince the doubting press corps that the shortage of legislative proposal and accomplishment since Mr. Nixon's inauguration is a consequence of careful, systematic, ultra-intelligent planning and not of any lack of social and other concern. From my notes on Ehrlichman's remarks: "The mood of the country has changed a good deal . . . less stridency . . . a lowering of the voices . . . considerable success in the administration's effort to restore the credibility of the Establishment." Counsellor Moynihan's big pitch is that "the President has repeatedly said to us, this is a reform administration" and it should be judged as such. The aim has been to educate the principal officers of government — former professor Moynihan was then a regular instructor of the assembled cabinet — in the mechanics and verities of "a systematic relationship in which everything you do relates to everything else." There had in fact been a beginning — a reduction of low-bracket income taxes, a start at mass transportation subsidies, the outlines of a family assistance plan that Mr. Nixon and a weird collection of congressional liberals were going to sabotage but hadn't then. The point of the foregoing quotations is mainly that this was

how the best minds in a brainy White House were being used and how
their possessors were talking. (I have Moynihan more than
Ehrlichman in mind but I don't exclude him, either — John
Ehrlichman was by no means a total stupe at that time.) Arthur Burns
was also on stage, though not at the 1969 briefing. It wouldn't have
done to have him and Moynihan publicly assailing each other. They
did that in private, though not so privately that their differences were
concealed and unreported.

As a matter of rank, one's recollections of some of the people
around the President should begin with Haldeman. As a matter of
interest and fondness, mine begin with — of all people — the late
Murray Chotiner. He was, in his brief White House period, a squat
and pallid figure in immaculate white shirts, composed, full of talk
about the early years in California, when he helped Nixon with his
races for Congress and the Senate and saw him through the agony of
his near-parting with Dwight Eisenhower in 1952. Chotiner was
relegated to a small office in the East Wing, which in symbolic
eminence rated far below the limited office space in the West Wing
and below the corner offices in the Old Executive Office Building
across West Executive Avenue. A comfort to him was that a
competing professional pol on the Nixon staff, Harry Dent, was also
housed in the East Wing. Chotiner never discussed his dislike of Dent
but it was known. His contempt for the way in which Harry, in
Murray's opinion, botched the Florida arrangements that led in 1970
to the defeat of Congressman William Cramer, then and in 1974 a
close friend and associate of Gerald Ford, for nomination to the
Senate and put President Nixon in the absurd position of seeming to
prefer none other than G. Harrold Carswell, his discredited and
rejected Supreme Court nominee, for the same seat, was expressed in
scowls and sniffs that defied reporting. Looking back on it, I don't
know why I valued access to Chotiner as much as I did and why I took
advantage of it as frequently as I did. Perhaps it was because I, as a
White House man for *The New Republic,* was assumed by many of
my press colleagues to have no access to such as Chotiner and to rely
upon such in-house liberals as Pat Moynihan. As sources, I always
preferred tough reactionaries to talky liberals. Chotiner seldom told
me anything really useful in the way of news. He did indicate to me, in
remarks that had very little meaning at the time but came to have a lot
of meaning, that he couldn't understand why his friend and sometime

pupil in politics, Mr. Nixon, relied to the extent he did upon the political judgments of three men whom Chotiner regarded as abysmal amateurs: Attorney General John Mitchell, H.R. Haldeman and John Ehrlichman. When Chotiner was ejected from his White House niche in 1971, and I reported that his reputation for the practice of dirty politics in earlier times made him unsuitable for the approaching 1972 reelection campaign, he complained that I'd hurt his feelings and injured him in a way that he didn't seem to think I had when I'd previously written that he was capable of lying. He joined an intensely political Washington law firm and was deeply involved in the Nixon crowd's shabby and secret preelection dealings with the milk industry. In early 1974, when he was fatally hurt in an automobile collision, he was telling me at intervals of his difficulty in believing that Richard Nixon could have entrusted his 1972 campaign to the amateurs and scoundrels who, in Chotiner's view, got him into the Watergate horror. Chotiner being Chotiner, one had to suspect that he knew more about that many-faceted affair than he ever let on. But there was no doubting that President Nixon excluded him from the inner circle in 1971-72 and that the President would have been wiser and better off if he hadn't.

Another of the professionals whom I liked and saw a good deal of was Chotiner's nonfriend, Harry Dent. Murray's decline and Harry's rise in presidential esteem were signaled by Dent's removal from the East Wing to a munificent corner suite in the Old Executive Office Building. It was there, it turned out later, that he and an assistant named Jack Gleason collected and disbursed several million dollars in funds for the midterm 1970 campaign and in doing so neglected to comply with certain technicalities of the ambiguous federal law that then governed such activities. The last time I saw Dent, in December 1974, he had just pleaded guilty to a misdemeanor and got off with a month's unsupervised probation. He appeared to reporters in the federal courtroom where this occurred to be downright jubilant. When I met him a few moments afterward in a corridor, on my way to Judge Sirica's courtroom for an afternoon at the big Watergate trial, Harry wasn't jubilant. He was trembling. His right hand shook when he held it out to me and I grasped it. There was no time to thank him then, though maybe I will if and when I get down to Columbia, S.C., where he practices law, for the hints he kept throwing at me in 1972, before and after the election, that there was and had been something dreadfully wrong in the way that campaign was conducted. The hints, never specific but strong enough to have been picked up and followed up if I had been as bright and alert as I thought I was, took the form of such remarks as that his lifelong rule in politics had been "*Never get cute.*" The implication was that unnamed White House colleagues had gotten cute and that they and their master, the President, were going to pay for it. Dent made it clear in December 1972 that he wanted out and was determined to get away from the Nixon White House. Mr. Nixon wanted to install him full-time at the Republican National Committee's headquarters in Washington. Dent, obviously unhappy and uncertain, warned in advance that he'd probably give in, as he did, to the President's persuasion to the extent of becoming general counsel to the committee and dividing his time between Washington and Columbia. It was evident that he didn't want to do even that much for the President. Harry Dent was one of several lawyers at the White House who were beginning at the turn of 1972-73 to realize that they risked disbarment or worse (if there be anything worse than disbarment for a lawyer) if they stayed in the vicinity, in capacities that made it impossible to escape some knowledge of what was going on and had gone on. Harry was among those, I perceived later than I should have, who were beginning to realize that a time was near when knowledge would be equated with responsibility, as it came to be when the Watergate disclosures led to the establishment of the Special Prosecution Force.

One who may not have recognized the peril later than Dent did, but acted on it later, was Leonard Garment. One of Garment's minor handicaps at the White House was that he was assumed to be my friend and a prime source. He was my friend. He never was a very productive source. He knew better than to be. Over the Nixon span he was much less useful to me than were two of his conservative colleagues, Patrick Buchanan and James Keogh, who will shortly be discussed in a bit more detail. Leonard Garment had been a partner in the New York law firm that Nixon joined before Nixon joined it and he retained a basic loyalty to Nixon after that became a difficult thing to do. Mr. Nixon appointed Garment acting White House counsel, or chief staff lawyer (as distinct from the Attorney General) to the President, on April 30, 1973, the day that counsel John Wesley Dean, staff chief H. R. Haldeman and domestic affairs adviser John D. Ehrlichman were fired. Ehrlichman and Haldeman pretended until they went on trial before Judge Sirica in 1974 for obstruction of justice and related offenses that they more or less forced their resignations upon the President for his and the country's good. Ehrlichman in effect abandoned the pretense at his trial. He said, as I had reported in May of 1973, that Nixon demanded his resignation. He didn't say, as I had also reported, that he and Haldeman begged the President to keep them or at least let them take leave without the onus of obviously required resignation. But that is an aside. Returning to Garment: he perceived in late 1973 that he simply had to get away from involvement in the Watergate aftermath, especially in the handling of the catastrophic Nixon tape recordings, if he was to escape disbarment at best and criminal involvement at worst. Gen. Alexander M. Haig, Jr., who on May 4, 1973, had succeeded Haldeman as the President's staff chief, understood Garment's plea and problem and enabled him to get as far away from the mess as any lawyer in Nixon's service could. Garment's services to the President before and during the concluding tragedy in 1974 are but dimly understood and probably never will be fully reported. Suffice it to say here that Leonard Garment, liberal and Democrat and thoroughly decent man that he was, never betrayed his President's confidences to me or, so far as I know, to any other reporter, and did his President the final service of helping Haig and a few others convince Richard Nixon that he had to go. His last service of substance to Mr. Nixon, one that to my knowledge has not been previously reported, was to assist in persuading President Ford that he should grant to Richard Nixon a full and absolute pardon for any offenses that he had committed or may have committed while he was President. It was a wise and right thing to do. Mr. Ford suffered grievously for doing it, and Leonard Garment deserves more credit than he is likely to receive for it's being done.

It may appear to the reader that I keep shying away from my acquaintance with Bob Haldeman and John Ehrlichman. Not really. I liked Haldeman and saw a fair amount of him from around May of 1969 into the summer of 1970. I did him what he acknowledged to be the favor of underrating him in print at first, judging him to be a factotum without the authority of Pat Moynihan, Arthur Burns and Henry Kissinger. How silly that was! After I had begun to appreciate his authority and importance in the Nixon establishment, he talked to me a few times about his role and about his sensitivities. I was the first journalist, I believe, to report on my authority (not Haldeman's — I seldom quoted sources) that he had and occasionally exercised the power to return Kissinger papers to Kissinger for what Haldeman thought to be necessary revision. He was stern in manner and appearance, his hair was crew cut, but he resented the building image of him as a German Mafia type. The essence of his story, now dimly recalled and not put into written notes at the time, was that he was more Swiss than German. In June of 1970, when the President took the necessary step of replacing Robert Finch at the Department of Health, Education, and Welfare, and Finch appeared in tears in the White House press room, Haldeman told me in private a story that I wrote in essence and still believe to be true. Haldeman didn't deny that Finch was crying; he couldn't. He did say that Finch recognized the troubles and deficiencies that had marred his performance as department Secretary at HEW and was grateful for transfer to the White House staff in lieu of outright dismissal. This was my last conversation with Bob Haldeman, excepting occasional hellos when we passed on the White House grounds. In the fall of 1970, after the President's trip to the Mediterranean, Britain and Ireland, I wrote an account of a press session that Mr. Nixon had in Ireland when I was abed with a cold in Limerick. Mr. Nixon was at his queasy worst and I said so. I wrote that I wasn't there, that I had to rely upon the accounts of other reporters. The point worth noting here is that Haldeman, the sometime advertising and public relations expert and vice president of the J. Walter Thompson agency, damned rather than credited me for acknowledging that it wasn't a firsthand report. He said it was "the shittiest piece of journalism I ever saw" and never forgave me for reporting that he'd said it. His remarks to Press Secretary Ronald Ziegler and to other reporters indicated, when they were relayed to me, that what he couldn't understand was that I'd admit not being at the Nixon session and would write about it as I did. Only a shit, he said, would do that. I could never make out whether it was the admission or the writing that offended him most. I'll say this for Haldeman: he generally had Lawrence Higby, his man Friday, return my telephone calls and say Mr. Haldeman was sorry he couldn't find time to see me. There came a time, in and after the summer of 1972, when John Ehrlichman didn't do that much.

Ehrlichman! I find it difficult to be fair about and to John Ehrlichman. Here I should note that in 47 years of reporting I have never thought that public officials were obligated to give me their time and confidence. I have considered that it's been my job to persuade them to do that. Ehrlichman was the first among the chief assistants in the early Nixon White House to give me some of his time and confidence and I appreciated it. There was a quality in him, a pomposity, that I never liked. But it didn't deter me from seeking and welcoming time and talk with him. He was immensely helpful to me in Mr. Nixon's nominations of Clement Haynsworth and Harrold Carswell to the Supreme Court. He did not conceal from me the fact, and it was a fact, that John Mitchell's poor advice and performance in those two miserable episodes first caused the President to doubt Mitchell's capacities and to give Ehrlichman a certain oversight responsibility in Department of Justice matters. This was the origin of Ehrlichman's and Mitchell's detestation of each other and of Ehrlichman's inclination, in the secret 1973 stages of the Watergate unfolding and later in public at his trials, to blame Mitchell and encourage Mr. Nixon to blame Mitchell. A few episodes in my acquaintance with Ehrlichman — it of course was never more, and it was a reporter's flimsy acquaintance at that — seem worth recalling here. I was waiting for him in 1970 in his West Wing office just over the President's Oval Office, when Ehrlichman, his wife and a friend from his home city of Seattle entered. They were convulsed in laughter. Trudie Osborne, my wife and a first-rate writer, had given me a book entitled *All I Know About Nixon.* Its pages were blank. The Ehrlichmans and their friend had seen it on my desk in the White House press room, had opened it, and were laughing about it. In the summer of 1972 at San Clemente, during one of the President's visits, Ehrlichman spent the best part of an hour on the sunny patio outside his office telling me that he had practically nothing to do with planning for the reelection campaign and barely knew Howard Hunt, one of the recently arrested Watergate conspirators. He had a great deal to do with the reelection campaign, as I observed and reported at the Miami Beach convention that August. During the campaign, I came upon Ehrlichman and Donald Bacon of the Newhouse Newspapers at the rear of the Regency Hyatt Hotel in Atlanta. I had a small Sony recorder in my hand and a Sony microphone in my jacket lapel. Bacon said, "You're really wired for sound, Osborne." I glanced at Ehrlichman. He was transfixed, staring at the microphone and the wire trailing from it with an unmistakable look of horror.

Recorders were customary equipment of reporters. It occurred to me then that there was something extreme and abnormal in Ehrlichman's expression. I suspect now that he was already using recorders in his own office, though he's said since that he started doing it much later and didn't know about Mr. Nixon's recording system for months after that encounter in Atlanta. After the 1972 election Press Secretary Ziegler started producing Ehrlichman in the White House press room for occasional question-answer sessions. He had a habit then that he displayed in 1974 when he testified as a defendant under cross-examination. He corrected his questioner's questions and insisted on answering his own questions. I told him once at the White House that I had a right to an answer to my question and was not interested in his answer to his questions. It was the beginning of a dislike of John Ehrlichman that hardened before Mr. Nixon fired him. At his trial in Washington I found that the pity I'd once felt for him and others in his indicted company didn't come to me as readily as it once had.

Two others of my White House acquaintances and contacts, James Keogh and Patrick Buchanan, were mentioned earlier in this account. Although Keogh and I had worked for Time, Inc., I first met him when he took leave and served Mr. Nixon as his chief speech writer in the 1968 campaign. Afterward, when Keogh was chief of the White House writing staff in 1969 and 1970, I saw a good deal of him and greatly valued his conveyed feel for the atmosphere around Mr. Nixon. In October of 1970, a few months before he quit the White House staff to write a book, *President Nixon and the Press*, in which the media as a whole were thoroughly damned for their mistreatment of Mr. Nixon, the curtain dropped. Keogh stopped returning my telephone calls and receiving me in his office. I was puzzled, a bit hurt, since I didn't recall violating his confidence or using anything he told me against his boss. I couldn't have done the latter, since he never said anything against his boss. Anyhow, at the end of a telephone call I made to him in connection with a review of his book, I asked him why he had stopped seeing me or doing me the bare courtesy of returning my calls. He answered: "It wasn't just you, John. I stopped seeing you and other reporters because nothing I told you came out the way I wanted it to." Keogh returned to federal service as director of the U.S. Information Agency in 1973. I didn't try to call him or see him.

Pat Buchanan is the last of the early White House contacts and sources whom I shall discuss as such. I've already said that I generally preferred as sources the conservatives and reactionaries to the people who passed for liberals on the Nixon staff. When I review the appendix to Volume 10 of the printed Ervin Watergate committee hearings, as I occasionally do, I ask myself how I could possibly consider that bastard Buchanan a friend of mine. In this appendix are laid forth the documents that tell of the formation of the Nixon "enemies list" and of Buchanan's frequent and loving contributions to the same. I was on what I call the "B" list, with 56 names, as compared with an "A" list of 20 names (Mary McGrory of the Washington *Star-News,* Dan Schorr of CBS among them) and a "C" list of several thousand names. I thought the whole thing a rather bad joke, never mentioned the honor in *The New Republic,* and never went beyond asking Buchanan to spare me his protestations that it wasn't really an enemies list. It was. It was a goddamned disgrace and it reflected the worst qualities of the Nixon administration. But my presence on it, albeit only the "B" list, made it impossible for me to take the whole thing as seriously as I should have. It was utterly impossible to dump Buchanan from my list of speaking acquaintances. Intelligence is to be valued, wherever found, and Pat Buchanan is a very intelligent man. He was also a useful contact, a factor that any reporter worth his pay is bound to take into account. He, though not he alone, enabled me to write the first published account of the "attack group" that claimed more credit than it probably deserved for doing in George McGovern in 1972. My view remains that McGovern did himself in and needed no help in that endeavor. I differed with practically all of Buchanan's strictures upon the liberals in the Nixon White House and in the Democratic opposition and I felt that his substantial contributions to Vice President Agnew's spewings in 1969 and 1970 were disservices to the nation. But I had to recognize as a technician that Buchanan as a technician did his job extremely well and to respect the skill with which he presented his views to me and (I was told) to Mr. Nixon. I argued to Buchanan and in print that he overdid his indictments of liberal bias in the national media. But who could deny that the bias was there and that it affected the coverage of Mr. Nixon and the administration? It didn't bring Richard Nixon and his people down — their sins did that — but it did becloud the reporting of what was good or at least defensible in the Nixon performance. All this aside, though, a tiny incident at the very start of the Nixon administration obtrudes upon my memory and impression of Pat Buchanan. Shortly after noon of January 20, 1969, I saw him and Shelley Scarney, a lovely blonde girl whom he later married, walk up the White House driveway to the West Wing of the White House and pause outside the portico, staring upward. The pride, the hope, the anticipation in their faces were and remain unforgettable. It's the sort of memory, atop all that's happened, that even in December of 1974 brings me close to tears at times.

Alex Butterfield — Colonel Alexander Porter Butterfield of the U.S. Air Force — spent a small and surely the least important part of his time in early 1969 keeping me away from Haldeman. Butterfield said Haldeman wanted time to "get his ducks in a row." After that, Butterfield arranged initial access to Haldeman. Butterfield was nominally a deputy assistant to the President and actually a principal assistant to Haldeman in Haldeman's capacity as the closest of all assistants to the President. In November 1969, when Vice President Agnew vacated the corner office in the West Wing that had been assigned to him, in the course of the usual and invariably futile pretense at the start of administrations that Presidents expect their Vice Presidents to do serious substantive work, Haldeman moved to Agnew's corner from a smaller office adjoining the President's Oval Office and Butterfield moved into the smaller office. There, in roles as cabinet secretary and general factotum to both Haldeman and the President, Butterfield observed and otherwise learned more than anyone else on the White House staff, possibly excepting Haldeman, about how Mr. Nixon did his job. On July 16, 1973, four months after he had left the White House to head the Federal Aviation Administration, Butterfield disclosed to Senator Ervin's Watergate committee the existence of the Nixon taping system — a subject that we return to later. On July 2, 1974, in testimony before the House Judiciary Committee during its impeachment hearings, Butterfield gave a unique account of Mr. Nixon's working habits. Amid the welter of Watergate evil, that part of Butterfield's testimony was largely ignored and I learned of it only when I read the printed record of the committee proceedings.

The Butterfield account interests me for two reasons. It is among the several factors, some of them known to me and noted by me at the time and others, like the Butterfield account known afterward, that

caused me to write in *The New Republic* of May 12, 1973, that the
President "evaded . . . elided . . . lied" when he said in his first major
Watergate speech on April 30: ". . . I decided as the 1972 campaign
approached that the presidency should come first and politics second.
To the maximum extent possible, therefore, I sought to delegate
campaign operations, to remove the day-to-day campaign decisions
from the President's office and from the White House." More
effectively than his direct testimony that Mr. Nixon "absolutely" ran
the 1972 campaign and "made the big decisions" affecting that
campaign, Butterfield's account of the President's minute preoccupation with detail confirms other evidence and impressions that he
could not have left and did not leave the direction of the campaign to
others as he said he did. The failure of the Ervin committee and of its
chief counsel, Samuel Dash, to explore and expose this patent flaw in
Mr. Nixon's Watergate defense — the very basis of his defense,
indeed — seemed to me in 1973 and still seems to diminish the value
of much of the committee's work. My second reason for interest in the
Butterfield testimony about to be quoted is that it includes some of
the first support for and intimations of concern that Richard Nixon
was of less than sound mind during and before the Watergate period.

Now to the testimony. John Doar, the Judiciary Committee's chief
counsel, had perceived — as Sam Dash seemingly never did — during
preliminary conversations with Butterfield that here was an
important and relevant piece of the Watergate-Nixon story. Doar
asked Butterfield for "an indication of the President's work habits
with respect to attention to detail." Butterfield's long answer was
introduced with the explanation that in anticipation of the question
he had drawn upon his memory of "hundreds and hundreds of
memoranda" and of his years of work "directly with the President
and Haldeman" and had "written it out." Obviously aware before he
began his recitation of the details that it was going to sound at least
mildly odd, Butterfield said: "These are typical items which are of
considerable concern to the President. I hope you understand I don't
say [*sic*] them at all in a derogatory manner, in fact, quite the
contrary. I say them in a complimentary manner because thanks to
his close attention to these kinds of details, the White House staff
functioned better." Somewhat condensed, with ellipses omitted for
the reader's ease, the body of the relevant testimony follows:

"The President was concerned whether or not the curtains were closed or open, the arrangement of state gifts, whether they should be on that side of the room or this side of the room, displayed on a weekly basis or on a monthly or daily basis. He was deeply involved in the entertainment business, whom we should get, for what kind of group, small band, big band, black band, white band, jazz band — whatever. He was very interested in meals and how they were served and the time of the waiters and was usually put out if a state dinner was not taken care of in an hour's time. He wanted to see the plan, see the scenarios, he wanted to view the musical selections himself. He was very interested in whether or not salad should be served and decided that at small dinners of eight or less, the salad course should not be served.

"Guests were of great interest to him. He did review all the guest lists very carefully. Who are the reporters, the press people invited to this? He would review all of these lists personally and approve them personally. [Very few journalists were invited.] He was very conscious of the criticism of the worship services, yet he wanted to continue having the worship services. There was criticism that he was using them for political purposes, so he purposely invited a number of Democrats, people who might be considered enemies. He debated having worship services on a monthly basis or bimonthly or whatever or not at all. [They were discontinued in 1972.]

"Ceremonies — he was interested in whether or not they should be public on the south grounds or whether we should have only administrative personnel; the details of the drive up the walkway [to the south portico of the White House]; whether the military would be to the right or left, which uniforms would be worn by the White House police, whether or not the Secret Service would salute during the "Star Spangled Banner" and sing, where the photographer would be, and such things as that.

"He wanted to note who was going to be on hand [from the White House staff] to record [meetings]. He suggested after awhile that we nominate a number of anecdotists to go to these events at which some human interest item might occur, little vignettes of human interest. He wanted those recorded for the President's file, for history. [John Andrews, a White House staff writer who resigned with several blasts at the Watergate evil that he belatedly noticed around him, was one of these anecdotists.]

"Cabinet meetings — he debated always about the frequency of cabinet meetings, the agenda. He wanted the members to talk up more and not sit there silently as many of them so often did. He was interested in where the cabinet members were and eventually required cabinet and subcabinet members to get approval for foreign travel from me, speaking for him, and Henry Kissinger speaking for the Department of State.

"White House furniture, the appearance of the White House, his desk and the history of his desk, photographs of former Presidents in the Executive Office Building — he wanted to make sure he knew whose office had photographs — all of this, I think, understandable. He wanted to convert some offices to other offices and he would actually sort of outline the plans for those conversions. We had some paintings put up in the west lobby [of the main White House office wing] and he wanted us to log the comments made about each painting to see how popular it might be to guests who were awaiting appointments. He wanted to know who was going to sit where in the cabinet room, not meetings of the cabinet but meetings of others in the cabinet room.

"He worried a good deal about Secretary Connally. He liked Secretary Connally immensely and wanted to make sure that he got enough time off — that Camp David was made available to Secretary Connally and Secretary Connally and his wife were invited hither and yon.

"He spent a lot of time on gifts — gifts for congressional leaders, gifts for people who came into the Oval Office. He actually looked at the inventories of cuff links and ash trays and copies of Six Crises. He worried about gifts being appropriate for people. All of this I charged up to his being especially thoughtful in that way.

"He was interested in wines. He wanted me to find out the best Bordeaux-type California wines, the best German wines, the best vintages, to talk to the connoisseurs. He followed this and did buy some excellent wines from his own personal funds.

"He was very interested in the grounds at Key Biscayne, Camp David, San Clemente, the cottage, the house, the grounds, where the Secret Service were, how many Secret Service were on duty at a time, how sinister or casual Secret Service agents were acting around him, all for the sake of appearance.

"He was interested in whether we should have a POW wife or another girl be the receptionist in the West Lobby. He debated this

Devalued currency

point a number of times and issued instructions with regard to who
the receptionist would be and how she would operate." [The
previously mentioned Shelley Scarney, eventually Mrs. Patrick
Buchanan, was the principal receptionist when Mr. Nixon resigned
and for some months afterward.]

"He was interested in the plants in the south grounds and whether
or not we should retain the tennis court or move it. Memorandums
went on about the tennis court for over a year's time.

"And Washington, D.C. — He even did a memorandum in
Belgrade, Yugoslavia, having been impressed by the fine restrooms
along the way there, or at least the structures along the way, and
having the feeling that back here on the Mall we had some rather
shabby wooden restrooms which he had seen during the time of those
[antiwar] demonstrations. He had me look into this project when he
returned from Yugoslavia, having dictated the memorandum in
Belgrade. Thinking always about detail.

"In my mind, all of these things are understandable. I think they are
all typical of a thoughtful and careful and well-disciplined man, but
they certainly do bring out the fact that he was highly interested in
detail."

Perhaps "all of these things" were indeed "understandable."
Certainly many of them were and many could be matched with other
Presidents' minor preoccupations. Democratic majority counsel
John Doar let the Butterfield testimony stand without comment or
examination. Albert E. Jenner, Jr., the chief Republican minority
counsel, showed more concern about its possible implications than,
in the opinion of Nixon assistants who considered him a traitor, he
showed about other testimony that was much more directly
damaging. Jenner pressed Butterfield to reiterate his already
volunteered statements that he intended his testimony about the
Nixon obsession with detail to be complimentary. Butterfield
responded "not necessarily" to one of these demands. Under
questioning by Jenner, Butterfield remarked that President Nixon
had far more leisure time than any President is popularly supposed to
have and continued: "He had no hobbies. The presidency was his
hobby . . . . He seemed to me to be preoccupied with his place in
history, with his presidency as history would see it . . . . I would guess
that the concept is normal, but the preoccupation probably is not."
Jenner leaped at the reference to "preoccupation" — did Butterfield

think the preoccupation was "insidious?" Butterfield answered: "No, I just say that my honest opinion is that it was a bit abnormal."

In a conversation with Butterfield on November 13, 1974, I recalled his saying that he thought Mr. Nixon's preoccupation with detail was "a bit abnormal" and asked:

"Did you think he was a little crackers?"

Butterfield: "Ah, no."

Osborne: "You wouldn't be the only one around there who had come to think so."

Butterfield: "Oh, no. Yes, I know that. No, I didn't think that, necessarily. It was just that a tremendous amount of time was taken up with all of these little things — so much time that I knew if it were ever, if the whole world could know what's going on in there, because you assume that when the President is busy behind the closed door great affairs of state are being discussed, big decisions made, policy outlined and that sort of thing. And almost always what was really going on were these kinds of things. Oh, they might be kicking around a trip he was going to take, but they'd get right into the nuts and bolts, the details, the lobby of the hotel, what it looked like; the President liked to talk about when he was there before. You know, just sitting around chewing the fact, that's what he liked to do. But I didn't — *abnormal?*"

Osborne: "You did use that word."

Butterfield: "Well, I thought it was strange that he would dictate a letter from Belgrade about the lousy restroom facilities we had around the Mall. And the dog [presumably King Timahoe, a handsome red setter] — a lot of time with the dog and when the dog was going to have his hair cut, and all that sort of thing. But no, I didn't think he was crazy at all."

It must be obvious that I would not have given this much space to Butterfield's testimony about detail and to my subsequent conversation with him if I did not agree with the senior Nixon assistant who on the day before Mr. Nixon's resignation on August 9, 1974, confided his conclusion that the President must have been suffering from some mental defect that preceded the Watergate affair by many years. A psychiatrist denounced me and the assistant (whom I have never identified) in a letter to *The New Republic* for presuming to make judgments that no layman could be qualified to make. Without laboring the matter further at this point, I trust that readers who finish this account will perceive that I and the assistant were not alone. I may add that I never read any of the numerous studies of the Nixon mind and mentality by psychiatrists and other alleged authorities who never met Mr. Nixon or discussed him with people who knew him. I regard these types with the contempt that *The New Republic's* aforementioned psychiatric correspondent expressed toward me.

Alex Butterfield made a mistake when he disclosed the existence of the Nixon taping system to the Ervin committee on July 16, 1973. He said then that it was installed, all at once — in two Nixon offices, in the cabinet room, and on four Nixon telephones — in "approximately the summer of 1970." A White House lawyer told the Ervin committee the system was installed in "the spring of 1971." Mr. Nixon twice spoke of starting it up in the summer of 1970. Butterfield has tried in executive sessions with congressional investigators and federal prosecutors and in two public forums to set the facts straight on the basis of later information. He said during our previously quoted conversation that even in his last public testimony, at the trial of five Watergate defendants, including his friend and White House sponsor, Bob Haldeman, he didn't have or get it quite straight. The straight of it, Butterfield said, is that there were two separate and successive installations. The first, in February 1971, was that of the microphones in the President's Oval Office and in the cabinet room. About two months later — Butterfield was still uncertain of the precise time — he was instructed by Lawrence Higby, another assistant to Haldeman who on both occasions relayed the orders from Haldeman, to have the Secret Service's technical security detail put microphones in the President's second office across West Executive Avenue from the White House proper, in the Old Executive Office Building, and to bug the President's telephones in the Oval Office, the Lincoln Study in the executive mansion, the EOB office and the cottage ("Aspen") where Mr. Nixon stayed when he was at Camp David in the nearby Maryland mountains. This sequence has a certain importance, since it bears upon whether the system was operating (it seemingly was not) when such nefarities as the original deal in 1970 to increase federal milk-support levels in return for milk-industry campaign contributions was initiated. A minor note is that more than the generally assumed and reported four Nixon telephones may have been attached to one of the two sets of central recorders.

Butterfield, who rather casually supervised the taping operation until he left the White House in March of 1973 and turned the responsibility over to still another Haldeman assistant, Stephen Bull, is certain only that the telephones in four places were hooked into the recording system. There were two or more telephones in some of these places.

The installations and their timing are of less interest to me than *why* they were put in and *why* they were kept in operation after April 30, 1973, when the President fired Haldeman, John Ehrlichman and counsel John Wesley Dean and even after (for a short time, nobody has ever established just how short a time) Butterfield made their existence public. The answers to these *whys,* it seems to me, tells or would tell much about the Nixon mentality, his own and his White House community's. I say "would" because I do not have and doubt that anybody else has *the* answers. All I have is some answers, now to be summarized. They come from such people as Gen. Alexander Haig, who replaced Haldeman as the President's chief of staff; Henry Kissinger; Butterfield in his open testimony; Lawrence Higby and Stephen Bull; Leonard Garment; J. Fred Buzhardt, sometime counsel to the President and chief White House listener to the tapes once they were exposed; former Press Secretary Ronald Ziegler and several of his assistants; James St. Clair, the Boston lawyer who was the President's chief Watergate defender in 1974 (in his public statements; St. Clair never talked privately to me); Ken W. Clawson, Jr., Mr. Nixon's most aggressive propagandist from February 1972 to the resignation in August 1974; Patrick Buchanan and Raymond K. Price, Jr. (the latter a "liberal" Nixon writer-thinker and good friend whom I have done the kindness of neglecting in this account); and quite a few others who worked for Mr. Nixon and saw enough of him to have some understanding of him, his ways and his quirks. Partly because many of the discussions were on the condition that they would not be quoted, and partly because I prefer to write on my own authority anyhow, the following distillation of what I heard about the tapes and all that they signified is presented with minimal attribution to persons.

Alex Butterfield said something on the House Judiciary Committee's public record that goes a long way to explain the phenomenon and contains the gist of much that was said to me in private. He was explaining why he didn't see anything either wrong or extraordinary

in his toting a satchel containing $350,000 in cash from Bob
Haldeman to a friend of Butterfield's who had agreed to hold the
money until it was needed for unstated purposes (most of it
eventually went to the original Watergate defendants, the burglars
and tappers organized and headed by Howard Hunt). Butterfield
took the cash to his friend on April 7, 1972. After saying he'd been
told since then by Leonard Garment that his action was not illegal,
Butterfield continued: "I certainly didn't think so at the time. And
people don't seem to realize that during this time there was no scandal
in government and everything that everyone did was in the aura of —
of course it's legal, of course it's normal, where the President is only
20 feet away and that sort of thing."

In his last newspaper interview and his clearest statement of how
the taping system came to be installed, Mr. Nixon told columnist
James J. Kilpatrick in May 1974 that Bob Haldeman rather casually
suggested that a full record of what remained of the Nixon presidency
should be made and preserved for history and that he, the President,
agreed without giving it much thought. Mr. Nixon also said he
promptly and literally forgot that the system existed and was
recording all that he and others said in hearing of the microphones
and telephone pickups. Butterfield testified to his certainty that the
President was "totally oblivious" of the system after it was installed.
Haig, Ziegler, Buzhardt are among many who said the same thing.
They may have believed this. But it probably was never true and it
certainly was not true in and after early 1973. Published tape
transcripts have shown that Mr. Nixon not only was aware that
Ehrlichman and others around him were taping their own telephone
callers but instructed Ehrlichman to tape John Mitchell and spoke of
taping in his EOB office. He also said in this period, regarding a fear
that John Dean might have been taping *him*, that he had his own tape
to throw against Dean's if it came to that. In a taped conversation
with Haldeman in late April 1973, less than a week before Haldeman
was made to resign, Mr. Nixon asked for reassurance that the fewest
possible number of trustworthy people knew about the taping
system. A friend who has heard this tape (it had not been publicly
disclosed in late 1974) told me that it has Mr. Nixon speaking
approximately as follows to Haldeman: "Jesus Christ, you know it
would just never do for that to get out, that the President was taping
conversations with people in the Oval Office, that would be terrible.

Of course if anything did happen, we'd just have to say that we only recorded, that we only retained those things which had to do strictly with national security, for the record, business of state and that sort of thing, and that all of the rest was destroyed." My friend said Haldeman answered approximately, "Well, of course, that's what it was used for."

Mr. Nixon may have had this conversation in mind when a friend of mine — it really was another friend — called on him at the Bethesda Naval Hospital in July 1973. The President was being treated for viral pneumonia that had him spitting blood on his pillow at the executive mansion before Gen. Haig and the White House physician, Maj. Gen. Walter Tkach, succeeded at the end of a day of effort in persuading him to enter the hospital. Mr. Nixon was low in body and spirit, reflective, regretting. He recalled that around the time of the conversation quoted in the preceding paragraph he urged Haldeman to remove the taping system and have the accumulated tapes destroyed. He said that Haldeman argued against it and that he, the President, regretted that he had given in to Haldeman's persuasion and had not ordered Haldeman to do what the President then thought and by midsummer was convinced should have been done.

It was not done, then or ever. At least six members of the Nixon staff — Gen. Haig, Ronald Ziegler, Larry Higby, Stephen Bull and two lawyers, Buzhardt and Garment — knew in mid-June of 1973, a month before Butterfield testified, that he would disclose the existence of the taping system if he were asked about it. He had warned them that he wouldn't lie about it. Higby and Bull were also prepared to disclose it if they were asked. A theory developed afterward within the staff that somebody, perhaps Haldeman and later Haig, figured that the act of destruction would be bound to become known and would cause a greater stink than the tapes themselves would cause. So far as I know, nobody in authority actually said this. Long after the actual taping was ended at least some of the microphones remained in place, disconnected but damningly findable. The stacks of boxed tape reels remained in storage at the White House and the EOB. In early 1974 the recordings of 43 Nixon White House conversations and three others concerning but not including the President were transcribed, edited, and on April 29 released with a statement from Mr. Nixon saying that they

contained the whole Watergate story. They didn't, of course. I wrote
at the time that they *had* to be complete, so far as they pretended to
be. Special Prosecutor Leon Jaworski and his staff, federal Judge
John Sirica, and the staff of the House Judiciary Committee, already
preparing its impeachment proceedings, would inevitably be
reviewing the same tapes or copies of them and — I reasoned — even
the Nixon people could not be stupid enough to risk serious deletion.
They did risk it and not, I am convinced, simply and only from
stupidity. Gen. Haig, Ken Clawson, James St. Clair, Fred Buzhardt,
Pat Buchanan, Raymond Price, Richard Nixon, many others who
were involved in that operation were not stupid in the simple and
literal meaning of the word. The answers to "why," to this and related
questions that I heard then and later, were more interesting and more
complex than that.

You have to go back for the essence of it to Alex Butterfield's
reference to the aura around the presidency. All sorts of pejorative
terms — arrogance, the imperial notion, the sheer and crawly evil that
came to pervade the Oval Office in the Nixon period — are brought to
mind by the answers and explanations that I heard. But no one of
these terms or even all of them, taken alone, really suffice. You have
to hear or anyhow be exposed to at least a little of the several answers
in order to get anything near an adequate feel for how it was. Here is
my attempt, drawn from thousands of words in notes, from scores of
conversations in the last Nixon months, to convey my feel for how it
was to an extent that I couldn't or failed to do in my *New Republic*
columns at the time.

There was, first of all, a sense of absolute security. The President
was supreme; the presidency was inviolable. True, he'd lost his
Attorney General and his deputy Attorney General in the process of
getting rid of the first special prosecutor, Archibald Cox. His claim
that all presidential communication (whether preserved in memories
or on paper or on tape) was constitutionally protected had been
eroded. But it had not been destroyed; *the claim* had not been
decisively rejected. The US Court of Appeals for the District of
Columbia had validated it in its basic aspects, allowing for
qualifications having to do with criminal investigation and liability
that the Nixon people were neither inclined nor conditioned to weigh
as seriously as they should have. A fascinating fact in this connection
is that the sense of absolute security was first and for some three

months in mid-1974 eroded for only one man, the President. He and (so far as I know) he alone called for and heard on May 5 and 6, 1974, the three June 23, 1972, tape recordings that convicted him on their face of conniving in the concealment of presidential responsibility for Watergate crimes and, three days after they were disclosed with his permission on August 5, brought him down. As I reported after the fall and probably will be repeating here, a sense that something was horribly wrong spread very slowly during the months that followed through his upper entourage.

At least two separate efforts in December 1973 and the period of January-February 1974 to warn the President that his danger was so serious that he ought to resign hardly dinted the sense of security and inviolability that surrounded him and shielded him from reality. Special Prosecutor Leon Jaworski, who had succeeded Archibald Cox, told a Nixon associate on December 7, 1973, that evidence previously accumulated by Cox and supplemented since Jaworski came aboard was so damning and so deeply involved some of the President's closest associates that Mr. Nixon himself could not survive the coming indictment and trial of these people and the reflection that would inevitably be cast upon him even if he himself were not indicted or named a co-conspirator. Jaworski's deputy, Henry Ruth, delivered much the same message and warning to a Nixon assistant in early 1974. It seems likely that Ruth's warning was never passed to the President and there is reason to suspect that Jaworski's wasn't, either. Gen. Haig, told of Ruth's warning, shrugged it off as "the line that Jaworski's peddling" and left the assistant who received and conveyed it under the impression that Haig didn't think it worth repeating to the President.

There also was a sense of mingled rightness and injury. Hard though the fact may be to accept now, Mr. Nixon was served and surrounded by people who believed in him. This belief in him survived into and through July of 1974. It emerges strongly from notes of conversations with Gen. Haig, Ken Clawson and Ronald Ziegler during the President's visit to his Florida home in April 1974. The gist of these conversations, reflected in pieces at the time, will not be repeated here except to recall that bitter resentment against his attackers and detractors and a feeling that Republicans inadequately defended him dominated the White House end of those conversations. There was absolutely no sense conveyed that the impending

release of the White House tape transcripts would be the disaster for
Mr. Nixon that it turned out to be. And why should there have been?
James St. Clair said afterward that Mr. Nixon personally edited the
transcripts and personally ordered or approved the deletions from
them. I've suspected since then but don't know that St. Clair's rapid
departure from the White House after Mr. Nixon resigned resulted in
part from uneasiness about that operation. St. Clair's assertions of
ignorance of the content of the original tapes and his implied
suggestion that somebody else — in the circumstances, the President
and Fred Buzhardt — had to be responsible for any and all obfusca-
tions and deletions seemed then and now, to me, to be open to doubt.

It's the related sense of injury that most interests and impresses
me when I review what I was told and knew of those last
Nixon days. The beginning day of those last days was July 24, when
the President was at San Clemente and the Supreme Court ruled that
he had to surrender the tapes of 54 conversations, including the June
23 conversations that completed the destruction of his presidency.
My story, the first in print or on the air, of how Mr. Nixon early that
morning telephoned Fred Buzhardt and told him to call for and
review the June 23 tapes, appears in one of my last Nixon columns.
Here are added facts that were unknown to me at the time.

Mr. Nixon was very late that morning in getting in touch with Gen.
Haig, James St. Clair, Ronald Ziegler and Ken Clawson, the
principal assistants who were more or less with him in San Clemente.
A story that he'd overslept doesn't jibe with the verified account of his
telephoned early morning instruction to Buzhardt in Washington to
listen to those June 23 tapes and report whether they were as hellish as
Mr. Nixon thought they were. Even so, there was something odd
about the President's lackadaisical behavior that day. He was slow
and his spokesmen were slow in their reactions. Concerning the day
and later events that preceded Mr. Nixon's resignation, Gen. Haig
said to me: "Only two people, President Nixon and Alex Haig, know
that story, and Alex Haig is not about to tell it." I hear that he's told
parts of it to other reporters. Before Haig left the White House to
assume, by grace and selection of President Ford, the US and NATO
military commands in Europe, some intimations of what passed on
that fatal July 24 in San Clemente were picked up from him and
others. The information that I couldn't or didn't report at the time is
summarized in what follows.

Ziegler saw very little — some who don't like him say nothing — of President Nixon that day. Haig is said to have told the President, who was at the residence two or three minutes' walk, or a one-minute golf-cart ride, from the Western White House offices, that Ziegler wished to come over and was told to tell Ziegler not to come. Mr. Nixon conferred with Haig and St. Clair at the San Clemente residence, in the square little study that was furnished at government expense (rightly, in my opinion) on the second floor overlooking the Pacific. It was in that study in 1969 that I saw and inexcusably failed to report what were not then known to exist, the reading glasses that the President used in private. On that fatal July 24, the President asked and asked and asked St. Clair and Haig whether there was "any air" in the Supreme Court decision. He meant, was there any way around complying with the finding that he had to give Judge Sirica, the special prosecutor and (in the sure though unstated end) the House impeachment committee those 54 recordings, including the ruinous June 23, 1972, recordings. He was told that there was not any air in the decision — no way around it. But Haig and St. Clair did NOT then tell the President that they accepted and believed Buzhardt's report back to San Clemente, after listening to the June 23 tapes, that they were conclusive and disastrous. I gather, though I do not know for certain, that Mr. Nixon was allowed by Haig and St. Clair to hope that Buzhardt could have been as wrong in his interpretation of the June 23 tapes as he had been (by his own admission) in his first reading of some 1973 subpoenas for other Nixon tapes. You have to understand that Haig and St. Clair profoundly detested Buzhardt and that St. Clair envied and feared him. It was Buzhardt (so the media kept reporting) that the President trusted for access to and knowledge of the tapes. It was Buzhardt (so St. Clair kept saying) who knew what was in the tapes if anybody did and St. Clair (so St. Clair kept saying) who did not know what was in them. All of this is pointless tragicomedy in a sense. St. Clair unquestionably remained the Nixon attorney in charge of the President's defense, to the very end. Mr. Nixon had heard the June 23 recordings on May 5-6 and he knew what was in them. This mix of facts — the President's knowledge, the calls for assurance, the doubts on Haig's and St. Clair's parts or perhaps their reluctance to acknowledge to the President that Buzhardt was right in his interpretation of the June 23 tapes — add up to collective irrationality. I wrote then that I didn't know whether Ziegler knew of Buzhardt's report on the June 23 tapes when he said for the President on July 27 in a formal, written statement that Mr. Nixon remained convinced that he was innocent of any impeachable offense. Ziegler said later that he wished I'd asked him about that before I wrote it. I spared him the fact that I'd tried and tried to get him and couldn't — he was incommunicado at that point. Ziegler said that when he issued the July 27 statement he knew nothing about the report from Buzhardt to the San Clemente White House at around noon of July 24. If Ziegler was telling the truth, and I'm inclined to believe him, the President had deceived Ziegler. Haig had deceived Ziegler. St. Clair had deceived Ziegler. The Nixon establishment had once again demonstrated its inexhaustible capacity for betrayal of those who were most loyal to it.

We end with the sense of injury. It was very evident and it persisted after Mr. Nixon was gone and pardoned. At his and four other defendants' trial for obstruction of justice and related offenses in Washington, Bob Haldeman was heard by reporters to say that the recordings of White House conversations played in court conveyed an incredibly wrong impression. What he and others were heard to say, he meant to indicate, wasn't as bad as it sounded. Recalling some of my own conversations, it's believable Haldeman and the others really believed this. Up to July 30 and 31, when a very few White House assistants were told what was in the decisive tapes, and up to August 5, when the transcripts of the June 23, 1972, tapes were released, a sense of profound, irresistible and undeserved injury to a good and great President prevailed at the Nixon White House. It prevailed in Washington after he returned and in San Clemente during the last July days at what was so soon to cease to be the Western White House. A sense that something catastrophic had happened began to spread through the San Clemente offices on the Coast Guard base there, adjoining the Nixon estate, on July 24 and afterward. Lou Cannon of *The Washington Post* reported it at a time when people at the office compound were telling me and other reporters that everything was fine. Partly because of the Cannon story, I got through by telephone on July 27 to one of the few assistants at the Nixon compound whom I could expect the truth from, if it could be expected from anyone. I hope that Dianne Sawyer, one of Ziegler's assistants and one of the brightest people in the Nixon White House, will forgive me for saying that she was the person I got on the phone. I was calling from a pay phone at the San Clemente Inn, my notes were scratchy, and I quote only in essence. The gist of what Dianne Sawyer said, in a wrenching tone of grief and belief, was that there was a feeling at the Nixon compound that something unknown had happened — that events were closing in upon a President who deserved better of the media, Congress, the public. It was plain that she, who was among the least gullible and the most intelligent of the Nixon people, felt that an enormous injustice was in process and was about to be inflicted upon her President.

So the end came. A penalty of resignation, disgrace and condemnation, by his successor among others, was laid upon Richard Nixon. The penalty was less than many citizens thought he should suffer and less than many of his servitors who did what they did because of their belief in and reliance upon him suffered in fines, imprisonment, disbarment, loss of repute and professional future. Dianne Sawyer and many friends of five and a half years at the Nixon White House underwent the agony of being compelled to recognize that they had served a false and lying master. A midlevel Nixon staffer who worked for one of the few assistants — Haig, Ziegler, Buchanan, Garment, Price, St. Clair — who saw something of the doomed President in his final days of falter and resignation spoke of how the disclosure of the June 23 tapes struck home: "I was sick, I was shocked, I told myself I couldn't believe it although I had to believe it. He had lied to me, to all of us. I think my first thought, before *that* sank in, was of those Republicans on the Judiciary Committee — Wiggins, Sandman, those men who had risked their careers to defend him. He had lied to them! You won't believe it, I guess, but at some point that afternoon when I first read the transcripts of those tapes (in this assistant's case, July 31) I said to myself that this has to be some sort of ghastly joke. I actually laughed aloud. I laughed and laughed. I know now that I was hysterical, of course. We all were, the ones who knew then."

The assistant whom I am quoting went through a change between July 31 and August 5, when a larger group of White House employees were forewarned and the transcripts were released. This assistant's boss told his staff how the President was reacting and his story of "the agony the President was in" had an effect. My informant described that effect: "I began to think of him as a man, of the agony he was going through, instead of as a President who had lied to me. What we

were told was so strange, so mystifying" — and here my friend
stopped, as if to go on would disclose horrors that did not bear
recounting. In the silence that followed, I thought of what another
assistant who was senior by several levels to the friend quoted here
had told me. The senior assistant said that Mr. Nixon, right up to the
morning of his resignation, had insisted that he was innocent of any
real wrongdoing. He recognized that as a practical political matter his
own words on the June 23 tapes convicted him of doing what he many
times had denied doing, which in essense was to authorize and
participate from the time of the Watergate burglary in efforts to
conceal the involvement of administration officials. He said to this
assistant that he realized that he would be impeached and convicted if
he did not resign and that he therefore had to resign. But the
President continued to say that he had not done anything wrong. In
the sense that they indicated he had, he said over and over, his taped
words were wrong. The assistant to whom the President had said this
and who was telling me that the President had said it looked at me as
if he were begging me to understand something that was left
unspoken. It was, I think, what my junior staff friend's boss had told
his group. It was, I think, that the President — their President — was
sick of mind.

Never once in the last Nixon days at the White House did I hear
mentioned Mr. Nixon's first Vice President, Spiro T. Agnew, and the
satanic fact that the two of them spent almost five years deceiving
each other. It's a fact that should be remembered, though I'm as
prone as others to forget it.

Vale, Mr. President and Bob and Ron and John and John and
Chuck and all the others, and thanks for the ride.

Washington, D.C.
December 31, 1974

I

Hanging in There

At the end of Mr. Nixon's fifth year and the beginning of his sixth year in the presidency, the overlooked news at the White House was that some people who work there were talking as if they actually believed that 1973 hadn't been utterly disastrous for him and that he really is going to be able to hang in there, as he keeps saying he is determined to do, and avoid either resignation or impeachment.

Two of the assistants who talk this way are Kenneth Cole, the executive director of the Domestic Council and one of its five associate directors, James Cavanaugh. Lest what they say be thought in this time of obsessive preoccupation with Watergate to be totally irrational, it should be explained before they are quoted that domestic legislation is high among their concerns and that the administration fared better in Congress in 1973 than is generally realized. One of 54 enacted bills signed by the President during the Christmas-New Year recess provided federal support for private, prepaid medical and hospital service plans that could revolutionize health care in the next few years. A public employment and manpower training law implements the President's belief that much of the control over federally supported social programs should be transferred from the federal government to state and local governments. An 11 percent increase in social security benefits is bigger and takes effect sooner than the administration wished and the law requiring the increase postpones the enforcement of regulations intended to tighten control over some social-service expenditures. In signing these and several other bills, Mr. Nixon accepted provisions that he disliked and might have rejected with vetoes in happier times. But the same legislation embodies some concessions to him and, on the whole, augurs well for the national health insurance, welfare revision and other domestic proposals that Cole, Cavanaugh and many others at the White House and in the departments are working up for the President to advance or at least mention in his pending budget and State-of-the-Union messages.

It's this view of the legislative record and prospect that Jim Cavanaugh has in mind when he says that *of course* he's staying on at the White House, saddened but not deterred by the Watergate scandals and effects, and that "we've got a lot of exciting things going on." Kenneth Cole reflected the same view when he said in December 1973, speaking of himself and his principal associates on the Domestic Council staff: "Most of us are staying. We're enthusiastic about the progress that's been made this year, and we're looking forward to next year. I've been saying for the last three months that it's been a good year, and it really has. I think we've had one of the better legislative years in my memory. We didn't get all the specifics that we wanted, but we at least preserved the principles."

A question that I always ask during such conversations is whether the assistant I'm talking to has any doubt whatever that the President is as determined as he says he is to remain in office and serve out his second term. Cole doesn't pretend to be one of the very few assistants who see the President regularly and alone. He was, however, with official and visiting groups that spent some time with Mr. Nixon on all but two of the working days in the fortnight preceding the conversation quoted here, and he was photographed with the President at the California White House on the January day when he said by telephone that he still felt as he did when we talked in Washington on December 20. Apart from the standard expression of belief that Mr. Nixon really does mean to hang in there, Cole's answer to my question added a bit by implication to the ample evidence that the President has been through and up from periods of profound depression and distraction since the full horrors of Watergate began to break upon him in March and April of 1973. Quoting Kenneth Cole: "I think that the President plans to stay here for the long haul and it's my judgment that he will. I think the President's spirits have picked up considerably in the last two months. He is very much his old self. He is interested in what is going on. He has a lot of suggestions and instructions as to how things ought to be approached and how to look into things."

Most of the visible Nixon performance since mid-October, the point from which Kenneth Cole seems to date a pickup in the President's spirits, contradicts the impression of strength and confidence that White House loyalists inevitably try to convey. Mr. Nixon's Christmas decision to travel by commercial aircraft from Washington to California, and his success in hiding that intention from the White House press corps until he was aboard a United Airlines plane, may have dramatized his dedication to the conservation of fuel and impressed the public as effectively as his spokesmen said it did. But it was actually a pathetic display of weakness, a confession that he had fallen so low in public esteem that he didn't dare do what he should have done. That was to travel when and wherever he wanted to travel in Air Force One, the magnificent jet aircraft that is provided for and befits the President of the United States. The only good thing about this episode and the indicated return to Washington in another commercial airliner was the constructive lesson the whole business taught the White House press corps, to the effect that it can get about on its own when it has to, without demeaning dependence on the White House staff for chartered planes and such attendant favors as hotel and hire-car reservations.

While the President was at his California home, he got himself a new Watergate defense lawyer. He first defied and then backed away from his defiance of the Senate Watergate committee's foolish and extravagant demand for hundreds of White House tapes and documents. After many weeks of preparation and several days of shilly-shallying, he had the White House staff release statements that purported to prove that he didn't reward the dairy industry with increased price supports and the International Telephone and Telegraph Corporation with favorable antitrust treatment because they contributed or promised large sums to his 1972 reelection campaign.

Mr. Nixon's attorney is James D. St. Clair, a Boston trial lawyer who is famed within the legal profession for his skill at defending difficult causes. The choice is the strongest indication to date that the President foresees that the House Judiciary Committee will submit a resolution of impeachment to the House of Representatives and that he is sure to be involved, though indirectly and marginally, in criminal indictments of former Nixon subordinates and associates that Special Prosecutor Leon Jaworski will soon be getting from a federal grand jury. A mistaken impression, derived from a reporter's inquiry, that Jaworski planned to have Mr. Nixon named as an unindicted co-conspirator in one or more of these indictments caused abject panic at the Western White House until assurances that Jaworski had no such intention were obtained. A collateral effect of the St. Clair appointment was to inspire a lot of misplaced and frequently hypocritical sympathy for Leonard Garment, a former Nixon law partner who has been acting counsel to the President since May 1973. J. Fred Buzhardt, who was replaced by St. Clair at the head of the Watergate defense unit of some 11 lawyers, replaced Garment as White House counsel and Garment became an assistant to the President. Anonymous "senior aides" encouraged press reports that Garment, who by comparison with most of his White House associates is a flaming liberal, had been demoted and rebuked for unsatisfactory work on Watergate problems. What the President thinks of Garment's Watergate work, I don't know. Garment has detested it ever since he had to take some of it on, intermittently and never with full responsibility for it. He'd been wanting out of it for many weeks and the only thing about the change of assignment and title that displeased him was that it didn't completely remove him from Watergate concerns. It's worth noting in passing, incidentally, that Garment the liberal softie has urged the President and is still urging him to stand absolutely firm in defense of presidential privilege and privacy, even though and when it invites a suspicion that he's hiding guilt.

All that I currently have to say about the dairy and ITT disclaimers is that they can't do the President much good. They demonstrate the fallacy of the notion, urged upon the President by many powerful Republicans, that disclosure for the sake of disclosure is or can be a solution for him. On its face the sequence of events set forth in the milk-funds paper sustains the President's contention that his knowledge that big contributions were promised and coming from dairy cooperatives had nothing to do with his decision to overrule his Secretary of Agriculture and raise price-support levels in 1971. But it remains true that the contention is believable only to the extent that Richard Nixon is believable. Both the dairy and ITT papers confirm and, in the President's defense, magnify the impression that powerful interests with major stakes in official and presidential decisions had an access to officialdom and to the President himself that beclouded the decisions. Beyond all else that might be said, these papers demonstrate that in such matters as the dairy and ITT controversies, complete disclosure is not possible for this President.

January 19, 1974

II

Peepers & Creepers

For awhile there, between January 11 and January 15, the White House news took one away from the Watergate scene and back to the halcyon time when it was possible to groan and laugh and marvel at the doings around Richard Nixon, including the examples of stupidity and chicanery that surfaced often enough to satisfy any but the most rabid critics, without fearing for the nation and having to conclude that the Nixon presidency deserved and was nearing its end. The brief holiday from horror ended on the 15th when six electronics experts told federal Judge John Sirica in Washington that 18½ minutes of a subpoenaed tape recording of a conversation about the original Watergate break-in and burglary in June of 1972 between the President and his staff chief, H. R. Haldeman, had been erased in a way that could only have been deliberate. The testimony concerned an erasure that had been known to the President since October 1 and concealed from the court and public until November 21. The erasure occurred on one of the White House tapes that the President said on July 23, 1973, he had taken into his personal custody, ostensibly to see that they were preserved intact and inviolate and actually to protect them from judicial, congressional and public scrutiny. The expert testimony indicated beyond supportable doubt that a specific crime had been committed on the President's behalf and conceivably by the President himself. A reporter at a public White House briefing asked Mr. Nixon's spokesman, "Did the President erase the tape?" In a tone and with a facial expression indicating awareness of the humiliation to which he and his President were reduced, the spokesman answered, "No." The damage to what was left of Mr. Nixon's repute and credibility made impeachment more likely than it already was, made the question of whether a sitting President is subject to criminal indictment a real and present question for Special Prosecutor Leon Jaworski, and immensely increased the pressures upon the President to resign.

The news that afforded temporary respite from such concerns was lightsome and relieving only by comparison with the accustomed run of Watergate news. It raised quite serious questions as to whether the President either deceived himself or knowingly deceived Congress, the courts and the public in 1973 when he said publicly on three occasions and privately on many others that vital issues of national security required him to withhold information about the White House surveillance and espionage outfit known as "the plumbers" that he set up in 1971. He also argued that national security matters handled by this outfit were so critical and sensitive that the Senate Watergate committee and the special Watergate prosecutor would cause grave harm to the nation if they probed deeply and extensively into the activities of his Special Investigations Unit. Even so, the news that emerged on and after January 11 was a relief in the sense that it had more to do with peepers and creepers in high places than it did with admitted felons and with characters who found it needful to say as the President said on November 17, 1973, "I am not a crook."

The thrust of the news was that military personnel who were assigned to Henry Kissinger's National Security Council staff at the White House spied upon him, rifled his and the NSC's files, and regularly conveyed stolen information and documents to the Joint Chiefs of Staff and specifically to the JCS chairman, Admiral Thomas Moorer. Rear Admiral Robert O. Welander and a young naval secretary-stenographer who was assigned to him, Yeoman 1st Class Charles Radford, were reported to have been doing the dirty work for their superiors at the Pentagon in 1970-71. Radford was said to have given columnist Jack Anderson the official, verbatim minutes

"Just following orders, sir"

of four meetings of an NSC subgroup, the Washington Special Action Group, at which Kissinger relayed and executed the President's command to "tilt" American policy in favor of Pakistan and against India during the India-Pakistan war in late 1971. There was much more of the same kind of stuff, all of it essentially trivial. Admiral Moorer said the notion that he would or needed to rely upon stolen data for knowledge of what went on in Kissinger's shop was "ludicrous and absurd." Yeoman Radford said that he wasn't Jack Anderson's source. These assertions were greeted with indulgent disbelief at the White House. In February 1972, soon after Welander and Radford were abruptly removed from the NSC staff and the NSC-Defense liaison office in Room 376-A in the Executive Office Building next door to the White House was stripped of its files and abolished, NSC staff civilians were told that Welander and Radford did supply Moorer and others in authority at the Pentagon with purloined information and that Radford had leaked the WASAG documents to Anderson.

Two circumstances lent these shenanigans an interest that they wouldn't otherwise have had. First, they were the subject of investigation and report to the President by his Special Investigations Unit. This was the fact that brought them to the attention of the Senate Watergate committee. Second, the military spying upon Henry Kissinger and the theft of documents from his files resulted from the extreme secrecy in which he conducted NSC business. He literally cut both the Defense and State Departments out of the main channels of information at a time when he was preparing the Nixon approach to Communist China and superintending the preparation of the US position to be taken in arms limitation talks with the Soviet Union. Military aides stationed at the White House and military people assigned to the NSC since the council was established in 1947 have always, as a matter of course, kept their service superiors informed about what was going on at the White House. The degree of secrecy practiced and required by Kissinger, along with his reach for power and control over both foreign and defense policy, drew responses from the Joint Chiefs and from Defense Secretary Melvin Laird that went beyond the accepted norms. Laird required all communication between the military services and the NSC staff to be conducted through his office, and during his last year at the Defense Department there was almost no communication.

In July 1973, when the Senate Watergate committee was looking
into the Nixon plumbers' activities, Senator Howard Baker of
Tennessee noticed that a paragraph was omitted from a White House
memorandum on the subject and demanded an explanation. Two
Nixon lawyers, Fred Buzhardt and Leonard Garment, briefed Baker,
the Republican vice chairman of the committee, and Senator Sam
Ervin, the chairman, in the deepest secrecy. Buzhardt and Garment
argued for the President that a thorough inquiry into the plumbers'
doings would be bound to lead to disclosures of secret information
that would gravely damage the national interest. What the damaging
information was the lawyers didn't say, with one exception. They told
Ervin and Baker about the internecine rivalries, secrecy and thievery
that marked the relationship between Kissinger and the Joint Chiefs
and maintained that revealing this unpretty picture at committee
hearings wouldn't do anybody any good. The President referred to
this briefing when he said on November 17 that one piece of the
information involved "was so serious that even Senator Ervin and
Senator Baker agreed it should not be disclosed." It wasn't quite that
way. Ervin's principal reaction was that the behavior of Kissinger and
his military antagonists was none of the committee's business and
that the committee therefore should and would refrain from
thorough investigation of the Nixon plumbers. Baker thought the
committee probably should disregard the White House argument but
he didn't press the issue. Mostly he brooded about the singular fact
that Admiral Welander and Yeoman Radford were not penalized or
punished and that Admiral Moorer remained chairman of the JCS
although the President knew or believed that he had authorized and
benefited from military spying upon Henry Kissinger. During a talk
with the President in mid-October, Baker asked him, "Why don't you
proceed against these people?" Mr. Nixon answered, "If we did, we'd
have to disclose the contents of the documents." Baker indicated to
me on January 16 that he's willing to believe, but would like to have it
proved, that in this matter the President really is concerned with
national security and not about the effect that full inquiry into and
disclosure of the operation would have upon him.

January 26, 1974

III

Last Try

A last effort to save the Nixon presidency took shape at the White House during the week of January 21. The associates, spokesmen and supporters who participated in the effort didn't call it a last try. But that is what it was and the President himself, with something he said to a group of Republican congressmen, made it clear that he understands that he and his presidency are finished if the effort fails. He authorized Representative Peter Frelinghuysen of New Jersey to quote the language he used in saying that he intends to resist the House Judiciary Committee's impeachment inquiry. Mr. Nixon said: "There is a time to be timid. There is a time to be conciliatory. There is a time, even, to fly and there is a time to fight. And I'm going to fight like hell."

In a curiously haphazard and slipshod way, the strategy for salvation was discussed and more or less decided upon while the President was in California, at his San Clemente home and at the Palm Springs estate of his wealthy friend, Ambassador Walter Annenberg, between December 26 and January 12. Most of the discussion that involved the President was with the two assistants upon whom he has been principally relying since last May, staff chief

Alexander Haig and press secretary Ronald Ziegler. The problems and possibilities of survival came up with other assistants who flew from Washington to San Clemente for consultation. Among them were counsellor Bryce N. Harlow, who had intended to quit toward the end of January and was persuaded to stay awhile longer, and Roy Ash, who is both an assistant to the President and director of the Office of Management and Budget. They did most of their consulting with Haig. Harlow met once with the President during four days in San Clemente. Ash, there for a day, didn't see the President at all. Another assistant was struck by the relatively little time, much less than reporters were led to believe, that the President spent with Haig and Ziegler. Mr. Nixon spent a lot more time in seclusion at his home adjoining the Western White House office complex and was often with his Florida friend and benefactor, C. G. (Bebe) Rebozo. The only tangible result of the talks in California, with and without the President, about how to survive was essentially negative. It was a decision to terminate the issuance of defensive and explanatory documents like the ones on the President's taxes and personal finances with two and only two more such attempts at apologia, the statements on the dairy industry's political contributions and the ITT antitrust settlement that were released January 9. It was decided *not* to publish the summaries of seven subpoenaed White House tapes that had been prepared and temporarily intended for release in late December. No satisfactory explanation of the decision to withhold these summaries, including the only documented accounts of some of the President's conversations with his former counsel and most formidable accuser, John Dean, has been offered publicly or privately. This leads me to suppose that the Dean recordings do not support the President's claim of innocence and ignorance in the Watergate affair as strongly and believably as he and others say they do. An odd and possibly revealing circumstance accompanied the release of the dairy and ITT statements. Those responsible for the release, presumably including the President, were determined that the statements be published before Mr. Nixon returned to Washington. It was true, as explained, that he wanted to get away from the miserable weather that prevailed along the California coast during his stay at San Clemente. But the final four days that he spent in the desert sun at the Annenberg estate were added to the California visit so that the dairy and ITT papers could be issued, published and dissected by his critics while he was away from the White House. A small fact that a Nixon spokesman wanted published, for some obscure reason, was that on one of the days at Palm Springs the President and Bebe Rebozo played 27 holes of golf on Ambassador Annenberg's private course.

The nature of the revised strategy was clear enough from what happened and was said after the President returned to Washington. He would admit nothing more, explain nothing more. In person and through staff assistants and others speaking for him, he would try to discourage and frustrate the mounting calls for his resignation by insisting that he absolutely would not resign and that if necessary he would see the Watergate crisis right up to and through an impeachment trial in the Senate. He would counter the spreading assumption that he couldn't govern by governing in the busiest and most spectacular ways that he and his aides could think up. So much and more was plain for all to see in publicized meetings at the White House; Secretary of State Henry Kissinger's somewhat labored display of his initial successes in promoting Arab-Israeli negotiation; much activity and some early proposals to Congress on oil and other energy shortages; and unprecedented eagerness to reveal in advance details of the 1975 budget and of the President's State-of-the-Union message.

A good deal of insight into the motives and reasoning behind this spate of counteraction—more insight, probably, than was intended—emerged from an extraordinary briefing that Press Secretary Ziegler gave in the White House press room on January 22. It was extraordinary in several respects. Ziegler, who has been doubling as an assistant to the President since last June, had briefed the press very rarely since then and had last done so on November 29. The many evasions and the occasional, downright lies that he used on the President's behalf in 1972 and 1973 to cover up the White House cover-up of the Watergate scandals had long since cost him the trust of White House reporters. Well along in the January 22 session, Ziegler remarked that "I will be having more regular briefings. I intend to give more briefings." In a tone of cold and brutal scorn, a reporter asked: "Do you think your credibility has been restored?" Let it be said for Ziegler, he didn't flinch. Evenly, with the air of one who believes what he's saying and knows that he isn't being believed,

he answered: "I think that credibility is always a question which has
to be determined by those who are listening. I do know this: that those
who are speaking know within themselves that if they have proceeded
in a way that they have always attempted on every occasion to
provide information that they were able to get and which they knew
to be the fact at the time, then a man can walk out and stand before
members of the press and address issues and address what the office
of the presidency is doing in very good conscience."

That's the way Ronald Ziegler talks and, more importantly, it
reflects the way he and many others in the Nixon White House think.
Here, condensed and put together from several answers to several
questions but not distorted, is some more Ziegler talk on the 22nd. It
bespeaks the fervor and weakness of the President's hope that he can
forestall the ruin that either resignation or impeachment and removal
would bring upon him. Ziegler speaking: "I don't intend or want to
get into an intensive discussion of the entire Watergate matter today.
I would like to talk about the business the President is working on
and what the President is doing in terms of running the government
. . . . The President is determined to devote his time to matters
relating to legislation and to the running of the government. That is
what he is determined to do. He is determined not to become
consumed for another year by the Watergate matter. He fully intends
to complete his three years in office and is not entertaining at all the
subject of resignation . . . . I think the President feels we have had
almost a year now of extensive investigations of the Watergate matter
and it is time to wrap this matter up, conclude it . . . . I am not
surprised by the poll figures. If you look over the last year at the many
charges that have been leveled against the President, there would
have to be, as there has been, an effect on the polls and on public
opinion. A lot of that has been the result of the constant, constant,
constant, constant charge, charge, charge against the President. Our
view is the way to see those figures go up is to not constantly be
devoted to proving the negative and constantly being on the defensive
about charges that are leveled against us." And, after saying 1973
when he meant 1974: "Excuse me. 1973 has had quite an impact on
me. I can't get it out of my mind."

February 2, 1974

IV

Between the Acts

At this writing, after a fortnight when there have been no major Watergate shocks and while the President is getting ready to deliver his State-of-the-Union speech and message, his annual economic message and his fiscal 1975 budget, it seems appropriate to catch up with some points and thoughts about the Nixon situation and the Nixon White House that have been minimized or overlooked in my recent reports.

Accounts of Mr. Nixon's declared determination to hang in there, fight off impeachment and put himself and the nation through the agonies of a Senate trial if it comes to that, rather than resign, seldom reflect and convey what to me is the most interesting impression that the inquirer gets from the few assistants who see enough of the President to have a worthwhile version of his state of mind and attitude. The impression that he gives them and that they pass along is that he is absolutely convinced that he is in the right and that his detractors are in the wrong in the whole gamut of issues and allegations that Watergate connotes. His continuing rejection of suggestions that he resign and his defiance of the impeachment process are said to be based upon considerations that transcend mere calculations of what he can and cannot get away with.

The President is comforted, to be sure, by the reports he gets from such advisers as counsellor Bryce N. Harlow and departing counsellor Melvin Laird to the effect that at the turn of January-February a majority in the House of Representatives is not prepared to impeach him, regardless of what the House Judiciary Committee may recommend, and that a two-thirds majority in the Senate is not prepared to convict and remove him. Mr. Nixon is said to understand, as his advisers and informants do, that House and Senate attitudes could change. What fortifies him and moves him to hold fast, according to the assistants who are quoted here, is the certainty in his mind that there is no valid reason for either resignation or impeachment. He tells his people that resignation would be wrong, a disservice to the country, and that impeachment by the House and conviction by the Senate are inconceivable. He is said to say with every indication of genuine belief that either resignation or impeachment and conviction would deprive the country of a President who has served it well and who is obligated to go on serving it well. This sort of thing comes across with a horribly tinny ring when the President and his apologists talk in public about his carrying out the mandate that he thinks he got with his reelection in 1972. It comes across to the assistants who hear it in private from the President as a belief deeply held, a sense of obligation and duty truly and profoundly felt. Gen. Alexander Haig, the White House staff chief, said in a recent interview and continues to say in conversations that Richard Nixon will be adjudged on his record, once the memory and obsessions of Watergate have faded, as a good President and may be adjudged a great one. Although Gen. Haig is capable of forming his own judgments, this one doesn't come to him from nowhere. It comes from Mr. Nixon.

In White House conversations of the kind reflected here, the President's chances of survival are generally discussed in terms of what the public seems to believe and want, and of what Congress is likely to do. The most heartening indicator recently reported to Mr. Nixon and, it's said, taken by him to be a reliable indicator is that congressmen seemed to return from their year-end recess with no sense of a popular command to get rid of this President. The characteristic reaction reported to the President was that a depressing number of voters would welcome his voluntary departure and that his continued incumbency would be a heavy liability to Republican candidates in the 1974 midterm elections, but that the same or equivalent majorities dreaded and shied away from the prospect of impeachment. The net effect upon senators and representatives was thought to be a wish that Nixon and the problem personified by him would go away, but not that the problem had to be exorcised by driving him away. A measure of the low state of presidential and White House confidence is that this judgment was taken to be a plus for Mr. Nixon.

Unless the inquirer brings the point up, no discussion is heard of the effect that the terms and language of the indictments of former Nixon associates that Special Watergate Prosecutor Leon Jaworski will soon be announcing may have upon the President. Jaworski has said that the President is a target of his investigations, that any evidence involving him has been or will be presented to grand juries. The last indication from Jaworski's office was that Mr. Nixon wouldn't be named in the indictments unless he himself were indicted, and that the prosecutor still had to decide whether an incumbent President is indictable. The fact that the Nixon problem is discussed in these terms around the special prosecutor, though not at the White House, is a sufficient measure of the peril from that quarter in which Mr. Nixon stands. Even if he is not explicitly implicated in allegations against others, the implication of involvement is bound to be there and the consequences for him could be decisive. The thunderous silence upon this aspect of the problem at the White House is a further measure of its gravity. A Nixon spokesman said on January 30 that 13 White House lawyers are working full time on the President's Watergate problems. The cost in salaries and expenses must run at a yearly rate well above $500,000. It's a figure to keep in mind when weighing the possibility of resignation. Without the immunity from prosecution that an incumbent President is assumed to have but may not have, an ex-President in the only circumstances that might conceivably lead to Mr. Nixon's resignation would have to meet legal expenses that he, with his known resources, could not meet without assistance.

A statement of the President's personal resources issued last December 8 said that he had $466,000 in cash or other liquid assets as of May 1973. He owed $471,000 on his Florida and California homes. What makes these facts relevant is the President's tax situation. His spokesman said in the course of the December 8 disclosures that he would pay any federal or other taxes that he was found to owe during reviews of his 1969-72 returns. Saying this was a lot easier than paying will be for Mr. Nixon if he has to pay all that he may turn out to owe. If the gift of his vice presidential papers to the National Archives in 1969 and the resultant deduction of $576,000 from his taxable income *(not* from taxes due, as many reports indicate) are found to be invalid, he could owe $234,000 to the federal treasury and it could be many thousands more, with penalties. Capital gains and California income taxes that he could also be found to owe could bring the cost of fulfilling his December promise to well over $400,000. Perhaps of graver consequence to him, the tremendous increase in federal income tax that he will have to pay if the vice presidential papers gift and deduction are invalidated could wreck his plans to leave office in 1977 free of debt and a certified millionaire. If the gift is found to have been fraudulently arranged, and there is evidence that it may have been, the hirelings who devised it for him could be indicted and he could be indicted, too, before or after he leaves office.

It was against this background that an argument over what to do about the President's taxes swirled around him in late January. The question was whether or not to anticipate findings by the Internal Revenue Service and the joint Senate-House Committee on Internal Revenue Taxation, both of which are reviewing the President's tax record at his request, that he's evaded taxes that he should have paid and to pay up before such findings are announced. The argument for paying in advance was that it could diminish, though nothing could banish, the harm already done and certain to be done to the President's reputation. The argument for awaiting the expected adverse findings, and then paying up, was that the sums found to be due and the terms in which the findings were stated might be more and worse, or less and better, than was anticipated in January. There could be no sadder commentary upon Richard Nixon and his presidency than the fact that this argument was raging among his lawyers and advisers when he prepared to tell the nation how it was doing and why it should trust him to manage, among other things, the spending of more than $300 billion in fiscal 1975.

February 9, 1974

_____

For the consequences of the decision to await the official findings, see Chapter XIII. Obvious though the arithmetic later became, the foregoing report was among the first nationally published analyses of this aspect of the President's problem. A White House lawyer estimated at the time that the legal services the President was getting could cost him $2 million a year as a private citizen. The reported sense of rightness and of injustice done persisted to the end.

V

Cornered

Despite the sense of confidence and rightness that was noted in my last report and that the President tried once again to convey in his State-of-the-Union speech, the overwhelming impression that this inquirer continues to get at the White House is that Mr. Nixon is a cornered President with, in the foreseeable end, no way to go but down and out. Several events during the last days of January and the first week of February, including the President's delivery of "a personal word with regard to . . . the so-called Watergate affair" at the close of his State-of-the-Union address, strengthened the impression.

Only an underlying desperation could have induced the President, whether in person or through assistants, to persuade Sen. Hugh Scott of Pennsylvania to do what he did for Mr. Nixon on January 20. Scott, the Republican leader in the Senate, said that he had seen secret White House material that convinced him that John Dean, the President's former staff counsel, lied under oath when he told the Senate Watergate committee that Mr. Nixon knew about attempts to cover up the Watergate scandals before March 21, 1973, when the President says he first learned about these attempts at the White

House and elsewhere. Sen. Scott refused for days to say what the material was that he had seen. Nobody else, speaking for the President, would say what it was or that Scott was right in interpreting it as he did. Scott, angered and disturbed by the failure of White House spokesmen to back him up, disclosed that Gen. Alexander Haig, the President's staff chief, had shown him summarized transcripts taken from taped recordings of some of Mr. Nixon's conversations with Dean and others. Gen. Haig had previously been understood to say that he'd had nothing to do with the Scott performance and didn't think it was a good idea. It was a poor idea, as a matter of fact. It risked alienating a powerful senator whose support is vital to the President. The summaries, like the tapes from which they were derived, were known to be equivocal and inconclusive, open to interpretations that might or might not be deemed to favor the Nixon cause. Thus it is that persuading Sen. Scott to defend the President and denounce John Dean the way he did may fairly be called an act of desperation.

Mr. Nixon knew when he delivered his Watergate peroration on State-of-the-Union night that a related development was about to compound his peril. The special Watergate prosecutor, Leon Jaworski, had on that day asked the President's chief Watergate lawyer, James D. St. Clair, for some more White House tapes and documents and St. Clair had indicated to Jaworski that Mr. Nixon was in the mood that he expressed when he said: "As you know, I have provided to the special prosecutor voluntarily a great deal of material. I believe that I have provided all the material that he needs to conclude his investigations and to proceed to prosecute the guilty and to clear the innocent. I believe the time has come to bring that investigation and the other investigations of this matter to an end. One year of Watergate is enough." The President's third assertion since November that he isn't going to quit and his qualified promise to cooperate with the House Judiciary Committee in its impeachment inquiry "in any way that I consider consistent with my responsibilities" obscured the indication in his reference to the special prosecutor that a confrontation similar to the one that ended last October with the dismissals of Archibald Cox and Deputy Attorney General William Ruckelshaus and the resignation of Attorney General Elliot Richardson could be in the offing.

Two happenings after the President spoke fired up Sen. Scott and

"And now, a man of great ideas . . . a natural born leader . . ."

entangled him in the differences with Cox's successor, Special
Prosecutor Jaworski. A Jaworski assistant, Richard J. Davis, told a
federal judge in Washington that "we have no basis for believing that
Mr. Dean has committed perjury in any proceeding." This observation was addressed only to a claim that Dean would not make a
believable prosecution witness in subsequent Watergate trials. It had
nothing directly to do with Sen. Scott's statements that Dean had lied
under oath about the President's knowledge of and involvement in
Watergate offenses and therefore was a perjurer. But it stimulated
derisory speculation, already rife in the senator's home-state press,
that Scott had let himself be made a White House dupe. He insisted to
the President and afterward to Gen. Haig that a Nixon spokesman
speak up for him, firmly and fast. The second event that magnified
Scott's anger and insistence was Leon Jaworski's appearance on
ABC's "Issues and Answers" TV program.

   Jaworski, coming over from the tube to this viewer like a parboiled
statesman of the law, carefully confined himself to citation of his
assistant's declaration in court that no basis had been found "for
believing that Mr. Dean has committed perjury." With a fine
distinction that probably escaped many viewers, he differentiated
between fallible memory and unintended errors and the sort of
deliberate lying that a conscientious prosecutor or judge treats as
punishable perjury. His meaningful remarks, the ones that shook the
Nixon legal establishment headed by James St. Clair, had to do with
the President's and his press spokesmen's assertions that Mr. Nixon
had "voluntarily" given the special prosecutor all the tapes and
documents "that he needs to conclude his investigations." Jaworski
said that he'd had to insist upon getting what he needed from the
White House and replied as follows to the President's contention that
the special prosecutor already had the evidence he needed: "Simply to
say that I have sufficient evidence to indict certain individuals is not
enough. That is not the criterion, as I see it." This view of the duty laid
upon him has to be read along with Jaworski's indication that he and
his staff have just about concluded that a sitting President cannot be
indicted. Jaworski seemed to be saying that, beyond indictments and
trials of Watergate offenders, he is obligated to determine and to say
whether in his opinion Mr. Nixon has committed or been responsible
for offenses for which he cannot be indicted but should be impeached.
   Jaworski said he'd been promised that he'd be told on the following

day whether he'd get from the White House the additional tapes and documents that he had requested. White House reporters, awaiting that news, got instead a written statement from the President's press spokesman, in the name of James St. Clair, asserting with studied contempt that "the Special Prosecutor and members of his staff have seen fit to discuss in public their views regarding John Dean's veracity." St. Clair said that "the tapes and other evidence furnished to the special prosecutor . . . do not support sworn statements made by Mr. Dean" and do "support what the President has said." The President's chief defender also said that the matter shouldn't be discussed "in the public media." Inasmuch as he, the President, Press Secretary Ronald Ziegler and Sen. Scott had been discussing it in the media, this seemed to be a rather dim way of giving Sen. Scott the support he'd been demanding, if that was what was intended. Scott understood that it was what was intended and his press spokesman said the senator appreciated the support.

Vice President Gerald Ford had said that he was offered a look at the summaries that Scott was shown and said no thanks. On CBS' "Face the Nation," he was asked why he refused to look at the evidence and responded: "Supposing I had looked at it, and supposing I was of a nature that I wanted to help myself get a higher position? I could interpret that information to my own personal good, and to harm the President. I don't think I should be in that position. I think it would be a very bad position, being number two, to misinterpret some information that might make it more difficult for the President and more beneficial to me." This extraordinary statement fascinated me for two reasons. It showed that Gerald Ford is thinking, as of course he must, about becoming Number One. The second reason is that Ford's statement was made in part upon the advice of White House counsellor Bryce Harlow, who has heard some of the recordings and read the summaries that sent Hugh Scott plunging out on his limb. So far as I know, Harlow has not lost confidence in Mr. Nixon and his chances of survival. But it's interesting that he's telling his friend the Vice President to take it slow and easy.

February 16, 1974

VI

Travels with Jerry

Vice President Gerald Ford was near the end of a long day of travel in Michigan, raising money for the state and national Republican party, when he briefly addressed some 6000 scoutmasters, den mothers and other adult leaders and supporters of the Boy Scouts of America in the Detroit area. The sight of several thousand grown men in Boy Scout uniforms, dining with their ladies and a smattering of actual Boy Scouts in Cobo Hall, a cavernous community center in Detroit, didn't faze Gerald Ford. The occasion pleased and stimulated him. It inspired remarks that seemed to me to tell more about the kind of man he is and the kind of man who soon could be President of the United States than anything he said at three press conferences, three receptions and a $100-a-plate dinner.

After Gov. William G. Milliken of Michigan introduced Ford as "a former Eagle Scout," the Vice President told how he attained that eminence during his youth in Grand Rapids and failed to earn the highest of three decorations that are open to zealous Eagle Scouts. The quoted words, condensed here for clarity but not otherwise altered, communicate the feel of the occasion only if you imagine the man erect and stolid at the microphones, speaking in his customarily flat and earnest tone, framing what he said to suit his hearers but doing it with an air of total sincerity. He said: "In 1925, at the age of 12, I became a tenderfoot. Over a period of several months I gradually moved up the ladder and finally I was lucky enough to get to be an Eagle Scout and went on with other efforts but never got that last, final thing. I got involved in athletics and never finally made the one thing I really wanted (that third and highest decoration). But the point is that with the help of my mother, my father, my scoutmaster, I and a group of us who joined scouting in September of 1925 really moved ahead in a great, great movement. Without any hesitation or qualification or reservation, I can say that to whatever extent I have been lucky or successful, scouting has contributed significantly. The people who guided me had a significant impact on me and I cherish those many moments at Boy Scout meetings and at various other activities. I know of no other movement that has as great an impact for good as the Boy Scouts of America." Amid thunderous applause, the Vice President proceeded from that hall to another Cobo cave where 1200 souls had paid $100 apiece for a plate of soggy meat loaf and the privilege of hearing him say that "the prophets of doom and gloom" and "the devils of doubt and despair" are not going to bring down either Richard Nixon or Republican candidates in 1974.

Ford had survived nine weeks in the vice presidency in what appeared to be good shape and spirits, despite some petty irritations. He was having more trouble than was generally known in getting approval of the size of staff that he thought he'd need. His office next door to the White House, as distinct from his smaller Capitol Hill office, was budgeted for 30 positions, the level to which the departed H. R. Haldeman had cut Spiro Agnew from a previous total of 40 in late 1972. Ford's staff chief, a former reporter named Robert Hartmann, wanted about 10 more, several of them in high-salaried (over $30,000) slots. He had to appeal to the President's staff chief, Gen. Alexander Haig, from the ruling of the Office of Management and Budget that 30 people at a cost of $625,000 in fiscal 1975 were all the new Vice President needed. Five clerks and secretaries who were helping Spiro Agnew in his transition from glory to hell were being paid from what was now Gerald Ford's 1974 budget, a fact that did not enthuse his assistants. Ford persuaded L. William Seidman, a friend, accountant, attorney and banker from the Vice President's home town of Grand Rapids, to join the staff as a consultant and analyze the probable needs. The operation being as modest as it is, the thought occurred to me that Seidman might be surveying the White House set-up and preparing to advise Ford on his staff requirements just in case he succeeded President Nixon. Seidman was so thoroughly startled and shaken when I broached this thought to him that I had to conclude that he indeed was aboard only for 60 days or so and was solely concerned with the vice presidential staff. "No way, no way!" he all but shouted when I asked him about it.

Some reporters and commentators made overly much in mid-January of the rumor that Nixon assistants had gulled and goaded Ford into denouncing "the AFL-CIO, the Americans for Democratic Action and other powerful pressure groups" for "stretching out the ordeal of Watergate for their own purposes" and "waging a massive propaganda campaign against the President." It seemed to many people, including influential Republicans, that Ford had foolishly impaired his stature and usefulness by excessive identification of himself with the President and his plight. Dark assumptions were drawn from the disclosure that two Nixon writers, David Gergen and Aram Bakshian, drafted the incendiary speech. Bakshian, the principal drafter, did write into the speech language close to that used by Ford in the quoted passage. But Bakshian did it at the suggestion of Robert Hartmann and Paul Miltich, Ford's press spokesman, and Ford himself toughened the passage up. Hartmann tried to hire Bakshian away from the President's staff before this happened. Bakshian declined the offer. One experienced political ghoster, Milton Friedman, has joined up as a Ford speech writer and a second writer is being sought. Gergen, the chief Nixon writer, understands that his and his staff's help will continue to be requested and welcomed now and then.

Vice President Agnew had a plane and crew permanently assigned to him from the air force's VIP "Special Mission" fleet of five Boeing 707s, five other and less opulent four-jet transports, 11 twin-engine Lockheed Jetstars and two twin-engine Turbo-prop Convairs. Two of the 707s are assigned to the President. Whichever of them he uses is Air Force One when he's on it. Except for very special journeys, Vice Presidents and such get Jetstars and Convairs. Ford gets one of them on request, but not always the same plane and crew. He got a Convair for the Michigan trip. It seats 35, cruises at 300 knots and—this being a political trip—cost the Republican National Committee $662 per hour for about six hours in the air plus a minimum charge of $1324 (two hours' air time). If Ford had used a 707 the committee would have had to pay $1701 per hour. The committee will recover several hundred dollars of the Convair's cost from the one writing reporter, three broadcasters, one TV producer and three TV camera crewmen who accompanied Ford. Agnew usually traveled with a posse of assistants. Ford took only one assistant, Paul Miltich, with him to Michigan.

The fact that I'm running out of space and quoting very little of what Ford said in Kalamazoo, Saginaw and Detroit deprives the public of practically nothing that it needs to know. More hecklers than friends greeted Ford at the dedication of a local party headquarters in Saginaw. He received their boos and signs ("Bury My Heart at Watergate") with cool indifference and said of other hecklers in Detroit: "Oh, I always look at them. I appreciate the right that they have to picket me and I equally have the right to disagree with them." He said at each press conference, as he's said again and again, that he has no intention of running for the presidency in 1976. When he was asked whether that would be true if he succeeded Mr. Nixon before 1976, he replied that "I don't like to speculate on something that I don't think is going to happen." Although he'd been told that he invited a suspicion that he was afraid he'd find evidence against the President if he read the transcripts of taped White House conversations connected with Watergate he persisted in saying he refused to do it because "if I was so disposed, which I am not, I might utilize that information for my own personal benefit" and in a way that could "adversely affect the President."

Ford said over and over in Kalamazoo, Saginaw and Detroit that 1973 was "a pretty good year" for the Nixon administration and the Republican party and that Republicans ought to be grateful to Richard Nixon rather than leery of him and his expected impact on the 1974 elections. The Vice President's Michigan friends hoped to raise $500,000 at the three receptions ($1000 per couple) and the dinner. They grossed $270,000.

February 23, 1974

———

For evidence that Vice President Ford was indeed thinking about being President Ford, and Seidman's place in these prospects, see Chapter XII. It turned out that the press fares went to the air force, not the national committee, via the Vice President's office.

VII

Plugging Away

The President resumed his usual and munificent mode of travel when he flew from Washington to Florida for five days of sun and work at his home on Key Biscayne and back to Washington by way of Huntsville, Alabama, and Indianapolis. There was no more of the economy that he displayed after Christmas, in a rather silly show of leadership in the fuel shortage, with a flight to California on a commercial airliner and return to Washington on a small air force plane. Then a great point was made of requiring White House assistants and other officials to shuttle between Washington and San Clemente on commercial aircraft. Locally obtained motorcars were used by the President and his staff at San Clemente and when he and his party drove across the mountains to Palm Springs.

Mr. and Mrs. Nixon flew to Florida with a sizable staff in the magnificent Boeing 707 that I call Air Force One and that he calls The Spirit of '76. One of the President's Lincoln limousines was flown in a military cargo plane to Miami, then to Huntsville and then back to Washington. When Gen. Alexander Haig, the President's staff chief, suddenly wanted two White House lawyers in Florida, they were flown there and back to Washington and Boston in a military plane.

When Julie Nixon Eisenhower fell sick in Indianapolis and entered a hospital for surgery, a military jet flew Mrs. Nixon and Rear Adm. William Lukash, the assistant White House physician, from Florida to Indianapolis. David Eisenhower went from Washington to Indianapolis in another military passenger plane. When the Nixons returned to Washington with Julie and David Eisenhower aboard Air Force One, a helicopter transported the family from Andrews Air Force Base to the White House. Nineteen large, black and chauffeured Chrysler sedans from the White House fleet awaited other passengers from Air Force One. Four of the cars were for Alabama's Democratic senators and two of its Republican congressmen who had traveled north with the President. The other 15 Chryslers were for White House assistants. The 19 cars were parked quite a distance from the President's plane and, when they moved together toward it with headlights shining in the dusk, they resembled a clutch of crawling, luminescent beetles.

The White House press corps was in a poor position to object to this exercise in conspicuous consumption at a time of shortage for most people. The usual press plane wasn't chartered by the White House transportation office for the post-Christmas expedition to California. When I noted then that reporters, cameramen and technicians assigned to the White House beat got a useful lesson in arranging their own air passage, hotel rooms and hire cars, I flattered both the White House establishment and the White House press. Everything but a chartered plane was arranged as usual for the media in California and was welcomed as usual. For the Florida trip the White House transportation staff first chartered an airliner that was just big enough to accommodate the 76 working professionals who signed for the journey. A clamor arose for space enough for the family dependents who usually infest press charters on the Florida and California trips. The employers of the working passengers pay on a prorated basis for the plane and accompanying services at rates substantially higher than first-class fares. Dependents travel at drastically cut rates ($75 for the round trip to and from Florida, $150 to and from California for adults, $25 for children). The harried transportation staff finally found an available airliner big enough for workers and their loved ones, costing at least $1000 more than the smaller plane would have cost. As it happened 22 wives, one husband and 15 children, aged one to 17, were packed into the press plane with the working passengers—"like sardines," chief transportation officer Ray Zook said, overlooking the fact that sardines don't cry and occupy toilets. One of the parental beneficiaries of this system, emerging fron the press plane at Andrews AFB with his wife and young son in tow, literally choked up with outrage when he saw the 19 Chryslers. He growled that the spectacle was OBSCENE! He was right, but in the circumstances I managed to restrain my dander.

Mr. Nixon was trying to tell the country something with his return to what for him was travel normalcy. He was saying that he wasn't scared anymore or anyhow wasn't going to act as if he were scared. Not of Watergate and its dreadful effects upon him as a person and a President. Not of the energy crisis, with the political effects of its impact upon most Americans. When he chose or needed to travel, he was going to do it in presidential style (as I've written and continue to believe he should, maybe keeping those 19 Chryslers out of sight). What was seen during the recent days of rest and travel was a facet of the varied effort to demonstrate that Richard Nixon is confident of himself and his future, determined to serve out his second term and prepared to see the developing impeachment process all the way through House committee and floor consideration and, if need be, through trial in the Senate. Getting around among his White House people to the extent I can, I find absolutely no indication or admission that his determination is any other and any less than he says it is. Occasional glimpses of the President at the White House and the sight of him during two speeches on the recent trip make it impossible to believe that he is as confident of survival in office as he says he is and as the few associates who are enough with him to have a useful judgment say he tells them he is. This President appears to me to be a tortured man, intermittently close to collapse, not physically as healthy as his principal physician, Maj. Gen. Walter Tkach, said he was after putting him through a delayed examination before he went to Florida. The President had a tan that looked as if it were real at the beginning of his four full days in Florida. At the end of the stay, much of the daytime part of it spent strolling and sitting and talking in the sun with his friend and neighbor, Charles G. (Bebe) Rebozo, the tan had deepened. But something in the total look of the President seemed to me to attest a pain, a weariness, a state of body and mind that could result only from illness that Dr. Tkach says isn't there or from a subtler toll of the pressures that beat upon Richard Nixon.

The toll is the kind the President reflected when he spoke in his fifth State-of-the-Union address of "a new effort to replace the discredited President" and corrected himself. He'd meant to say and finally said "discredited present welfare system."

Mr. Nixon told us how he wants to appear to be, and perhaps how he believes himself to be, when he visited the Lincoln Memorial and spoke of Abraham Lincoln on his birthday, February 12. "No President in history," this President said, "has been more vilified during his time in the presidency than Lincoln." Mr. Nixon recalled that people who knew Lincoln well wrote that "he was very deeply hurt by what was said about him and drawn about him, but on the other hand Lincoln had that great strength of character never to display it, always to stand tall and strong and firm no matter how harsh or unfair the criticism might be." Perhaps more than anything else, President Nixon said, President Lincoln was admired for his "poise under pressure." At Huntsville on the following Monday, legally though not actually George Washington's birthday, the President again portrayed himself as he wants to be perceived when he addressed crippled Gov. George Wallace and a crowd, mostly of friends, that exceeded 20,000 and could have run to 40,000. The attempt at persuasive and suggestive portrayal came when the President said with typically confused syntax: "The American people are not a nation of quitters. We are a nation that will keep fighting on until we, as Winston Churchill once said, speaking in another context, he said, 'We did not journey all this way across the centuries, across the oceans and across the mountains and across the prairies because we were made of sugar candy.' " Apart from whatever good the President's appearance at Huntsville did him, Gov. Wallace's appearance usefully instructed journalists and others who may harbor the notion that he has an active national future despite his shattered spine. Watching him worn and wasted in his wheelchair and being lifted in visible agony to the microphone for a few words of welcome to the President, it was hard to believe that George Wallace can ever again campaign for national office or greatly influence the campaigns of others.

In Miami, dedicating a new hospital wing and promoting his revised national health insurance proposals along with the message that his survival in the presidency for three more years is essential to the peace of the world, Mr. Nixon showed himself as he really is under the stress of Watergate. How he appeared in nationally televised snatches, I don't know. To me in his audience, standing within 50 feet of him, he seemed to be under remarkable control and in peril of losing control. An invited audience of some 2000 friendlies sat immediately in front of and on each side of him. His only truly public audience consisted of about 250 people in the street in front of him and beyond the roped enclosure. Perhaps 50 of these people were friendly. Two hundred were loudly and cruelly hostile. Many of them carried "Impeach Nixon" signs and chanted, "Impeach Nixon Now." He hated it and them. He had to look at their signs only when he faced straight ahead or to his left. Mostly he looked to his right, his face tight and drawn beneath the tan, occasionally gripping the podium with his hands in a discernible spasm of repressed reaction.

Before the President left Florida his assistants and lawyers had to deal twice again with the White House tapes issue. Special Prosecutor Leon Jaworski told the Senate Judiciary Committee that the President had refused to deliver 27 requested recordings of White House conversations. The President's chief Watergate defender, James St. Clair, said in an explanatory statement that the requested tapes and documents had been and would continue to be withheld because their surrender wouldn't importantly assist the Watergate prosecutions and would gravely breach presidential confidentiality. A *Washington Post* report suggesting but not actually alleging that two previously subpoenaed and surrendered White House tapes were possibly altered copies and not originals, as a court had been told, sent Mr. Nixon's chief assistant, Gen. Haig, up the wall in a condition of pointless and exaggerated rage that indicated the extent of paranoia, frustration and fear behind the White House facade of confidence. While damning and denying the *Post* report, Haig took occasion to say that a defective recorder had caused an 18-minute gap in a crucial tape. A day earlier Press Secretary Ronald Ziegler had said nobody at the White House knew what caused the gap.

Mr. Nixon left Florida, stopped in at Huntsville and flew to Indianapolis to retrieve his daughter Julie from the hospital on the day when a Democrat was winning a congressional seat held by Republicans for 63 years and by the new Vice President, Gerald Ford, for 25 years. At Huntsville, hours before this devastating news from Michigan was known, the President tried to boost the spirits of some

30 Alabama Republicans in a private chat. "You keep plugging away," he told them, "and I'll keep plugging away, and we'll all be all right." He wants to believe this. Maybe he does.

March 2, 1974

VIII

Desperation

If Mr. Nixon knew what a story going around Washington had him knowing when he strode into the East Room at the White House for his 36th press conference in five years, he showed it only in a most oblique and curious way. What the story had him knowing was that evidence gathered by the special Watergate prosecutor, Leon Jaworski, incriminated him so clearly and seriously that he would be in the shocking array of former associates and assistants who were about to be indicted by a Watergate grand jury if he were not the President. Jaworski was known to doubt that an incumbent President is subject to indictment and to have decided that it would be improper and unfair to name Mr. Nixon as an unindicted co-conspirator. The implication of these views was that any evidence in the hands of the special prosecutor and involving the President would be passed, in one way or another, to the House Judiciary Committee for its use in deciding whether to tell the House of Representatives that Mr. Nixon should be impeached.

One of the few White House assistants who is in close and regular touch with the President said after the press conference and a couple of days before Jaworski was expected to present a batch of Watergate indictments to federal Judge John Sirica that Mr. Nixon had not indicated in any fashion to anybody that he knew or believed the evidence involving him to be as serious and substantial as the cited story assumed. But it was a believable story, if for no other reason than that the President surely knew the import of the White House tapes and documents that had been given to the special prosecutor. I'm persuaded that Mr. Nixon was indeed reflecting the knowledge that the story assumed when he said with a show of total assurance at his press conference that he did not expect to be impeached and did expect to serve out his second term. Mr. Nixon's show of confidence seemed to me to be the performance of a President who knows that he is in desperate straits and has concluded that his only hope of salvation lies in pretending to the very last that he is safe and innocent.

Reporters who were seated along the aisle the President used when he walked to the East Room podium heard him breathing hard before he faced the microphones and cameras. The last time I heard him breathing that audibly was August 22, at a press conference in San Clemente, when he was still recovering from viral pneumonia. Mr. Nixon always sweats at press conferences, whether or not he is under television lights. This time sweat appeared on his upper lip sooner than usual, before he was done with a transparently wishful statement about the energy shortages to the effect that "while the crisis has been passed, the problem remains." The President told some of his assistants afterward that he thought the conference went well for him and he was probably right. With a couple of exceptions, the reporters failed to assist him on this occasion with the animal cries for recognition that aroused sympathy for him at his last conference on October 26. The generally moderate tone of the questions, including some tough ones, fitted with his desire to project an impression of quiet confidence. In his answer to one of the questions, a request for his "personal reaction" to the expulsion of Aleksandr Solzhenitsyn from the Soviet Union, the President reminded us of how effective he can be when he is stating a sound position. He said that he admired Solzhenitsyn for showing "such great courage" and continued: ". . . if I thought that breaking relations with the Soviets or turning off our policy of negotiation and turning back to confrontation would help him or help thousands of others like him in the Soviet Union, we might do that." He wasn't going to do that because the two nuclear powers must recognize their differences and also recognize "the fact that we must either live together or we will all die together."

It was inevitable, however, that his press conference would be remembered chiefly for Mr. Nixon's answers to questions about and related to scandals and conduct associated with Watergate, and for his manner when he answered some of them. His most interesting physical reaction occurred when he was asked whether he believed that the conduct that led to the resignation of former Vice President Agnew last October "brought dishonor upon his office, this Administration and the country." The president turned away from his questioner. Reporters who were seated where they could see him in profile saw him shudder. What seemed on the spot to be a very long moment passed before Mr. Nixon turned back and answered in part: "It would be very easy for me to jump on the Vice President (he noticeably didn't say former Vice President) when he is down. I can only say that . . . he rendered dedicated service in all of the assignments that I gave him . . . . Now at this point I am not going to join anybody else in kicking him when he is down."

Mr. Nixon was at his scabrous worst when he dealt with two questions about his tax situation and the huge deduction that he took for the donation of his vice presidential papers to the National Archives. He said with a faint but detectable leer that he'd be glad to pay state and local taxes in California if he were required to "and, of course, deduct that from my federal income tax liability." He said again that he'd taken his vice presidential papers deduction on the advice of Lyndon Johnson, who isn't around to say whether this is true, and that anyhow he'd only done what President Johnson, Hubert Humphrey, John Kenneth Galbraith and Jerome Wiesner among others had done. Galbraith took a modest deduction and Wiesner took no deduction for donations of papers. The question that brought on the snide reference to them was, "Now Mr. President, do you think you paid your fair share of taxes?" Mr. Nixon didn't answer it.

The President added nothing that wasn't known or anticipated to the defensive position that he is shaping up against impeachment and resignation. But the sum of his replies made his position and intentions clear beyond dispute. When he said, "I do not expect to be impeached," he reflected the guidance on present sentiment in the House of Representatives that he was getting from such informants and advisers as counsellor Bryce Harlow. Mr. Nixon omitted the qualification that was usually attached to this guidance: namely, that he's probably safe from impeachment IF nothing new and serious in the way of scandal or proof of his involvement develops. Whether the President is impeached may turn upon whether a House majority requires proof of criminal and indictable conduct before it will vote impeachment. Mr. Nixon at his press conference took the narrow and, for him, prudent view that "a criminal offense on the part of the President is the requirement" and indicated that his chief Watergate lawyer, James St. Clair, would soon submit a brief to that effect. A Justice Department study suggested that grave but not necessarily indictable offenses against the state could justify impeachment. In terms that were ominous for this President, the House Judiciary Committee's legal staff declared that the impeachment of a President should be "predicated . . . upon conduct seriously incompatible with either the constitutional form and principles of our government or the proper performance of duties of the presidential office." In short, in the staff's opinion, criminal and indictable conduct did not have to be alleged and proved.

In essence Richard Nixon relies upon the presidency to protect and preserve his presidency. He said that he'd cooperate with the Judiciary Committee's inquiry "in any way consistent with my constitutional responsibility to defend the office of the presidency against any action which would weaken that office and the ability of future Presidents to carry out the great responsibilities that any President will have." When he was asked whether he'd reconsider his determination never to resign if it became evident that his continuance in office doomed the Republican party to "disastrous defeat" in this year's elections, he answered: "No. I want my party to succeed but, more important, I want the presidency to survive, and it is vitally important in this nation that the presidency of the United States not be hostage to what happens to the popularity of a President at one time or another." Congressmen will be less likely to impeach, senators less likely to convict if they are convinced that "the popularity of a President" rather than the conduct of this President is the controlling factor. In the unlikely event that he gets by with his conception and defense of "the office of the presidency," Mr. Nixon may be enabled to withhold from the Judiciary Committee White

House evidence that would make impeachment certain, conviction
probable and resignation wise.

March 9, 1974

————

Jaworski had personally assured Gen. Alexander Haig back at the
turn of December-January that he shared the view of his predecessor,
Archibald Cox, that naming the President as an unindicted co-
conspirator would unfairly and simultaneously pillory him and deny
him the opportunity to disprove the charge. This remained
Jaworski's view into February and early March. The only believable
explanation I heard of why Jaworski finally permitted the grand jury
to name, without indicting, the President as a co-conspirator is that
he decided that his case against the indicted defendants could not be
constructed and sustained unless he did so. The issue eventually
became whether the others could be prosecuted if the President was
not also charged.

IX

Indictments

The White House story was that Mr. Nixon received in utter calm, with no discernible show of shock or disturbance or regret, the news on March 1 that seven of his former associates and assistants, including four men who were at the pinnacle of his administration among the closest to him during his first term, had been indicted by a federal grand jury. All of them were charged with conspiring and four of them were charged with acting to conceal the nature and extent of the original Watergate crime—the break-in and electronic bugging at the Democratic National Committee's Washington office—and to minimize its consequences for the President and his presidency. After all, the story of Mr. Nixon's glacial performance went, the indictment was expected. He and everyone around him understood that this indictment was going to be followed by others that could be even more damning in what they implied about him and the Nixon presidency. Twenty-eight people who had been associated in some way and degree with the Nixon White House or the Nixon reelection campaign in 1972 had already been indicted and 15 of them had pleaded guilty or been convicted. So there was nothing in the March 1 indictment to get all that excited or worried about. The very senior

White House official who said this to me had the wit and grace to add that the President, of course, was not *pleased* by the indictment. But he took it in stride, so it was said, and he was pleased—definitely pleased—with the Watergate situation as he saw it shaping up for him on the whole. Mr. Nixon was said to be pleased because facts were beginning to replace rumor and innuendo and, most of all, because both the judicial and congressional processes connected with Watergate were moving toward a conclusion.

Such was the response that the President evidently wanted inquirers to believe he had to the indictment of former Attorney General John N. Mitchell; H. R. Haldeman, the former chief of the White House staff; John D. Ehrlichman, who had been the assistant for domestic affairs; and Charles Colson, who during the latter part of his service as special counsel to the President and especially during the 1972 reelection campaign spent more time with Mr. Nixon than anybody on the staff except Haldeman. Robert Mardian, another of the indicted seven, had served the President at the White House, at the Justice Department, and at the committee that nominally managed Mr. Nixon's 1972 reelection. Kenneth Parkinson, also indicted, had been that committee's chief attorney. Gordon Strachan, the seventh and most junior of the March 1 defendants, had been on Haldeman's personal staff and had handled much of Haldeman's communication with the reelection committee. Haldeman said at his home in Los Angeles that he and the President talked by telephone after he was indicted. Mr. Nixon didn't want it known that he talked to any of the seven. Once the fact that he called Haldeman on March 1 was out, the President ordered a spokesman to say that he had congratulated Haldeman on his 25th wedding anniversary. The anniversary was February 19.

Haldeman was charged with conspiracy, obstructing justice and perjury. The three perjury counts affected the President in a direct and damaging way. They had to do with whether the President knew about, condoned and perhaps authorized the payment of hush money to the lawyers and families of men who organized and carried out the Watergate burglary and bugging. John W. Dean, the fired and indicted White House lawyer who managed this aspect of the Watergate aftermath, told the Senate Watergate committee last summer that Mr. Nixon knew all about it and remarked, during a conversation in his White House office last March, that raising a

"Snow White's still at large"

million dollars for the Watergate defendants wouldn't be a problem. Haldeman, who was present for part of the conversation in question and had listened to a taped recording of all of it, testified that "The President said, there is no problem in raising a million dollars, we can do that, but it would be wrong." Mr. Nixon said at a press conference August 22, 1973, that Haldeman's account was accurate, Dean's inaccurate and false. After hearing the same recording of the conversation that Haldeman had heard, the special Watergate prosecutor and the Watergate grand jury charged in the indictment that Haldeman lied under oath when he swore that the President had said that "it would be wrong."

If Haldeman had lied, the President had lied. Much was made of the fact, belatedly discovered and published by William Safire, a former Nixon speech writer who now writes a column for *The New York Times,* that Haldeman in his original, written statement to the Senate committee paraphrased the President and didn't put the "it would be wrong" line between quotation marks. The committee stenotypist and the drafters of the indictment put the disputed words between quotation marks. It was an interesting but essentially pointless point. The President either had or hadn't said that raising the million "would be wrong" (or "wrong"). It developed during the subsequent controversy that the President said it or something very like it, but not explicitly about raising the money. He said it about the related suggestion that he promise executive clemency to the Watergate seven. Mr. Nixon indicated at the August 22 press conference and said at another press conference on March 6, his second within 10 days, that when he said "it is wrong" he referred specifically to clemency but "meant that the whole transaction was wrong." If it be true, and what I hear at the White House and at the office of the special prosecutor inclines me to believe it is true, that the charge against Haldeman on this score is simply that he applied the questioned remark to the wrong part of the conversation, any reasonable person must conclude that the prosecutor was either irresponsible or after Haldeman and his confederates for something else. The something else is made clear in the indictment. It says that the following "overt acts" occurred immediately after the President, Haldeman and Dean discussed hush money and clemency. Haldeman telephoned Mitchell. Mitchell instructed Fred LaRue, a previously indicted Mitchell and Nixon associate to pay approximately $75,000 to an attorney for Howard Hunt, one of the convicted Watergate defendants. LaRue arranged this payment. The next day "Mitchell assured Ehrlichman that E. Howard Hunt, Jr., was not a 'problem' any longer." Ehrlichman thereupon told Egil Krogh, a previously indicted and convicted White House assistant, "that Ehrlichman did not believe that E. Howard Hunt, Jr., would reveal certain matters." These are allegations. They have yet to be proved. But, set forth as charged fact in the indictment, they chill this reader. It is impossible to believe that they don't chill the President.

At his March 6 press conference and during the five days preceding it, Mr. Nixon acted as if he were thoroughly atop his situation. He had his chief defender, James St. Clair, assure federal Judge John Sirica that all of the White House tapes and documents that had been provided to the special prosecutor and to the grand juries investigating various categories of Watergate offenses would be given to the House Judiciary Committee for its inquiry into whether a bill of impeachment should be reported to the House of Representatives. The grand jury had recommended to Judge Sirica that he turn over the same material to the committee, along with a summary of evidence that seemed to the jurors to bear upon the involvement of the President. Judge Sirica made it clear at a hearing that he was troubled by the arguments of the indicted defendants' attorneys that their clients' rights would be jeopardized if he surrendered the White House evidence and other evidence collected by the special prosecutor to the House committee. If the President and his lawyers were troubled by the same possibility, they suppressed the concern. The President's promise to give the material to the committee appeared to be unqualified. He resisted some of its demands for other White House evidence. But he offered to give sworn answers to written interrogatories and also to answer under oath, informally and at the White House, any questions that the committee's chairman and ranking Republican member might wish to put to him. Limited and reluctantly offered though they were, these were substantial concessions. They strengthened the impression, previously reported, that the President is frightened and has good reason to be.

March 16, 1974

X

Having Fun

It was good to see the President having fun in Nashville on March 16. Watching him at the airport, greeting Mrs. Nixon when she returned on her 62nd birthday from ceremonial visits to Venezuela and Brazil, and then at the new Grand Ole Opry House, lapping up the plaudits of performers who perpetrate and people who enjoy the many variations of the rhythmic rural whine known as country music, I was overwhelmed with a wish that the occasion could really be as happy for the President as he and his hosts tried to make it seem to be.

Of course it wasn't and couldn't be all that happy. Tennessee's Republican Gov. Winfield Dunn knew better than to settle for simply telling the airport crowd that it was about to welcome "our great and our beloved President." He was constrained to continue: "I know you will want to show our President every courtesy. But most especially let me ask you, my fellow Tennesseeans, for your thoughtful courtesy to his lovely wife—remembering that this is her birthday, remembering that she is the beautiful and charming first lady of America, and keeping this in mind when we welcome her as considerately and courteously as we possibly can." Thanks to the preparatory care exercised by the governor's state policemen and by local party loyalists, the crowd in the hangar where the initial ceremonies occurred was friendly and abundantly equipped with pro-Nixon signs. It cheered a country music singer and author, Fred Boyd, when he chanted in the nasal manner of his ilk: "Stand up and cheer for Richard Nixon/For he's the President of our great land./I've been hearing talk about impeaching/The man we chose to lead us through these times./But talk like this could weaken and defeat us,/Let's show the world we're not the quitting kind." Hundreds of sheets with the words of this ballad, sung to the tune of "Okie from Muskogee," were distributed in the hangar. The sentiments of a smaller but sizable crowd just outside the hangar and near the podium were expressed by such signs as "OPRY YES, NIXON NO" and "THROW THE BUM OUT."

Mrs. Nixon was received with admiring yells and screams and no audible rudeness when her husband escorted her from the presidential jet that had brought her from Brazil. She seemed to be happy and poised, and she was obviously clued in to the preferred theme of the day, when she told the crowd that the statesmen whom she met on her trip "wanted me to convey the message that they support us in our quest for peace." A few hours earlier she was anything but happy and poised. Reporters who accompanied her to the inaugurals of new Presidents in Venezuela and Brazil said that she grew angry when, on her plane near the end of the trip, she was asked how she had stood the strains of the past year. Her voice was said to be shaking with pain and rage when she answered, "No, I really don't wish to speak of it. It's just a personal thing, and why bring that into the trip?" Although shouts of "Impeach Nixon" and worse troubled the President as they always do, he didn't flinch and he didn't scowl as darkly as he usually does. He appeared to be enjoying himself, at the top of his form, and taking conscious pleasure in the skill with which he linked his wife's trip to Latin America with his trips in 1972 to Communist China and the Soviet Union, his labors for "a generation of peace," and the implication that it was his duty and his hearers' duty to "see to it that America is not only strong militarily but that we will be the world leader, which it is our destiny to be, because without our leadership there cannot be peace." After that he didn't need to say that without three more years of RN there cannot be peace.

At the new Opry House, a $15 million testament in red brick to the fact that country music is both a national habit and a thriving industry, the President's audience included Governors George Wallace of Alabama and William Waller of Mississippi, Tennessee's Republican senators and congressmen, and some 4500 citizens who were prepared to be nice to anybody who professed to share their liking for their favorite art form. Mr. Nixon not only professed to like it; he equated it with "faith in God . . . love of this nation, patriotism, . . . those combinations which are so essential to America's character." At this point, so help me, the President managed once more to drag in his peace-and-strength-with-Nixon theme. This he did by saying that country music expresses the best in American character "at a time that America needs character because today— one serious note—let me tell you, the peace of the world for generations, maybe centuries to come, will depend not just on America's military might, which is the greatest in the world, or our wealth, which is the greatest in the world, but it is going to depend on our character, our belief in ourselves, our love of our country, our willingness not only to wear the flag but to stand up for the flag, and country music does that."

Mr. Nixon's principal greeter and adorer on the stage was Roy Acuff, a veteran practitioner of the art who has been a guest and performer at the White House. Reporters who follow the President will never forget Acuff at a 1972 campaign rally in North Carolina, bellowing over and over in his raspy drawl: "FOH MOH YEHS! FOH MOH YEHS!" He didn't call for three moh yehs in Nashville, but at the end of the Acuff-Nixon performance he did lead a gaggle of country singers in a plea to "stay around a little longer." He twice called the President to the piano, once to play "My Wild Irish Rose" and the second time to play and sing "God Bless America." It's one of Mr. Nixon's favorite acts—he'd done it three nights before at the White House, after a dinner for the nation's governors. This time, though, he put on the act with more verve and less pretense at embarrassment and reluctance than he usually displays. His arms flailed at the piano with great abandon and he looked as if he were having a really splendid time. Presented with a copy of the yellow yo-yo that Acuff flips and twirls when he sings, the President made a show of his awkward attempts to master it and elicited a burst of laughter from the enthralled audience when he said to Acuff, "I'll stay here and try to work this yo-yo. You go back and try to be President."

When he moved about the stage, from his chair to the piano and the microphones, Mr. Nixon walked with the odd, mincing prance that he frequently affects in moments of exuberance. There have been times and occasions, such as his appearance at a veterans' convention in New Orleans last August, when the sight has inspired reporters in his party to make some extremely unkind cracks. This time it didn't. The reporters took it to be one more sign that Mr. Nixon really was having fun.

The Nashville visit was one of a series of public performances that the President and his staff advisers expect to help him mightily in his struggle for survival. It followed press conferences on February 25 and March 6 and fell between question-answer sessions at the Executives Club in Chicago and the 1974 convention of the National Association of Broadcasters in Houston. He challenged Congress to "get off its duff" and enact the legislation that he thinks he needs to deal with fuel and other energy problems. He warned the European members of NATO and the Common Market that they can't indefinitely enjoy US military and nuclear protection and at the same time indulge in "basic hostility" toward the US in political and economic matters. He warned the governments of Arab oil countries that they can't bludgeon the US into friendship for them and hostility toward Israel with their oil embargo and rocketing oil prices. This and more of the same comprised, quite obviously, a studied endeavor to show the nation a bold, vigorous and confident President who was not and never would be intimidated by Watergate troubles and pressures. Much of it, particularly the harsh warning to Western Europe, struck many people as a contrived and dangerous departure from prudence and a crass appeal for conservative support against the critics in Congress and elsewhere, including a growing number of Republicans, who would impeach him if they couldn't drive him to resignation. But the notion that it was all contrived, faked and worse than useless was mistaken. French Foreign Minister Michel Jobert, hitherto the most hostile and obstreperous among European opponents of American policy, responded with unaccustomed mildness to the President's strictures. A frequent domestic critic, *The Washington Post,* said editorially that Mr. Nixon's stance toward Europe was "right on the merits." The chief Arab oil producers lifted their embargo, though with a warning that it will be restored this summer if the US shows what the Arabs consider to be undue favoritism for Israel. On balance the President's attempt at a display of tough realism seemed to have done the country no harm and may have done it and him some good.

So much could not be said for Mr. Nixon's show of toughness in dealing with his Watergate problems. It was acknowledged at the White House, quietly and with manifest reluctance, that the President in person directed and to some extent orchestrated the aggressive defense that he and his spokesmen undertook with ever-mounting vigor and acerbity. His communications director, Ken W. Clawson, accused the House Judiciary Committee's chief attorney, John Doar, of trying to "hoodwink" the committee and deceive the public with a false and understated account of the volume of evidence the committee was demanding from the White House. The President's chief Watergate defender, James St. Clair, broke out of his hitherto total isolation from the media and "went public" with a series of newspaper and television interviews. His themes were that his client was the presidency rather than this particular President; that the Judiciary Committee already had or was getting from the White House all the tapes and documentary evidence it needed to conclude its impeachment inquiry quickly and fairly; and that, in any case, the committee had no right to demand and get more evidence until it evaluated what it already had and, beyond all else, defined what it would and wouldn't hold to be impeachable offenses. Clawson and staff counsellor Bryce Harlow, normally a cautious and soft-spoken fellow, denounced Rep. Wilbur Mills of Arkansas, chairman of the House Ways and Means Committee and vice chairman of the Joint Committee on Internal Revenue Taxation, for saying, in terms that implied a suspicion of fraudulent conduct, that the joint committee report on the President's tax behavior would complete his disgrace and force him to quit.

Doar had indeed and substantially understated the committee staff's demands for White House evidence. Mills said in a tone of apology that he hadn't meant to suggest that the President was guilty of tax fraud, though others in his service might be. But the main effect of the Nixon tactics was to stiffen Wilbur Mills in his attitude of scorn and distrust and to highlight his opinion that the President had been foolishly and fatally shoddy in his tax practices. The effort to divide Judiciary Committee Republicans from committee Democrats, committee moderates from committee radicals, and the committee as a whole from its Democratic and Republican staff attorneys, proved to be a miserable failure. John Doar, Republican attorney Albert Jenner, Democratic chairman Peter Rodino and the senior Republican member, Edward Hutchinson of Michigan, concluded in unison that the President had been trying to trap them into the premature issuance of a subpoena for additional White House evidence. Had such a tactic succeeded, it could have had the effect of drawing the impeachment issue on grounds of procedure and executive confidentiality rather than upon the more critical and, for Mr. Nixon, dangerous grounds of presidential behavior.

There were increasing indications that the President knew about and may have authorized payments of Republican campaign money to the original Watergate conspirators and burglars in order to keep them from revealing higher level involvement. Mr. Nixon said in a statement August 15, 1973, that his fired, indicted and convicted White House lawyer, John Dean, didn't tell him on March 21, 1973, that payments for silence had been made. The President said at his press conference on March 6 that Dean did tell him that hush money had been paid. The heated discussion of this clear contradiction overlooked Mr. Nixon's statement at a press conference in California on August 22, 1973, seven days after he had said he hadn't been told of payments for silence, that "Basically, what Mr. Dean was concerned about on March 21 was not so much the raising of money for the defendants but the raising of money for the defendants for the purpose of keeping them still. In other words, so-called hush money." Although the President in this statement stopped short of saying that he'd been told of hush money payments, he acknowledged in it that he was told that this was the intended purpose. The Watergate indictment returned on March 1 charged that a payment of $75,000 in hush money followed the March 21, 1973, conference within hours. The grand jury that returned the indictment asked federal Judge John Sirica to give the House Judiciary Committee the evidence on which it was based and a report summarizing some of that evidence. Judge Sirica, announcing on March 18 his decision to give the evidence and report to the House committee, identified "the person on whom the report focuses" as "the President of the United States." The judge said that the report "draws no accusatory conclusions," thereby seeming to confirm published suggestions that it lists and summarizes but does not evaluate evidence that involves the President. In obvious though unstated awareness of authoritative rumors that Special Prosecutor Leon Jaworski would have asked the grand jury to indict the President if he had believed, which he didn't, that an incumbent President is subject to criminal indictment, Judge Sirica said that the report "is not a substitute for indictments where indictments might properly issue." That observation deserves a lot of pondering. It suggests that Mr. Nixon won't be having fun much longer.

March 30, 1974

———

My editors noted at the end of the foregoing article that I had won the George Polk Memorial Award for outstanding magazine reporting.

XI

Rays of Hope

An outsider at the White House during the last fortnight of March had cause to wonder whether the real world was the one from which he came or the world within the West Wing and the Executive Office Building across the street. The impression in the outer world was that the President's Watergate troubles deepened by the day and that the consequent pressures upon him to save the country from the agonies of impeachment by resigning steadily increased. In Mr. Nixon's White House world the predominant and conveyed impression was that his situation and his prospects of survival in office were steadily improving. The rays of hope were rather faint and they tended to flicker as the inquirer went from office to office. But the hope existed, it was seldom noted in the continuing torrent of Watergate and related reports, and it therefore is dealt with here at some length.

A chief source of what confidence there is at the White House— and, in simple truth, there is more of it than the public is led to suppose—is the President's demeanor and behavior as they are observed and sensed when he and his people are out of general sight. At such times, of course, the President and his assistants are out of a reporter's sight, too, and the available accounts come from interested parties. This circumstance must not be allowed to invalidate everything the reporter hears from interested parties. What follows about the President's private demeanor and behavior, and their effect upon the few who serve and observe him at close quarters and the many who serve him at a distance, is a distillation of what I'm told and find believable.

Mr. Nixon has not been acting of late like a frightened and preoccupied President. His attention to business and particularly to domestic business, which is likely to be more indicative than his ballyhooed concern with and oversight of Henry Kissinger's conduct of foreign affairs, is said to be close, continuous and knowledgeable. Kenneth Cole, who succeeded departed and indicted John Ehrlichman as the President's assistant for domestic affairs in early 1973, usually communicates with Mr. Nixon and gets directions from Mr. Nixon through either Gen. Alexander Haig, the White House staff chief, or counsellor Bryce Harlow, who says he will soon be going back to private employment as Procter and Gamble's Washington lobbyist. In the month or so preceding March 30, Cole is said to have been in more frequent and direct communication with the President than ever before. Mr. Nixon's main interests in the fields with which Cole deals have been in legislation concerned with education, housing, transportation, legal services, the minimum wage and campaign reform.

For example, the President has insisted that he be kept in detailed touch with the progress of legislation that, in its House version, would restrict busing for purposes of racial integration in the public schools and, in the Senate version, would sustain and promote busing where it's deemed necessary. Mr. Nixon prefers the House version and has said he would veto the Senate version. With the busing part of this legislation—there are other important facets of it, including consolidated federal grants with minimal federal control—the President is back on a line of popular appeal that he exploited before the Watergate scandals broke upon him. It is currently calculated to hold the conservative support he desperately needs. Aside from merits and motives, however, the point here is that he appears to the subordinates handling the legislation to be very much atop the problem and in close command of White House and departmental efforts to get it resolved in his way. In a related situation, cited by White House officials to make the same point, the President allowed the civil rights division of the Department of Justice to sue to break up Louisiana's system of basically segregated white and black colleges only after he had been shown in detail and convinced that the course taken was the less offensive of two undesirable choices. The alternative was to move administratively to cut off federal funds for Louisiana colleges. As anyone familiar with the President's views would expect, he would have preferred to let well enough alone and avoid any action. So, in fairness to him, would black educators who resist and deplore the erosion of black colleges in the name and for the sake of integration. Once Mr. Nixon was convinced that the law and a court decision required some federal action to bring about the consolidation of Louisiana's dual system, he chose litigation because it offered both black and white proponents of the existing system a better chance to preserve it than arbitrary administrative action would have offered. Whatever this choice may say about the President, it said to his White House assistants that he had taken the time to deal in detail and in person with a problem that a totally isolated and preoccupied President might never have heard of. For them, what they knew and were told of his conduct in this and other instances was more effective than the Nixon rhetoric about preserving the presidency for future Presidents and refusing to let his presidency and the country be dragged down by Watergate.

Some of the notions and attitudes that accompany a surprisingly high level of White House confidence seem to me to defy rational explanation. What is one to say, for instance, of Nixon assistants who interpret federal Judge John Sirica's opinion of March 18 to be a good omen for the President? This was the opinion in which Judge Sirica explained his decision to forward a Watergate grand jury's report and supporting evidence to the House Judiciary Committee. The assistants in question rely for their optimistic reading of the opinion upon Judge Sirica's statements that the grand jury report "draws no accusatory conclusions . . . is not a substitute for indictments where indictments might properly issue . . . is a simple and straightforward compilation of information gathered by the grand jury, and no more." Remembering, as of course they do, that the Judiciary Committee is considering the impeachment of the President, Mr. Nixon's assistants and lawyers would do better to take very seriously indeed Judge Sirica's statement that "the grand jury states it has heard evidence that it regards as having a material bearing on matters within the primary jurisdiction of the committee in its current inquiry and notes further its belief that it ought now to defer to the House of Representatives for a decision on what action, if any, might be warranted in the circumstances." Judge Sirica's reference to the report not being "a substitute for indictment" should have been read, but seemingly was not read at the White House, in the light of Special Prosecutor Leon Jaworski's advice to the grand jury that its authority to indict an incumbent President was so much in doubt that it ought not to think about indicting Mr. Nixon. Read in this light, Judge Sirica was saying in this passage that the report *is a substitute for indictments where indictments might not properly issue.* It's inconceivable that the President's chief Watergate attorney, James St. Clair, failed to read this and other passages in the opinion as extremely ominous portents for his client. Yet assistants who are advised and guided by St. Clair misread the opinion and cited it among indications that Mr. Nixon's prospects are improving.

Among other grounds for confidence was the fact that the special prosecutor has not asked for and obtained grand jury indictments in connection with the administration's disposal of the ITT antitrust case, the raising of milk price supports after getting and being promised massive campaign contributions from the milk industry, and the solicitation, concealment and use of 1972 campaign funds. It's true that Jaworski indicated in a New Year's statement that indictments in these and other scandal areas were coming in February or March and that the ITT, milk and campaign funds indictments, have not appeared. But Nixon assistants who take this to mean that the threat of more indictments, with their damaging implications for the President, is fading away are deluding themselves. The criminal process apart, the impeachment process moves relentlessly toward a vote of impeachment in the House and trial in the Senate. The staff of the joint Senate-House Revenue and Taxation Committee advised Washington correspondents to expect its report on the President's shabby tax record and behavior during the first week of April. The report can't help Mr. Nixon and may do him more harm than any other single development. Which is the dream world? It is Mr. Nixon's White House world.

April 6, 1974

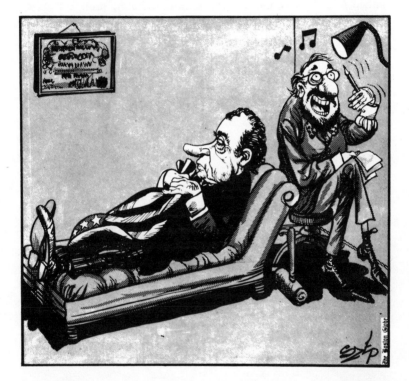

"Pack all your troubles in your old kit bag and smile, smile, smile"

———

Friends on the Nixon staff were pathetically grateful for the first part of the foregoing report. My brethren in the press room thought it one more indication that I can be a gullible sap. I and my staff friends didn't know what we were soon to learn: that the grand jury had named Mr. Nixon a conspirator without indicting him.

XII

Ford's Future

Gerald Ford continues to say publicly and in private that he expects to be Vice President and expects Richard Nixon to be President of the United States until January 20, 1977. The Vice President also continues to say that he has no intention of running and no plan to run for the presidency in 1976. But he concluded some weeks ago that it was foolish to go on pretending that there is no possibility that he, the first Vice President who was appointed to the office, may become President by succession before Mr. Nixon's second term is finished and that he may be the Republican nominee in 1976. During an interview with Henry Brandon of the London *Sunday Times* in late February, for instance, Ford said with utter calm that if he were President and running for reelection he would prevent a repetition of the Watergate campaign scandals by relying upon the regular Republican organization rather than a separate reelection committee and would monitor his campaign managers much more closely than Mr. Nixon supervised his managers in 1972. At a quiz session with Harvard students and a press conference in Boston on March 11, he said in a tone of gratitude that Mr. Nixon has "given me an opportunity to see firsthand the responsibilities not only of the Vice

President but the President as well" and noted that such activities as inspection of Strategic Air Command facilities "have helped prepare me if the unfortunate should happen." When a student asked Ford whether he would resign if President Nixon were impeached and removed from office, the Vice President answered matter-of-factly that under the Constitution he would have no alternative but to succeed to the presidency.

With such views and responses on the public record, the fact that Gerald Ford has done a lot of very specific thinking about his possible and maybe probable future should not surprise anyone. What follows is an account of his thinking as I've been led to understand it. This report is presented solely upon my authority, and readers will just have to assume and believe that I haven't made it up out of nothing.

Of course the Vice President thinks about a midterm succession to the presidency. He doesn't expect it to happen, he doesn't want it to happen, but he realizes that it could happen. This being so, he naturally thinks about who he'd want to have with him in a Ford administration and at a Ford White House if it does happen. His vision of a Ford Cabinet is far from complete but it is fairly precise so far as his thinking about it has gone. He is certain, he has been assured, that Henry Kissinger would be his Secretary of State. He has said publicly that he considers Kissinger to be "a superb Secretary of State" and he really does. Kissinger was recently understood and reported to have told several members of Congress that he could no longer serve effectively and would resign if President Nixon were impeached or otherwise compelled to leave office. Kissinger immediately got in touch with the Vice President and assured him that the report was erroneous. Kissinger said he would be happy to remain as Secretary of State if Ford became President and hoped that Ford would allow him to remain. Ford assured Kissinger that he would be not only allowed but asked to remain.

There's George Shultz, who recently resigned as Secretary of the Treasury and expects to leave office as soon as a successor is confirmed. Ford thinks Shultz is a great public servant who has been a tremendous asset to the administration and the country. Ford as President would want and welcome Shultz back in government, at the Treasury or elsewhere, if he were willing to return. The Vice President esteems Secretary of Labor Peter Brennan and would want him to stay. Ford thinks Rogers Morton has been an excellent

Secretary of the Interior and would hope to keep him in that office. Ford is aware that James Lynn, the Secretary of Housing and Urban Development, has an excellent reputation. The Vice President assumes that Lynn deserves the reputation and would retain the office if he wants to. The Vice President hasn't seen enough of Transportation Secretary Claude Brinegar and doesn't know enough about him to know whether he'd be asked to remain.

The Nixon cabinet member with the big question mark over his name is Secretary of Defense James R. Schlesinger. Ford thinks that Schlesinger is in many respects an excellent Secretary of Defense. He admires Schlesinger as a person and as an official. He agrees with Schlesinger's policies (although, quite apart from the information on which this report is based, I'm not certain that the Vice President agrees entirely with the administration's and Schlesinger's approach to strategic arms limitation and negotiation). Ford's reservation about Schlesinger has to do with Congress. In the Vice President's opinion, Schlesinger doesn't understand Congress and doesn't know how to deal with Congress. Ford holds that one of any administration's biggest problems in the foreseeable future is going to be dealing with Congress on defense matters and that an effective Secretary of Defense has to know how to deal with Congress or, if he doesn't know, have somebody at Defense who does know how. Ford spent most of the last week of March working on a problem in Congress that, in the Vice President's opinion, Schlesinger simply didn't know how to handle and was not equipped to handle. The problem was how to resolve a serious controversy between Chairman George Mahon of the House Appropriations Committee and Chairman F. Edward Hébert of the House Armed Services Committee over which of the two committees should determine the level of US military assistance to South Vietnam. Hébert's committee had authorized $1.6 billion in the current fiscal year and had attempted to nullify the Appropriations Committee's vote to cut it to $1.1 billion. The Nixon administration wanted $1.6 billion and was afraid that it wouldn't get approval of even $1.1 billion if opponents of aid to South Vietnam joined with defenders of the Appropriations Committee's prerogatives to block any amount. Ford realized at the end of the week that he hadn't resolved the controversy but he felt that he'd done more to bring Mahon and Hébert into agreement than Schlesinger and his people could have done. The President thought the issue was very important and Ford agreed. The Vice President felt that with his work on it he'd done more to earn his pay than with anything else he'd done since he succeeded Spiro Agnew in the vice presidency last December 10. Ford was a member of Congress for 25 years, so it's not surprising that the experience left him in some doubt about Schlesinger at Defense.

Ford has also thought about the staff he'd want with him at the White House. He knows who among his present staff of more than 40 he'd take with him into the presidency. One of them is Robert Hartmann, who worked for him in Congress and is the Vice President's chief of staff. Ford has concluded, and understands that Hartmann agrees, that Hartmann isn't up to staff management on either a vice presidential or presidential scale. L. William Seidman, a friend, lawyer and accountant from Ford's home town of Grand Rapids, Michigan, has been surveying the Vice President's staff needs on a temporary assignment and has just agreed to join and manage the permanent staff. President Ford would want Seidman on his White House staff. Another Grand Rapids friend whose name comes up in this connection is Philip Buchen, who was Ford's first law partner and for many years has been among Michigan's and Grand Rapids' leading attorneys. Buchen considers himself to be on temporary and part-time duty with Ford, setting up a staff to draft proposals for the protection of citizens' privacy. He'd probably wind up with President Ford. Bob Orben, a New York writer of material for comedians—Red Skelton has been an Orben client—has joined Ford's staff as a provider of the lightsome touch and he'd be in demand at a Ford White House.

Former Congressman, Defense Secretary and White House Counsellor Melvin Laird, who recently left Mr. Nixon for the *Reader's Digest,* and outgoing Counsellor Bryce Harlow would be asked to return to the White House staff under President Ford. He understands that both of them have had enough public employment for awhile and would be reluctant to resume it. But the Vice President is confident that he as President would be in a position to ask many people, Laird and Harlow included, to do things that they may not particularly want to do. A Nixon assistant who definitely would not be asked to stick around is Press Secretary Ronald Ziegler. An assistant who would be asked to stay is Gen. Alexander Haig, who succeeded H. R. Haldeman as President Nixon's staff chief last May. Ford thinks that Haig is a great manager and that he's done a tremendous job for Mr. Nixon in staving off staff collapse and chaos under Watergate pressures. Just how Bob Hartmann, William Seidman and Gen. Haig would fit into one White House staff isn't clear. My guess is that Gen. Haig would resolve his part of that problem by resuming his army career.

Vice President Ford's notion of how he as President would use Gen. Haig provides an insight into how President Nixon uses Haig and handles himself. Ford is under the impression that Mr. Nixon takes up so much of Gen. Haig's time in small talk, jawing away at him in the Oval Office or in the President's hideaway quarters in the Executive Office Building, that Haig the superlative manager doesn't have enough time to manage. Ford would leave Haig alone to do his intended job and absorb no more of his time than the job requires him to spend with the President. Ford is a pleasant, easy, surprisingly facile conversationalist in his off hours. But he doesn't like small talk in business hours. It bothers and offends him and he thinks the President is much too given to it. Although in his experience the President's small talk is always about big things, in Ford's opinion it can and does waste a lot of other people's time. Ford has heard that the President and Ron Ziegler spent a lot of time with each other after Watergate began to overwhelm the presidency last year. The Vice President has the impression now, however, that Mr. Nixon wants and demands much less of Ziegler's company than he did for awhile. Ford, as previously indicated, could and would do entirely without Ziegler's company. Recent reports that he doesn't get as much time with the President as he needs and would like to have genuinely puzzle Ford. The hours that he's had to spend with the President, mostly listening to Mr. Nixon talk about this and that, have on a few occasions driven the Vice President close to distraction. He's brought himself recently to break off their conversations, pleading that he's got to go someplace or do something important right away.

This impression of Ford's impression of Richard Nixon indicates that the President has undergone a change of personality in the past year or so. The late President Eisenhower, among others whose admiration for Richard Nixon was limited, felt that one of Mr. Nixon's serious personal defects was his abhorrence of small talk and his inability to practice or endure it for long. Of late, it would appear, Mr. Nixon can't do without it. The Vice President is not the only acquaintance and associate who perceives that the President is under some inner compulsion to let himself go in previously unaccustomed ways with people whom he knows and thinks he can trust.

Ford doesn't quarrel with journalists, among them some of the best political reporters in the business, who write after traveling with him on his rounds of party fund-raisers, press conferences and speeches to Republican groups that he's running hard for the GOP presidential nomination in 1976. He realizes that he's behaving as if he were after the nomination and that it's probably asking too much of the reporters who trail him about the country to expect them to believe that his sole interest is in doing what he can to save the Republican party and its candidates from disaster in the 1974 elections. His thinking about 1976 encompasses a possibility that inhibits him from flatly and conclusively ruling out the nomination for himself— something he has not done and doesn't intend to do. The envisioned possibility is that the leading active candidates—Rockefeller, Reagan, Percy come to his mind—may be in such close competition for the nomination that the 1976 convention will be threatened with deadlock and ruinous division. What if Vice President Ford or President Ford, as the case may be, is then offered the nomination and urged to accept it for the party's sake? Ford foresees that it would be hard indeed, perhaps impossible, for him to refuse the nomination in such an event. The cynics who will inevitably deride this projection as a tricky cover for Ford's actual purpose and ambition may be right, of course. All I know is what I'm told, and that is that this is the one and only circumstance in which Gerald Ford might accept the 1976 nomination.

Ford knows that he has to live with the impression, now practically universal, that he is drawing away from Mr. Nixon to the maximum extent that he thinks feasible without explicitly repudiating the President. When in Chicago on March 30, and again in Florida that night, he denounced the "arrogant, elite guard of political adolescents" who ran the President's 1972 reelection committee and charged them with "a failure to reinforce the President's impressive victory with enough Republicans in the House and Senate to ensure the success of his programs," he was attacking and had to know that he was attacking Mr. Nixon's concept and conduct of the campaign.

He didn't expect to be believed when he said with the utmost blandness at a subsequent press conference that he wasn't doing any such thing. He just wanted to be heard saying that he wasn't, for the record. In truth he is not totally convinced that Mr. Nixon is a total liability to the party this year. When it was suggested, a couple of days after the Chicago performance, that the President might go into Michigan's eighth congressional district and campaign for the Republican nominee for the House, Ford recommended that Mr. Nixon do so. The Vice President said that a visit by the President to Michigan wouldn't hurt and might help the candidate.

April 13, 1974

————

This piece created an enormous stink: Unelected Vice Presidents are not supposed to think about succeeding the President who nominated them. Mr. Ford handled the uproar generously and decently, on the whole. He could have and didn't deny the views attributed to him. He said instead that he was indeed the source of the article but had understood that he was not talking for publication. Our understanding that he was talking on what I called in preliminary conversation a "background-for-use" basis was clear to me, and, I am quite sure, to him. What he missed, I conjecture, was the conventional "sources close to the Vice President said" sort of dodge. I don't deal in that kind of crap.

Anyhow, Messrs. Ford and Schlesinger made it up, at least temporarily. Quoters of the piece universally overlooked the point that Kissinger had asked to be kept on. Laird, Harlow and Shultz did not join President Ford's staff in its early days, though Laird and Harlow were prominent among his unofficial counsellors. President Ford fired Ziegler and kept Haig for the transition.

XIII

A Taxing Time

The announcement that Mr. Nixon would pay the taxes that the Internal Revenue Service and the Senate-House Joint Committee on Internal Revenue Taxation said he owed on his income during the first four years of his presidency was couched in the familiar Nixon style. It began with a whine and ended with an assertion that if anybody was at fault in the matter it wasn't Richard Nixon.

However tedious it may be, a summary of the forgotten arithmetic and history of the Nixon tax situation is necessary if a finding of error and liability that is without precedent in the history of the American presidency is to be understood. Mr. Nixon reported a gross income of $1,122,347.37 in the four years of 1969-70-71-72. Claimed deductions from his gross income reduced his taxable income to $147,826.42 in 1969, zero in 1970, $5358.06 in 1971 and $19,707.77 in 1972. He paid a federal income tax of $72,682.09 for 1969; $792.81 (the inescapable minimum) for 1970; $878.03 for 1971; and $4298.17 for 1972. The biggest of the many deductions that enabled him to reduce his taxable income and his taxes to the foregoing extent was for a gift of his pre-presidential papers to the National Archives. The President maintained that the delivery of these papers to the archives on March

26-27, 1969, effectively and legally completed the gift on those dates. A law that Congress enacted and he signed in December 1969 allowed federal tax deductions for such gifts only if the gifts were legally completed by July 25, 1969. A justified suspicion in late 1968 and early 1969 that outgoing President Lyndon Johnson intended to make a series of gifts of his papers that would free him of federal income taxes for the rest of his life was partly responsible for the passage of this law. Mr. Johnson's Commissioner of Internal Revenue and personal tax consultant, Sheldon Cohen, told me in 1973 that he advised his patron not to try to beat the impending deadline and Mr. Johnson had sense enough to follow the advice. It appears that Mr. Nixon didn't get that sort of advice and that, if he had gotten it, he wouldn't have followed it. He said in October that after his election in 1968 he learned from President Johnson that a public official could cut his income taxes way down by donating his papers to the government and deducting their appraised value from his gross income. One of the less believable elements of the Nixon story is the suggestion that Richard Nixon, a lawyer and a former US representative, senator and Vice President who was paid hundreds of thousands of dollars a year by wealthy and tax-conscious clients, didn't know about this before Lyndon Johnson enlightened him.

A professional appraiser valued the donated Nixon papers at $576,000. Provided that the gift was legally completed by July 25, it entitled the President to deduct the appraiser's figure of $576,000 from his gross income over the five years beginning with 1969. Mr. Nixon deducted $482,018 over the four years 1969-72, thereby reducing the federal income taxes that would otherwise have been due by $234,000 and leaving $93,982 available for deduction from his 1973 and 1974 income. As I reported months ago, an Internal Revenue Service computer seeking out the returns of people who paid low taxes on high incomes horrified the incumbent commissioner of Internal Revenue by spitting up the names of Richard and Patricia Nixon early in 1973. The commissioner, now departed, checked with a Nixon assistant and was told to go ahead and audit the returns. The IRS auditors did so in a perfunctory fashion and found nothing wrong. A district IRS director has been pilloried in the press for sending the President a form letter complimenting him on "the care shown in the preparation of your returns." By the lax standards of review then and previously applied to presidential tax returns,

"I tried to beat them for 70 bucks . . . How about you?"

nothing was wrong with them. I remain unexcited by the news that
the IRS official who sent the letter was promoted in 1974. Things
were about to change, and change drastically, but had not yet
changed when the Nixon returns were audited in May 1973.

A *Washington Post* reporter, Nick Kotz, wrote in June of 1973 that
the President had claimed a big tax deduction on the basis of his
papers gift and raised questions about the validity of the claim. The
Watergate scandals were swirling, the Senate's Watergate hearings
were about to begin, and reports of large federal expenditures upon
the President's Florida and California homes were stoking a national
inferno of allegation and suspicion. On December 8, 1973, the
President made what he called "a full disclosure of my financial
affairs." He correctly said that "no previous President . . . has ever
made so comprehensive and exhaustive a disclosure." No previous
President needed to. The Nixon disclosures included the President's
1969-72 tax returns and a lot of other information, some of it
previously revealed, about his finances and the arrangements that
made the acquisition of his Florida and California properties
possible. The data showed that an increase in the President's and
Mrs. Nixon's net worth from $307,141 to $988,522 between January
1, 1969, and May 31, 1973, was mainly though not entirely due to
huge deductions for tax purposes from his gross income and the little
federal income tax that he paid in 1970, 1971 and 1972.

Mr. Nixon said in a statement accompanying the December 8
disclosure that "there may continue to be public questions about the
tax consequences" of two transactions. One of the transactions was
the gift of his papers. His second reference was to his claim that no
capital gains tax was payable upon the sale in 1970 of about 23 acres
of his San Clemente estate to his friends Robert Abplanalp and
Charles G. Rebozo. Mr. Nixon announced that he was asking the
Joint Committee on Internal Revenue Taxation to examine the
papers gift and the San Clemente sale and "decide whether, in their
judgment, my tax returns should have shown different results." He
said in the next sentence of the statement: "I will abide by the
committee's judgment."

What is known of the preliminaries to the President's decision to
submit his tax record to the joint committee and statements at four
White House media briefings that accompanied the December 8
disclosure indicate that Mr. Nixon and his advisers were confident

that his tax record and behavior would be vindicated. He had impressive legal advice that his record and behavior should be vindicated. Two distinguished attorneys, H. Chapman Rose of Cleveland and Washington and Kenneth Gemmill of Philadelphia, were assisting him without fee on his tax problems. At White House briefings on December 7 and 8, Gemmill said again and again that the papers gift and the tax deduction that derived from it were valid. When he was asked whether his examination of Mr. Nixon's records satisfied him that "the President has not profited personally in any illegal way," he answered, "I am satisfied 100 percent." Mindful that the briefing rules were that the briefers, including Gemmill, could not be quoted by name, Press Secretary Ronald Ziegler said, "You can quote him directly on that." In a remark that White House assistants would hate to have quoted back to them now, about the President's decision to refer the papers gift and the San Clemente property sale to the joint committee, Gemmill said: "Really they have a great committee and they have a wonderful staff . . . . Whatever the report they come up with, the President will abide by and that is that."

This brings us to the whine that was mentioned at the start of this report. The joint committee staff reported that the President underpaid his 1969 income tax by $171,055; his 1970 tax by $93,410; his 1971 tax by $89,667; and his 1972 tax by $89,890. The staff report made a persuasive showing that the 1969 Nixon papers gift was not legally completed before or by the July 25, 1969, deadline and that indictable fraud may have been committed in the effort to demonstrate that it was completed in time to justify the tax deductions that the President claimed. The White House whine emerged with the complaint that the joint committee had decided "to release a staff analysis of the President's taxes before the committee itself has had opportunity to evaluate the staff views and before the President's tax counsel could advise the committee of their views on the many legal matters in dispute in that report."

The interesting point, the point overlooked in the run of news accounts, is that the Nixon whine was in some part justified. It was true that the joint committee refused to give a hearing to the President's attorneys, Gemmill and Rose. It also was true that the committee permitted release of the staff report before it could have known of and approved the content of the report. This inquirer was advised to distinguish between the committee's and the committee staff's treatment of the President's lawyers. It was said for the committee staff and its director, Lawrence Woodworth, a fellow who is greatly revered by the Washington press corps, that the staff accorded the Nixon attorneys a courtesy and consideration that the committee did not accord them. In a literal sense this was true. But there was no denial that the Nixon attorneys' only communication with the joint committee was through the committee staff. Gemmill and Rose submitted their principal brief on February 19. It was an argument that the 1969 papers gift and the tax deduction derived from it were valid. Sen. Carl Curtis of Nebraska, the President's only all-out defender on the committee, said that he saw this brief on March 31. It was this sort of thing that lent force to the view of Arizona Rep. John Rhodes, the Republican minority leader who succeeded Gerald Ford, that any congressional committee ought to keep its staff under closer control than the joint committee does.

The crusher for Mr. Nixon came when the Internal Revenue Service told him, the day before the joint committee staff published its report, that he had underpaid his 1969-72 income taxes by $432,787.13 and owed the government that amount, plus interest that according to a White House computation would bring the total to about $467,000. The White House story was that the President fell into a hell-with-it mood and decided to pay the amount billed by IRS when he learned that the joint committee wouldn't hear his attorneys before its staff report was released. This story is of a pattern with the Nixon tactic of trying to discredit any and all critical entities, whether they be congressional committees and staffs or the special Watergate prosecutor's staff, on the ground that they are prejudiced against the President and dedicated to his destruction. The President's attorneys are right when they say they could present a strong defense of his tax position. They could present a strong defense, that is, on strictly legal grounds. They must know and the President must know that they would be in trouble if they had to defend him on factual grounds. Mortimer Caplin, President Kennedy's Commissioner of Internal Revenue, knew whereof he spoke when he said of the joint committee report that "it is a very disturbing report. Item after item makes one wonder."

April 20, 1974

———

Edward L. Morgan, one of the ablest attorneys on the Nixon staff, pleaded guilty in late 1974 to falsifying the date of the vice presidential papers gift.

XIV

They Done Him Wrong

When the attitudes that are described in this report were expressed
to me, the Republican leaders in the Senate had sent word to Mr.
Nixon—typically they had not been invited to tell him in person—
that he was going to be impeached if he didn't halt the delaying tactics
that he had been practicing since February 25 and comply
immediately and fully with the House Judiciary Committee's request
for White House tapes and documents. His response had been more
delay and in consequence he had become the first President to be
served with a subpoena by a congressional committee. Lawyers and
advisers were struggling with the problem of how to raise the
$467,000 that he'd promised to pay in hitherto denied or evaded
federal income taxes, the additional $100,000 or more that he's likely
to be owing on last year's income, and the $225,000 installment that is
due this summer on his San Clemente estate. Reports of criminal

investigations involving or at least touching his two brothers, his friends Charles G. (Bebe) Rebozo and Robert Abplanalp, the lawyer and accountant who have prepared his tax returns since 1969, and his confidential secretary and executive assistant, Rose Mary Woods, contributed to an impression and atmosphere of impending ruin.

So it seemed at a distance from the President and to some extent at the middle levels and outer fringes of his White House establishment. There the inquirer encountered a meld of stolid, defensive indifference and of controlled anxiety that was indicated by such qualifying references to future possibilities as "whatever happens" and "whoever is President then." Closer to the President, among the small group of assistants who see something of him with fair frequency and spend much of their time discussing his problems with each other, the discerned atmosphere was very different during the period in review here.

It was the week when the President dashed off to the tornado-stricken city of Xenia, Ohio, so suddenly that there was no time to assemble and accommodate the usual press entourage. He flew the next day into Michigan's eighth congressional district, ostensibly to help a Republican candidate for Congress and actually to help himself with a show of gutsy confidence. He conferred at the White House with the President of Algeria and Soviet Foreign Minister Andrei Gromyko, as if to say to the world that he's still looking after it. Finally he changed his plans within an hour and flew off to his Florida home on Key Biscayne instead of, as he had intended, passing the Easter season at Camp David, the mountain retreat for Presidents near Washington. He was said to have had a good time in the sun during a kindly weekend with Mrs. Nixon, his daughter Tricia and her husband Edward Cox—and with Bebe. The President's personal doings were cloaked in even greater secrecy than they usually are during his Florida stays. The fact that his beleaguered friend and next-door neighbor, Bebe Rebozo, was around during the Nixon stay was acknowledged only in private, with sour reluctance. Rebozo was with the President and the family when they attended an Easter Sunday service at the Key Biscayne Community Church. Mr. Nixon, departing afterward, exchanged cries of "Happy Easter" with the crowd. On these trips the President often visits Robert Abplanalp's weekend home on Grand Cay in the Bahamas, a short helicopter flight from the Florida coast. This time he didn't.

Now back to the discerned atmosphere around the President. "Discerned" is a necessary qualifier because, of course, reporters must rely upon what they are told about a milieu that they never really penetrate. The innermost White House milieu discussed here is peopled by Gen. Alexander Haig, the President's staff chief; Dean Burch, the Arizona lawyer and friend of Sen. Barry Goldwater who recently left the Federal Communications Commission chairmanship and became a White House counsellor; Bryce Harlow, a perennial assistant to Republican Presidents who has returned to the employ of Procter and Gamble in Washington but, judging from past performance, will remain in the Nixon circle; James D. St. Clair, the Boston trial lawyer who heads up the President's crew of Watergate defenders; and Press Secretary Ronald Ziegler, one of the few proteges of departed H. R. Haldeman who remain on the Nixon staff. J. Fred Buzhardt, a durable infighter, preceded St. Clair at the head of the Watergate legal staff and now, with the title of White House counsel, oversees the complex task of monitoring and transcribing critical tapes. He sits in on some of the inner sessions but doesn't begin to match St. Clair's influence over final policy decisions. Two lawyer-friends of the President, Kenneth Gemmill and H. Chapman Rose, have been helping without cost to him on his tax problems and join the inner council on occasion. "Chappie" Rose, a frequent unofficial counsellor to Mr. Nixon, has been involved in the search for ways to ease the President's acute money problem without drawing again upon his millionaire chums, Rebozo and Abplanalp. It is this group, varying in its composition somewhat when dealing with different problems, whose attitudes are reflected in the remainder of this account.

The attitudes that impress this inquirer more than any others are absolute confidence that Mr. Nixon will overcome and survive his difficulties and a conviction, embittered and profound, that his difficulties are mainly the work and fault of two kinds of people. There are the people—John Ehrlichman, John Mitchell, Maurice Stans, Herbert Kalmbach and his California law partner, Frank DeMarco, are among the many who come to mind and tongue in this connection—who were trusted by the President and are thought to have let him down. There also are the people, remote from and mostly unknown to Mr. Nixon, who are considered to be remorselessly and venomously committed to his destruction. The staff of the Senate

Watergate Committee, the special Watergate prosecutor and his staff are in this category. John Doar, chief of the House Judiciary Committee impeachment staff, ranks high in it and his Republican counterpart, Albert Jenner, is held to be only slightly less culpable. A recent addition to the club of supposed destroyers is a Nixon appointee, Internal Revenue Commissioner Donald Alexander. His qualifications for membership illustrate the state of mind depicted here.

Frank De Marco and the President's Los Angeles accountant, Arthur Blech ("a little man named Blech," I heard him called the other day), bear the immediate onus for the flaws in the Nixon tax returns for 1969-72 that have recently been exposed and acknowledged. The fact that Mr. Nixon personally set forth the philosophy of maximum attainable deduction that characterized these returns, in a 1969 memorandum to John Ehrlichman, is naturally overlooked. What one hears now are denunciations of DeMarco and Blech for foisting unconscionable deductions upon their client, the President, and virulent criticism of IRS officials who failed to warn Mr. Nixon that trouble lurked in his returns. When I heard this said about the IRS, I assumed that the reference was to an admittedly lax audit of the President's 1970-71 returns in May 1973. But no, the complaint went back to 1969 and it was only part of the indictment. The whole bit ran as follows. There were all these IRS types, see, who were embarrassed by the disclosure of their failure, year after year, to alert the President. Being embarrassed, they were resentful. He compounded their resentment by referring questions about his 1969-72 returns to the Joint Committee on Internal Revenue Taxation instead of to the Internal Revenue Service. With Commissioner Alexander's evident consent, the offended IRS officials determined to get that son-of-a-bitch Nixon and did so with a railroad job on his returns. Among the several items that this reading of IRS motivation overlooks are the facts that the joint committee found that the President owed considerably more in unpaid taxes than the IRS did, and that Commissioner Alexander went out of his way to say that the service found no evidence of fraud in the Nixon returns. The joint committee staff reported several indications of possible fraud and left further investigation to IRS and the House Judiciary Committee.

Hear now (in synthesis) two conversations about the President's problem with those White House tapes and the never-ceasing demands for access to them and related documents. It seems impossible (the talk at the White House goes) to lay out the dimensions of the problem so that it's understood. Nobody seems to believe that the President feels as deeply as he says he does that he has a duty to protect the presidency, not just himself, from unconstitutional invasion. He feels this very deeply and his position on the tapes will never be understood unless this is understood. And the taping system itself! How *could* those yahoos (meaning the people who conceived and installed it) have put in an uncontrolled system? Previous Presidents, Johnson for instance, recorded conversations. It was a way to preserve history. But it was under their control. It wasn't voice-activated, for Christ's sake, picking up bits and pieces of everything. A lousy system, operated by a bunch of ex-GIs who didn't have sense enough, sometimes, to replace the tape reels when they ran out. Voices from some parts of the EOB office (the President's second office in the Executive Office Building) weren't picked up at all. It was better in the Oval Office, but it wasn't really good anywhere. Listening to the tapes now, transcribing them, is a tremendously difficult job. There are gaps. It's impossible to identify some of the voices. We aren't stalling, we really aren't, when we say it takes time. The President? Sure he knew about it, he authorized it. But he didn't get into the details, he didn't know what kind of system it was. He forgot it. He became totally oblivious to it. And that's part of the problem now.

Continuing: the Republicans on the House Judiciary Committee— what a bunch! Christ! They won't stand up for the President. They're letting the Democrats run them off the court. They're complaining that the White House, not the committee, is responsible for the delays. They're falling for the line that the number of tapes given up, not the facts, is the issue. John Doar is determined, absolutely determined, to get a bill of impeachment. He knows that he doesn't have the evidence to get one now, and that's why he's getting the committee to demand more and more tapes and documents. He isn't through; he'll be after more if he gets all that the committee is calling for now (a reference to the recordings of 42 conversations subpoenaed April 11). He tells the Republican members of the committee very little, practically nothing. Jenner is no help. He sits in with Doar at the meetings with St. Clair. But he won't communicate separately with St. Clair or with anybody else at the White House.

He's done nothing to present the White House case to the Republicans and support the White House case. So the President's people feel that they don't get through to the Republican members very well and are completely cut off from the Democrats.

Now I leave the White House talkers to their plaint and conclude with two points derived from what they say. The central point, made over and over with the utmost urgency, is that after nearly a year of investigation by the Senate Watergate Committee and two special prosecutors "nothing will be proved because it can't be. The facts to prove anything against the President just are not there. The facts that are there"—meaning, in the White House transcripts and other documents—"prove that he's in the clear." The second point entitles the inquirer to wonder how the senior assistant who said the foregoing could be all that sure. When Gen. Haig, St. Clair, Burch, Ziegler and one or two others discussed St. Clair's letter of April 9 to John Doar, telling him in essence that it would take a while longer to review demanded tapes and documents and decide what to give the committee, the conferees anticipated that reporters would assume that the review began on or soon after February 25 and would ask why it wasn't completed by April 9. Thought was given to telling the simple truth. That would have required a spokesman to say that there was no intention whatever of providing anything in response to the February 25 demand, in the form it was put, and that the laborious monitoring and transcribing of the demanded tapes began only in late March when it became apparent that Doar would submit a revised request. The group authorized the spokesman, Deputy Press Secretary Gerald Warren, to say only that the review process took a lot of time and had yet to be completed. At this writing on April 17 it is nearly but not quite completed. When it is completed Fred Buzhardt and a few other staff lawyers will have spent some 300 hours listening to tapes. A crew of White House secretaries, bound to secrecy and unidentified because of fear that they might be subpoenaed, will have spent many more hours transcribing the portions of the tapes that Buzhardt and his assistants consider relevant to the committee request. Subject in event of doubt to the President's final approval, James St. Clair will decide what to give the committee in response to its subpoena.

April 27, 1974

XV

Haig's White House

On the night of April 16, flying back to Washington with the Nixons after a long weekend at the President's Florida home, Gen. Alexander M. Haig, Jr., was in relaxed conversation with several other members of the White House staff on Air Force One. A military aide, Lieut. Col. William Golden, remarked that on the previous Friday in Washington, before the party left for Florida, Sen. Mike Mansfield of Montana telephoned the President and Mr. Nixon returned the call. Gen. Haig shot up from his seat as if he had been ejected by rocket. "What did you say?" he growled to Col. Golden. Golden repeated the remark. "Why didn't you tell me that?" Haig asked his executive assistant, Maj. George Joulwan. Joulwan said he hadn't known about the call. Haig, normally calm and at ease, was angry, serious—*formidable.* He glared in turn at Golden, Joulwan, Press Secretary Ronald Ziegler and others in the group and said: "I run this White House and don't you ever forget it. Don't ever let that happen again." After a pause to let the message sink in he repeated "I run this White House" and sat down.

During the year since April 30, 1973, when the ordered world of the Nixon White House fell apart with the resignations of H. R.

Haldeman, until then the staff chief, and John D. Ehrlichman, the assistant for domestic affairs, there were times when survivors on the staff doubted that Haig or anybody else was running the place. They missed the firm and unquestioned authority with which Haldeman controlled access to the President and practically all communication, written and oral, with him. Even those who came to blame Haldeman for letting the Watergate horrors gather over and descend upon the President remembered with nostalgia the cool efficiency that seemed to be his and his regime's hallmark. For a time after Haig, previously Henry Kissinger's deputy and briefly the army's four-star Vice Chief of Staff, reappeared at the White House on May 4, 1973, in Haldeman's job, there were complaints that he wasn't taking hold. Haig himself admitted later to some uncertainty during that initial period. He assumed for a while that he was on temporary duty and destined for early return to the army. Although he had known and been respected by Haldeman's and Ehrlichman's subordinates when he was running the National Security Council staff for Kissinger, the thought of dealing directly with them in Haldeman's role made Haig uneasy. He brought aboard an army friend and associate, retired Maj. Gen. John C. Bennett, to be his deputy and a buffer between him and the civilians over whom the President had put him.

The uncertainty is long past. The only surprising thing about the little story at the start of this report is that Haig felt it necessary for him to say to anyone on the staff, "I run this White House." One of many signs of the total assurance with which he operates is the recent reorganization of his immediate staff. Gen. Bennett has gone. Haig, behaving in a way that is reminiscent of his experience in his first 18 months with Henry Kissinger, when Kissinger refused to grant Haig or anyone else the status of deputy assistant, has decided to do without a deputy. He looks to Maj. Joulwan and to a civilian, Jerry Jones, to do for him what a deputy would otherwise do.

Joulwan, aged 34 and a 1961 graduate of West Point, wants it known that he has a master's degree in international relations from Loyola University, Chicago, and that he majored in the history and nature of the presidency when he won the degree in 1968. He's served with Haig off and on over the past eight years, in Vietnam and at the Pentagon among other places. Haig says that he and Joulwan know each other so well that he, Haig, doesn't have to waste time explaining what he means and wants to Joulwan. He therefore regards Joulwan as "a perfect communicator" with other people and uses him for that purpose. Jerry Jones, also 34, is a former businessman and personnel specialist who came to the White House as a protege of Frederic V. Malek, then chief personnel officer and later deputy director of the Office of Management and Budget. Jones was Malek's deputy at the White House and, in 1972, at the Committee for the Reelection of the President. He succeeded Malek as the head of the White House staff charged with recruiting executive personnel for federal agencies and it was in this capacity that he caught Haig's attention.

A seldom noted fact about Haig is that he regards himself as the President's chief recruiter and placer of high-level personnel. He is very proud of the job that he and Jones have done in this area since mid-1973. In transferring Jones from the personnel office to his staff, Haig appears to be formalizing and strengthening his interest in and authority over executive recruitment. In late 1972 and early 1973, before Watergate in its various connotations overshadowed all else, the acknowledged purpose of White House recruitment and assignment was to extend and secure the President's authority throughout the federal establishment. Haig is said to maintain that he has reversed this policy, from centralization to decentralization. Maybe he has. It must be noted, however, that Fred Malek perfected, if he didn't invent, the philosophy of centralization in the Nixon manner. At OMB Malek retains a good deal of authority over personnel matters and his sometime deputy and disciple, Jerry Jones, is the assistant who specializes in recruitment for Haig. Although the general impression at the White House is that Jones has the title and status of deputy to Haig, the actual title is staff secretary. The previous holder of that title was a Haldeman protege, Bruce Kehrli.

Apart from his own staff arrangements, Haig has a voice and usually the decisive voice in important organizational moves throughout the White House establishment. The newest White House counsellor, Dean Burch, was first approached by Haig and agreed with Haig to join the staff before Burch and the President discussed the appointment. Early this year, when the respective jurisdictions of Ronald Ziegler and Communications Director Ken W. Clawson were debated and redefined, the President seemed to be willing to give the aggressive and ambitious Clawson the inclusive sway that he wanted over every aspect of White House "public relations," the official euphemism for overt propaganda as distinct from what passes for information. Haig preferred to restrict Clawson's jurisdiction and Haig prevailed. There were indications in this period that Haig wished and expected Press Secretary Ronald Ziegler to resume his largely abandoned role as the regular briefer of the White House press corps and to put less of his time and energies into private discussion and consultation with the President. In this matter Haig did not prevail. Ziegler continues to be less accessible to reporters than Haig is.

Haig also failed to get his way in an episode that illustrates both his prestige and the weakness of the Nixon presidency. When Secretary of Defense James R. Schlesinger decided that he wanted Paul Nitze, a former deputy secretary of Defense and more recently a key figure in strategic arms negotiations with the Soviet Union, to be his assistant secretary for international security affairs, Haig was one of the two men with whom Schlesinger cleared the idea. The other one was Henry Kissinger. Haig and Kissinger approved the proposal. So did the President, in a routine and passive fashion. He became actively involved only when Sen. Barry Goldwater objected and threatened to block Nitze's nomination, apparently in the mistaken belief that Nitze is a softie who would concede too much to the Soviet Union. The President, desperately in need of conservative support, drew back and refused to nominate Nitze. Goldwater's intervention outraged Haig. He was heard to say that bigotry on the right is as offensive as bigotry on the left.

Haig and his predecessor, Bob Haldeman, are very different individuals. Haldeman was secretive, inaccessible, vengeful, a worker in the dark. Haig is open in manner, moderately accessible, much more visible than Haldeman was. Yet the White House with Haig isn't very different from the White House with Haldeman. The reason is obvious. It wasn't Haldeman's White House and it isn't Haig's White House. It was and is Richard Nixon's White House and that is the trouble.

May 4, 1974

———

I learned later that what enraged Haig on the plane ride from Florida, in addition to not being told about Sen. Mansfield's call, was that Col. Golden didn't put the call straight through to the President as Haig would have done.

XVI

Tactics

The President pretty well decided how to respond to the latest demands for White House tapes and documents during the weekend that he spent at his Florida home in mid-April. Well before that, by March 6 at the latest, he had determined to meet the House Judiciary Committee's request of February 25 for the recordings of 42 of his conversations with the very least in the way of documents and access to actual tapes that he and his chief Watergate attorney, James D. St. Clair, figured he could get by with. After March 6 the remaining question was what the very least that he could expect to get by with would have to include. A related decision on what to do about Special Prosecutor Leon Jaworski's request of April 15 for a federal court subpoena commanding the President to produce recordings of some 64 White House conversations was postponed. But it became clear in retrospect that the inclination from the outset was to withhold compliance with the Jaworski subpoena at least until federal Judge John Sirica had been asked and either agreed or refused to quash it and to delay the announcement of this intention until the response to the more pressing House committee's request and subpoena had been disclosed. The hope and expectation from mid-April on were that the information supplied to the House committee could be made to appear to be so ample, so massive, and so far beyond anything that this President or any previous President had ever consented to disclose that the public would sympathize with and support resistance to further demands.

In Florida and in Washington after the President's return from his weekend, there was a distinction between what was said and what was implied by his spokesmen and by the few functional assistants who knew anything worth knowing and would talk to reporters. Three things were said in so many words. They were that the President had decided to give the committee some information that it had not requested; that the total response would be so generous that the committee would have to accept it and fair-minded people would have to conclude that it was more than sufficient; and that it would fall short of complete compliance with the committee request and subpoena. It was implied that transcripts rather than tapes would be supplied to the committee as a whole and that some access to the tapes, limited but sufficient to demonstrate the accuracy of the supplied transcripts, would be permitted. If I were inclined to write ahead of events at the Nixon White House, a folly that I try to avoid, I would have written on April 17 that the President had decided to do what he announced on April 29 that he was doing, with one exception. On the basis of what I had deduced from what I'd been told, I would have written that the House committee chairman, its ranking Republican member, and its chief majority and minority attorneys, John Doar and Albert Jenner, would be allowed to listen at the White House to any tapes that they wished to check in person. Mr. Nixon offered this privilege only to Chairman Peter Rodino and to the senior Republican committeeman, Edward Hutchinson.

The interesting point about these preliminary indicators is that such assistants as Gen. Alexander Haig, Press Secretary Ronald Ziegler and Communications Director Ken Clawson thought in mid-April that everything about the response except incidental details had been settled. Ziegler and his deputy, Gerald Warren, tried to make capital of the President's declared intention to respond before April 25, the deadline set in the committee subpoena. On April 23 Warren announced that the President had asked the committee to give him five more days. He wanted time, Warren said, to review the response "in its entirety." A fair supposition was that the President had realized for the first time the full importance of this response and faced up to the possibility that anything short of total compliance with the subpoena could ensure his impeachment. When I first tried this supposition out upon the few assistants who were accessible and who had any knowledge of what was going on, the reaction was that it was mistaken. Mr. Nixon, I was told, was doing what he had always intended and been expected to do, which was to check for himself every substantial element in the response. The only reason for the delay, it was said, was that the enormous job of transcription and editing had taken more time than the President and Haig had expected it to take when they were in Florida. Only after the President had delivered his televised speech on the night of April 29, a year less one day after he first begged the nation to put Watergate behind it in 1973, did a believable assistant say that the supposition was partly correct. This assistant said that the transcription process and the drafting of two documents, the text of the Nixon speech and a summary of the submitted transcripts, required the additional five days of preparation. But it also was true, the assistant said, that the President after his return from Florida came to be impressed with the gravity of his situation and with the possibility of impeachment in a degree that he had not previously manifested to the few associates who saw enough of him in this time to have a useful measure of his mood.

Another tenable supposition was that the President delayed the response in the hope and on the chance that two sometime cabinet members, former Attorney General John N. Mitchell and former Secretary of Commerce Maurice Stans, would be acquitted by the federal jury trying them in New York before the extended period for reply to the House committee expired. Mitchell and Stans were acquitted and one of the prosecution's principal witnesses, former White House Counsel John Dean, was to some extent discredited by the acquittal. Some of the New York jurors said they didn't believe Dean's testimony and were not convinced by the circumstantial evidence on which the prosecutors of Mitchell and Stans also relied. Inasmuch as the cases against several of the President's former associates and by implication against him rest in part upon Dean's allegations and upon circumstantial evidence, the acquittal gave everybody at the Nixon White House a tremendous lift in spirits and hope. It also caused the drafters of Mr. Nixon's speech and of the

*"We have, of course, deleted all profanities, vulgarities and
irrelevancies, to make things easier for the committee"*

transcript summary to sharpen the suggestions in both documents that Dean is a liar, a traitor to the Nixon cause and a thoroughly unbelievable accuser of the President. I'm believably told, however, that shots at Dean's credibility were written into both documents at the President's order before the New York acquittal and would have remained if Mitchell and Stans had been convicted.

John Dean's credibility and White House estimates of it aside, the Mitchell-Stans acquittal should have given pause to important segments of both printed and electronic media. The Watergate atmosphere has fostered and to some degree sanctioned departures from decent legal and journalistic standards that would have been generally denounced 18 months ago. The tendency to equate suspicion and allegation with guilt and to report as established or assumable fact assertions, deductions and rumors whose sole virtue is that they discredit public persons—Mr. Nixon notably among them—has been carried way beyond tolerable bounds. The tendency should have been and probably wasn't somewhat checked by this reminder that innocence is possible and guilt has to be proved even in the Nixon community.

Two examples of the sort of stuff that I have in mind surfaced just before and just after the President made his response to the House committee. Rumors that whiffs of anti-Semitism had been detected in some of the taped Nixon conversations broke into print in early April. No reader of the excerpts from the Nixon transcripts that are printed in the May 11, 1974, issue of *The New Republic* could be sure that there isn't some truth to the rumors. But, how much truth? Jewish leaders, including some who support and some who don't support the President, have complained to Nixon assistants in the past fortnight or so that they are hearing that blatant epithets and remarks of the most repellent kind have been heard on the tapes. A report that such language is on the tapes appeared in the April 30 *Washington Post*. Leonard Garment, a Nixon assistant to whom many of the complaints have been directed, has told Gen. Haig, James St. Clair and staff Counsel Fred Buzhardt that he damn well wants to know whether the reports are true. He has been assured that the reports are untrue and that they are originating with congressional and other rumor mongers who couldn't and don't know what's on the Nixon tapes. In some instances the reports have been traced to editors and publishers who got the stories from Washington correspondents who considered them fit for gossip but not for print.

The other example is a run of news reports to the effect that James St. Clair, supposedly the President's chief Watergate attorney, has lost control of the handling of the tapes problem to Fred Buzhardt and, more recently, that St. Clair and Mr. Nixon differed on how to respond to the House committee. The St. Clair-Buzhardt rumor originated in Congress, where members and staff assistants who long to discredit and disrupt the Nixon defense team abound. It was nominally substantiated by a departed Nixon lawyer who during his few months at the White House was principally distinguished for his garrulity and isolation. The rumor was and is nonsense. Buzhardt has managed the monitoring and transcription of subpoenaed tapes and St. Clair relies substantially upon him for knowledge of what's on them. But the attorney to whom the President listens and upon whom the President relies for advice on what to do is St. Clair. The public record supports his assertion that there has been and is no serious difference between him and the President. There is reason, however, to suspect that St. Clair recommended to the President that the House committee's chief attorneys, Doar and Jenner, be invited to monitor questioned tapes along with Rodino and Hutchinson and that, though initially overruled, St. Clair was prepared to offer the added access as a chip in bargaining with the committee after it voted 20 to 18 that the transcripts alone were not enough.

Two passages in the President's speech of April 29 caused me to wonder whether he had brought himself for the first time to believe—really believe—that he may be impeached and removed and to consider—really consider—resignation before it comes to that. An assistant who worked with him in the fortnight preceding the speech said he saw no sign whatever that this had happened. But I still wonder. The passages that induce wonder are the President's reference to the "wrenching ordeal" that an impeachment trial would bring upon the nation and his concluding quotation of Abraham Lincoln: "I do the very best I know how—the very best I can; and I mean to keep doing so until the end. If the end brings me out all right, what is said against me won't amount to anything. If the end brings me out wrong, ten angels swearing I was right would make no difference."

The propensity of the shoddy, profane, scatological Nixon portrayed in the tape transcripts to identify himself with Lincoln offends many people. Ah, well. It was Lincoln, I believe, who said the presidency doesn't give a man enough time to shave or shit.

May 11, 1974

———

The supposition that Mr. Nixon was at last beginning to realize the extent of his peril proved to be more correct than I knew when the foregoing was written. The ultimate aim of the massive publication of White House transcripts on April 30, an event that was fully reported elsewhere in the May 11 *New Republic* and therefore was not recounted in detail in this piece, was to forestall disclosure of the June 23, 1972, tapes that completed the ruin of President Nixon.

XVII

Tapestries

There I was at the typewriter, trying to muster the courage to confess that I wasn't as outraged by the Nixon transcripts and what they told about the squalid inner atmosphere at the Nixon White House as I should have been and as such wavering apologists for the President as the Republican Senate and House floor leaders, Hugh Scott of Pennsylvania and John Rhodes of Arizona, were saying they were, when the telephone rang. The caller said that White House Counsel J. Fred Buzhardt, who had supervised the preparation of the transcripts and the monitoring of the tapes from which they were taken, was ready to talk about the way the Nixon taping system worked and maybe I should hear the story. Most of the story has been told before, in court and Senate testimony. Very little attention has been paid to it, but that isn't why it is presented at some length here. The reason is that the willingness—indeed the eagerness—of a senior Nixon assistant to spend upwards of an hour detailing the story to a single reporter, at a time when there was much else of much greater importance to talk about, says all there is to say about the apprehension that prevailed at the White House after the edited and truncated transcripts of 43 Nixon conversations were released on April 30.

On the day when I was invited to hear Buzhardt's story, the morning newspapers quoted Sen. Scott's statement that the transcripts depicted the President and some of his closest associates, past and present, in "deplorable, disgusting, shabby, immoral performances." John Rhodes was quoted saying that he wouldn't quarrel with the characterization. The front pages featured an announcement by James D. St. Clair, the President's chief Watergate attorney, that Mr. Nixon had decided not to give any more White House tapes, transcripts and other documents bearing upon the Watergate scandal to the House Judiciary Committee and to Special Prosecutor Leon Jaworski. Chairman Peter Rodino said he expected the committee to subpoena the withheld tapes and documents. Jaworski had already subpoenaed many of them. The President appeared to be inviting a constitutional confrontation with both Congress and the courts and to have knowingly increased chances that he will be impeached by the House and tried by the Senate. Sen. Barry Goldwater, whose support the President has hitherto deemed vital to his survival in office, said that he expects Mr. Nixon to resign if he is impeached and so spare the nation what the President himself had termed the "wrenching ordeal" of a Senate trial. The senator's statement came nearer than any previous public event had come to confirming rumors that Goldwater and several other influential Republicans, among them former Defense Secretary and White House Counsellor Melvin Laird, were bracing themselves to tell Mr. Nixon to get out for his own, the Republican party's and the country's good.

With news of this kind dominating the headlines and the network broadcasts, Fred Buzhardt and the White House friend who arranged our meeting chose to concentrate upon a secondary matter. This was a suspicion, reflected in some news accounts and pumped up by journalists who increasingly tended to behave as if they imagined themselves to be crosses between Special Prosecutor Jaworski and Jesus Christ, that the Nixon tapes had been tampered with and that hunks of incriminating presidential chatter had been removed from the Watergate transcripts before they were released. Expert opinion to the effect that an 18½-minute gap and buzz on one Nixon tape was caused by manual and presumably deliberate erasure has been delivered to federal Judge John Sirica. Only a fool bathed in innocence would put fiddling with the record beyond some people in

"I was sitting listening to the tapes . . . and my reel finally ran out"

the Nixon crowd, beginning with the President. For two reasons, however, I'll await hard evidence before I either assume or seriously suspect that these transcripts and the tapes from which they were drawn have been messed with. One reason is that 19 of the tapes in discussion, including recordings of eight of the most critical conversations, are in the possession of the House committee staff. Most of them were previously in the Jaworski staff's possession. If anything worse than minor discrepancies between the actual tapes and the released transcripts had been discovered, the fact would have been leaked to the media. There have been indications from the Judiciary Committee staff that some of the many "unintelligibles" and "inaudibles" on the White House transcripts are intelligible and audible when played back on the committee recorders, but not that material omissions or distortions have been detected. The other reason for caution is that the released transcripts are rich in damning language and passages, demonstrating among other things that criminal conduct was discussed in the most sleazy fashion by the President and his intimates. In this sense the published transcripts validate themselves. If the purpose in preparing these transcripts was to protect the President, a lousy job was done.

The reports that bothered Fred Buzhardt had it that the indications in the published transcripts of deletions because words and passages were unintelligible, inaudible or "unrelated to presidential actions" did not explain why the released wordage, enormous though it was, was much less than would normally have been spoken during the 33 hours of logged and taped conversations covered in the documents. Readers on National Public Radio, talking in normal tones at normal speeds, repeated every word of the published conversations in 22 hours. One of the troubling reports was that gaps of total silence occurred on the White House tapes. The implication was that the gaps had been caused by deliberate erasure before the tapes were transcribed by a team of White House secretaries.

In order to appreciate Buzhardt's way of dealing with these reports, you have to recall the known history and nature of the Nixon taping system. Alexander Butterfield, a former White House assistant, revealed its existence to the Senate Watergate committee July 16, 1973. He said that conversations in Mr. Nixon's Oval Office and the Cabinet Room in the White House, in the President's alternate office in the adjoining Executive Office Building, and on four telephones used by Mr. Nixon had been recorded on a central taping system since "approximately the summer of 1970." Buzhardt in a letter to the committee dated the taping from "the spring of 1971." Twice in late 1973 the President agreed with Butterfield that it began in 1970. The timing, never satisfactorily resolved, is important because recording of conversations before "the spring of 1971" might illuminate the President's role in such controversial episodes as the decision to increase the levels of price support for milk after officials of dairy cooperatives promised to contribute two million dollars to the 1972 reelection campaign. Perhaps only because I failed to ask him about it, Buzhardt didn't address himself to the timing when we talked. His interest was in demonstrating that the seeming gaps in the tapes and the holes in the transcripts, many of which appear at points where obfuscation helps the Nixon cause, are due entirely to the taping system and not to the tapers. First he summarized the bare and familiar basics of the system: a battery of Sony recorders kept in a locked and guarded basement room; power switches on the recorders tied in to the locator switches that Secret Service agents pressed whenever the President entered his Oval Office or his EOB office; and sound-activated switches that set the tape reels turning whenever voice or other sound entered the input lines. Here, condensed and tidied for clarity but not altered in essence, is the core of Buzhardt's case in Buzhardt's words:

"The recorder used throughout this system was a relatively stable, low-quality recorder—reel type. In order to get as much as possible on one reel and lower the load on the people who had to change the reels, the recorders were always at the lowest possible recording speed, which gives you the lowest fidelity—15/16ths of an inch of tape used per minute, I think it was. The system was set up so that there were a number of lapel-type mikes, spaced around the Oval Office and the EOB office. All of these were fed into a single input and recorded on a single track. There was a separate input to a separate track on recorders hooked to the telephones. All of the recorders had a switch that was geared to an audio input signal, so there had to be some sound coming into the system to make it start recording. Now there was another facet to this thing: Hooked into the system was something called an automatic gain control on each of the recorders.

That is a device that varies the impedance, I think it is, on the input line. In other words, the gain control compensated according to the volume of sound. If you had a conversation going that put a substantial sound into the system, the gain control would be down at a minimum level where you get the best fidelity. If the volume of the sound coming in was low, the gain control would step up the amplification on the input line and that would cause distortion.

"Now, let's say the President goes into the anteroom of his EOB office. A Secret Service agent pushes the locator button and that turns on the power to the recorder. The President walks across the anteroom and opens the door to his office. The sound of the door opening and the sound of walking start the recorder recording. He walks across the room and even with the carpet on the floor you get squeaks on the tape. There's enough noise to actuate the machine but unless somebody is with him that he's talking to, it's a minimum type of noise and you have the tape running with nothing recorded except background noise. If that noise is very low, it can put a segment on the tape that may seem like silence but really isn't. Somebody may come in, speak to the President in a firm voice, and the gain control goes down and the fidelity is good. Then the voices drop off, the amplification goes up, there is distortion. Or maybe all the talking stops, there is silence, the reel stops turning. Then the talking starts up again and the reel starts again but there is a delay of a second or two in the recording, and you get a swurping sound instead of the first two or three syllables. You have this array of microphones leading into a single input to a single track. Two people speak at once and although their words might only partially overlap, you get a combination sound that is simply unintelligible and you have another place where you just cannot discern what was said. Bass voices at low frequencies record poorly. Voices at higher frequencies record well. John Dean's voice was relatively high, flat, not much fluctuation. It recorded very well. Ron Ziegler speaks softly in a bass voice and you pick up a word here and there. Ehrlichman's voice had a great deal of range in it, from low to high and down again, and when he was with several people you had real problems. You have to pick out words that identify the speaker—Ehrlichman says 'now' in a way that nobody else says it, and that is a help."

There was more of the same, in support of the contention that electronic and audio vagaries rather than villainy gave rise to the doubts. All I'm certain of is that Buzhardt left me believing that he believed what he had been saying in defense of his President.

May 18, 1974

———

Many flaws in the White House transcripts were due to factors of the kind cited by Buzhardt. But the Judiciary Committee and special prosecutor staffs discovered scores of omissions and distortions that benefited the President. They constituted proof that some of the Nixon people were greater fools than I thought them capable of being.

XVIII

Down to the Wire

A uniquely qualified and influential student of Richard Nixon's character, inclinations and quirks is former Congressman, Defense Secretary and White House Counsellor Melvin R. Laird. The friends who welcome and respect his views on what the President should do and is likely to do in response to Watergate pressures include Vice President Gerald Ford and practically the entire Republican leadership in the US House of Representatives. In his current capacity as the *Reader's Digest's* grandiloquently titled "senior counsellor for national and international affairs" and author of forthcoming articles on the presidential veto and presidential abuse of national security powers, Laird wants it to be understood that he is concentrating upon his first private job in 30 years and is out of politics. He was in Europe on *Digest* business in April and early May and might be supposed to have had no part in the Republican ferment that preceded and followed Mr. Nixon's release of the edited transcripts of 43 of his Watergate conversations on April 30. Laird returned to Washington at the end of the week when the transcripts were released and he didn't pretend that he was detached from it all when we talked by telephone on May 14. He did not exactly confirm certain rumors that I'd been hearing about him in Republican councils and the advice that he had been giving his party friends since he quit the White House staff last February. But he gave reason to believe that the stories were close enough to the truth to be reportable.

An extreme version of the Laird advice as it had filtered through to me was that he was saying that the President would be willing and prepared to resign and so rid the Republican party and the nation of the Watergate incubus to the extent that he personified it, provided— and this was a very big proviso—that a spectacular success enabled him to leave office on a note of triumph. The dismal domestic prospects being what they were, Watergate aside, any such success would have to come abroad in some area of foreign affairs. A conclusive settlement of the Arab-Israeli conflict and/or major progress toward viable and expanded agreement with the Soviet Union on strategic arms limitation were the obvious possibilities. Laird was said to have told his friends that the President hoped for at least the beginnings of an adequate success in March and that the thought of resignation then was entertained. Success didn't come in March or in April or in early May, and at mid-May even a limited Syrian-Israeli accomodation still seemed to be eluding Henry Kissinger in the Middle East. To believers in this version of the Laird version of Mr. Nixon's expectations and calculations, the fact that success on the required scale continued to elude the President and Kissinger represented a multiple tragedy and compounded an overwhelming sense of a time and a scene gone mad.

Laird indicated that he has been giving Vice President Ford and such other friends as Representatives John Rhodes of Arizona and Robert Michel of Illinois, respectively the Republican floor leader and the chairman of the Republican campaign committee, a line of advice that resembled the foregoing but differed from it in degree. His own version was interesting in itself and for the fact that such people listened to it even if they did not necessarily heed it. Rhodes said on May 8 that the President should consider resignation if his situation continues to worsen. Michel said that he wants no part of the clamor for resignation. Ford keeps indicating that he's plenty worried but not by any suspicion that the President is guilty of anything. Inasmuch as Laird made a point of dealing on the record with reporters when he was an official, he presumably won't object to being allowed to speak for himself in the abridged but not distorted account of our talk that follows.

Q: Anything to these stories that you've been discussing the President's problems and the Watergate situation with a good many other people and that you are the architect of some of the thinking on what to do about it?

A: First, I want you to know that I have not been calling people. I have had people calling me—people on the Hill and political people. They have been trying to get me involved and I have been trying not to become involved. I really think that I've got to pay attention to what I'm doing here at the *Digest* for a period of time.

Q: Have you expressed the view to some of your friends that your reading of Mr. Nixon is that if he managed to bring about a major accomplishment, probably in foreign affairs, something that would enable him to leave office on a note of triumph, a peak of success, he then might be prepared to leave?

A: Well, I have said that would probably be the only condition under which he would reconsider his position. I believe that when he says he will not resign, I think that is his position and something very dramatic would have to occur before that position would change.

Q: Have you also told your friends, the prospect of any spectacular success being rather remote, that probably the President could not be brought to resign and resolve this impasse until sometime in the fall, maybe even after the fall elections?

A: Well, I am not sure about that. Back around February, I thought that there would be a majority in the House of about a hundred votes against indictment [Laird's term for impeachment]. The situation is changing, there is a momentum that's going against the President, and right now I think probably he would win in the House by no more than 20 or 30 votes against indictment. But I don't think there will be any action in the Congress before September so there will be a period of time when many things could take place.

Q: Have you been discussing these problems with Mr. Ford lately?

A: Well, you know I talk to Jerry Ford and I talk to people like John Rhodes and Bob Michel, people like that. But as far as having a big strategy worked out, I just don't have anything like that and I have not laid one out any place. I have talked frankly and openly to people like that in a sort of private way. But I don't want to embarrass anybody about that. I think Jerry would tell you that I talk with him and I do keep in touch.

The discernible atmosphere at the White House indicated that Laird's reading of the Nixon mind, however much it may be respected by his friends, is not shared and will be profoundly resented by the President's current associates. At levels up to and just below that of Gen. Alexander Haig, the President's staff chief, the attitudes that I came upon at mid-May can be summarized as follows. There was absolutely no sense or readiness to acknowledge that the President and the very few advisers who were consulted about the release of the Watergate transcripts had misjudged their impact upon the public and Congress in any substantial or blameable way. The transcripts had to be released for two reasons: first, to forestall "selective release" of the most hurtful of them by the House Judiciary Committee, and, second, to rally public sympathy for resistance to further disclosure. The public's romantic notions of what goes on in any President's private councils and the consequent shock of reality may have been underestimated. The hypocrisy of politicans like Sen. Hugh Scott, whining about "deplorable, disgusting, shabby immoral perfor- mances" with which they were perfectly familiar and in which they had often participated, was not adequately anticipated. Reactions of this sort stimulated an adverse public reaction that wouldn't have been so severe, it was said in quarters very close to Mr. Nixon, if jerks like Scott had kept their mouths shut. But so what? The worst of it would pass, it was already passing. So went the talk that I heard and that, I was told, Gen. Haig heard and encouraged at his senior staff meetings.

The President bespoke the sentiment reported by those around him when he said to friendly congressmen: "I'm not guilty and I'm not going to resign." One of his daughters, Julie Eisenhower, quoted him at family dinner on his professed determination to see the impeachment process through to the bitter end of Senate trial if that be the will of Congress. "It was a very great quotation, very quotable," Julie said. "He said he would take this constitutionally down the wire." Nothing goes wholly right at the Nixon White House nowadays. An assistant checked with Mrs. Eisenhower and reported that she'd meant to say, "down to the wire." Several publications that were yammering about errors in the Nixon transcripts reported what she meant to say instead of what she said.

May 25, 1974

———

The point that I thought I was conveying in this piece, namely that Melvin Laird was participating with Vice President Ford and others in discussions of ways to get Mr. Nixon out of the White House, didn't come across as clearly as I intended it to. In a remark that I didn't quote, Laird said he thought Gerald Ford and Nelson Rockefeller would make a great ticket in 1976. The poor fellow was trying to surface through me his preference of Rockefeller for the vice presidency and I didn't have the wit to let him do it.

XIX

Escaping Watergate

Between May 12, when the President read in *The New York Times* that he'd been heard saying "wop" and "Jew boys" on White House tapes, and May 22, when he greatly increased the chances that he will be impeached by telling the House Judiciary Committee that he won't obey any more of its subpoenas and demands for tapes and documents connected with the Watergate scandals, Mr. Nixon never abandoned hope that success in Henry Kissinger's efforts at mediation between the Syrians and the Israelis would make it possible for him to get away from the horrors at home with a trip to the Middle East. During a weekend holiday at his Florida home, the President had his spokesmen repeatedly remind the press that Secretary Kissinger was working for him in Damascus and Jerusalem and that any success achieved would be a Nixon success. The word on May 17 was that the President "spent most of the morning reviewing cables from Secretary Kissinger" and "sending guidance to the Secretary." On May 19 it was that "the President continues to send guidance to Secretary Kissinger, who is in Israel today." Back at the White House on May 21, when Kissinger was reported to be saying after 22 days in the Middle East that he really had to return to

Washington soon, Mr. Nixon had a spokesman say that "he has told the Secretary to stay there as long as possible" and that "both the President and the Secretary are eager to make as much progress as is possible." Egyptian Ambassador Ashraf Ghorbal said on the 22nd that his government still hoped to greet the President in Cairo in early June and I was told at the White House not to rule out the possibility, difficult though it would be to arrange a presidential journey abroad on short notice.

Whether Mr. Nixon would actually be going to the Middle East was not the principal point of interest. The point was the indication in all the talk about the hope and the possibility that the President and his people were desperately anxious for a success that would call for celebration with such a trip. Mr. Nixon's assistants continued to say that he was determined to revisit Moscow in late June. Ambassador Ghorbal understood that the Moscow trip was scheduled for the third week in June. So the thought occurred: What a journey, what an escape from Watergate a trip to Cairo, Damascus, Jerusalem, Riyadh in Saudi Arabia and then on to Moscow would be for Richard Nixon. It was no more than a thought, of course, and it may have been a fantasy. But it was the sort of fantasy that the people around the President liked to indulge, for relief if nothing else, in the last days of May.

There was much to escape from and, in remorseless fact, no way to escape from it. On a night soon after the "Jew boys" report appeared in *The Times,* Julie Nixon Eisenhower telephoned Leonard Garment, a Jewish assistant to the President, at Garment's home in a Virginia suburb. Mrs. Eisenhower said her father wanted Garment to come immediately to the White House. It was 10 o'clock when Garment joined the President and Julie at the mansion, in the Lincoln sitting room. Garment said afterward that the President wasn't bitter, wasn't angry. But he was vehement in his insistence that he never called federal Judge John Sirica a "wop" and never referred to lawyers at the Securities and Exchange Commission as "those Jew boys." Mr. Nixon instructed Garment to do everything he could to correct the report and, if possible, to persuade *The Times* to retract its story. Garment and another White House lawyer, Fred Buzhardt, made what seemed to me to be a persuasive case that the reported remarks did not occur on any of the three tapes on which they were said to have been heard. Garment and Buzhardt hoped for a while that federal Judge Lee Gagliardi, to whom the three tapes had been submitted for use in the recent trial of former Attorney General John Mitchell and former Secretary of Commerce Maurice Stans in New York, would say that he'd listened to the tapes and had not heard the President say what he was reported to have said. Gagliardi said nothing. The White House denials were duly reported, in *The Times* and elsewhere. But the denials were not enough to erase the story's ugly impact. The episode perfectly illustrated the President's dilemma. His assistants were believed when they admitted, as they had to and did, that he was prone to waspish remarks about "our Jewish friends" and to somewhat similar references to other ethnic groups. But, Nixon credibility on any subject being as near zero as it was, the same assistants were not believed when they asserted that the President never used what would commonly be considered racial epithets and that, in particular, he had not said "Jew boys" and "wop" during the three conversations in immediate question. The only way to have had this last claim believed and reported as true would have been to let reporters listen to all of the three tapes involved. White House lawyers vetoed a suggestion that this be done, arguing that it would destroy the last remnants of the President's tattered claim to privileged confidentiality.

How the President who sets such store by confidentiality and who relies upon it as strongly as this President does to shield him from further disclosure could have brought himself or been brought by others to install the Nixon taping system continues to be one of the abiding mysteries. In the only individual interview that he has granted since 1972, Mr. Nixon indicated to a columnist, James J. Kilpatrick, on May 16 that H. R. Haldeman first suggested that presidential conversation be recorded "for historical purposes." Alexander Butterfield, the former White House assistant who supervised the installation and operation of the system and revealed its existence to the Senate Watergate committee in July 1973, indicated in his testimony that the President wanted it "to record things for posterity." Butterfield said the President "seemed to be totally, really oblivious" to the fact that his private conversations were being recorded and observed that he was "certainly uninhibited by this fact." The President told Kilpatrick, "I must say that after the system was put in, as the transcribed conversations clearly indicated, I wasn't talking with knowledge or with feeling that the tapes were

there. Otherwise I might have talked differently." This appears to
have been true for at least part and maybe most of the time that the
system was working. But, questions of Watergate guilt and innocence
aside, one of the most interesting passages in the transcripts released
on April 30 shows that Mr. Nixon was vividly aware of tapes and
taping on April 14, 1973.

The President was talking in his alternate office in the Executive
Office Building with Bob Haldeman and John Ehrlichman.
Ehrlichman was to meet in his own office later that day with Jeb
Stuart Magruder, former deputy director of the 1972 Committee for
the Reelection of the President, and then with former Attorney
General Mitchell. Magruder had decided to quit lying and tell a grand
jury about his and others' responsibility for the original Watergate
burglary and bugging. The President, Haldeman and Ehrlichman
had concluded that Mitchell had approved the plans that led to the
Watergate bugging. They hoped to persuade him to admit as much
and thus keep the blame away from the President. From the
transcript:

E: I would like a record of my conversation with both Magruder and
Mitchell. I think personally that maybe I ought to get my office
geared up so that I can do that.

P: (Unintelligible) or do you remove that equipment?

E: Yeah.

P: I do here for my meetings with Henry but I don't know. . . . Why
don't you just gear it up? Do you know, do you have a way to gear it
up?

E: Yeah. I've done it before.

P: Well, go gear it.

The President then told Ehrlichman that he wanted to know what
Mitchell said, but didn't want to hear the record. Ehrlichman used an
IBM dictating machine to record telephone calls and a small tape
recorder to record office conversations. His record of the Mitchell
and Magruder talks was on an ordinary tape cassette. Stephen Bull,
who replaced Butterfield in charge of the central taping system, and
others at the White House, say they don't know what Mr. Nixon
meant with his reference to his "meetings with Henry." He certainly
did not mean that he "removed that equipment" or halted the central
taping when he talked with Henry Kissinger. The office conversations

with Kissinger were recorded and Kissinger's voice is said to be among the clearest on the Nixon tapes.

June 1, 1974

When this piece was written, the official line was that Mr. Nixon had abandoned hope of visiting the Middle East. When it appeared, he was practically on his way.

Leonard Garment and Ronald Ziegler proposed to let me listen to the entire tapes on which Mr. Nixon was supposed to have said "Jew boys" and "wop." Somebody, identified by them as "the goddam lawyers," vetoed the offer. What sounded to *The New York Times's* source like the President calling Judge John Sirica "a wop" sounded to the House Judiciary Committee's staff like the President saying what Garment and Ziegler said he said—that Sirica was the kind of tough judge *"I want."*

XX

Auguries

The President's prospects were never grimmer than they were when he was firming up his plans to visit the Middle East and to revisit the Soviet Union. His spokesmen's assertions that the trips were undertaken solely in the interest of peace and not to inhibit and discredit congressional and judicial inquiries into the conduct of his presidency became ever more ludicrous and pathetic. By continuing to withhold subpoenaed tapes and documents from the House Judiciary Committee, Watergate prosecutor Leon Jaworski and two federal courts, Mr. Nixon strengthened an impression that he was hiding evidence that, if disclosed, would subject him to impeachment by the House of Representatives, conviction and removal from office by the Senate, and trial in criminal courts when the presidency no longer protects him from indictment and prosecution. Although the Judiciary Committee had been told that the President would not comply and had decided, at least for the time being, not to try to enforce its demands with congressional contempt proceedings or with court orders, subpoenas and threats of more subpoenas continued to cast Mr. Nixon in the role of a scoundrel who was using his office and his claim of a constitutional right of privacy to save himself. He was dealt two blows when the US Supreme Court bypassed the Circuit Court of Appeals for the District of Columbia and accepted for early review prosecutor Jaworski's contention that a President has no constitutionally protected power to decide for himself what evidence he will and will not supply to prosecutors and defendants in criminal cases that may involve the withholding President. The summary rejection of Mr. Nixon's plea that the issue be left to the usual and full appellate procedure enhanced the feeling, already prevalent, that he must be wrong in this as in so many other positions that he has taken in matters related to the Watergate scandals. It also deprived him of review by a tribunal, the court of appeals, that had just said in a unanimous and powerfully stated opinion that the doctrine of executive privilege upon which the President relies is constitutionally based and sound and should be overridden only upon showings of the most urgent need.

A blow that could be the worst that Mr. Nixon has suffered, excepting the blow that he dealt himself when he released the edited but damning transcripts of 43 recorded White House conversations on April 30, came when Charles Colson pleaded guilty to a charge of obstructing justice. In return for the dismissal of three other charges in two indictments, Colson promised to tell the Watergate prosecutor, the courts and the House Judiciary Committee everything he knows that could be relevant to the impeachment inquiry and to the trials of other defendants in Watergate cases. Colson knows a lot. He was special counsel to the President from the autumn of 1969 to March 1973. During the last two years of that period he was closer to the President than any other domestic assistant, H. R. Haldeman alone excepted. After he left the staff and resumed law practice in Washington in March 1973, Colson continued to consult with Mr. Nixon and senior assistants. They sought and got his advice on how to handle the President's escalating Watergate problems. It was partly upon Colson's recommendation that James St. Clair, a trial lawyer who had known Colson in Boston, was hired in late 1973 to head the President's sizable and costly staff of Watergate attorneys.

The talents that earned Colson his reputation as the President's chief expert in dirty work were a source of pride and satisfaction to Mr. Nixon. He said in one of his recorded conversations that "Colson would do anything." This and other Nixon remarks in the released transcripts may be interpreted to indicate a fear that Colson might rat on him some day. In an unrecorded conversation at the White House several months after Colson quit, however, the President said in a tone of admiration and approval that Chuck Colson had been the toughest son of a bitch in his service. Mr. Nixon added that this status and honor had passed to Ken Clawson, a White House propagandist who was hired by Colson in early 1972.

Colson's plea of guilt stimulated much speculation, in print and in Washington chatter, as to whether his action arose from the turn to Christ that he announced last December and whether he is equipped and willing to sink Richard Nixon. Lacking knowledge that would sustain a judgment on either point, I settle for a supposition and a fact. The supposition is that the Watergate prosecutor had enough on Colson to jail him for the rest of his useful life. The fact is that the President was correct when he described Chuck Colson as a tough son of a bitch. In a statement explaining his plea and the bargain that preceded it, Colson said that he wants "to tell everything I know about the Watergate and Watergate-related matters . . . no matter who it may help or hurt—me or others." Although St. Clair said that he and the President aren't afraid of what Colson may testify to, it is impossible to believe that Mr. Nixon took comfort from his sometime devotee's promise to tell all.

Other Watergate developments, some bad for the President and some good for him, crowded upon each other so rapidly that Mr. Nixon must have had difficulty keeping track of them while he was arranging his escape into world diplomacy. A report drafted and leaked to the media by the staff of the Senate Watergate committee all but accused the President of accepting a bribe in the form of campaign contributions and pledges from the dairy industry when he was deciding to increase federal price supports for milk in 1971. Prosecutor Jaworski reported that he had found no evidence of criminal behavior by officials of the International Telephone and Telegraph Corporation (ITT) in the course of persuading the administration to drop a batch of antitrust suits in 1971. Members of the House Judiciary Committee, not usually given to leaking information that favors the President, confided that recordings of two of Mr. Nixon's discussions of the ITT matter supported his story that genuine policy considerations rather than hope of political gain moved him to order the Justice Department to settle the ITT cases in a way that, to say the least, was more satisfactory to the corporation than it would have been if the President had not intervened. Albert Jenner, the committee's chief Republican attorney, diminished the impact of this news and further lowered his low standing at the White House when he said that evidence in his possession indicated that Mr. Nixon knew at the time that some of his subordinates perjured themselves when they swore in 1972 that there had been no White House intervention. Jenner said that the President, in failing to report this knowledge to the proper authorities, could have been guilty of obstructing justice. Federal Judge John Sirica released the final report of six electronics experts who had previously said and now reaffirmed that the 18½-minute gap in the tape recording of a conversation between Mr. Nixon and H. R. Haldeman on June 20, 1972, three days after the arrest of the Watergate burglars and tappers, must have been caused by five manual erasures and could not have been accidental. A rival expert who was retained by the President's lawyer, St. Clair, differed with the panel's finding only to the extent of arguing that the possibility of accidental erasure should not have been totally excluded. Both reports were bad news for Mr. Nixon and for his confidential secretary, Rose Mary Woods, who testified under oath in 1973 that she may have accidentally erased about five of the 18½ lost minutes.

The best of the little good news for the President was marginal. Rep. John Rhodes of Arizona, the Republican floor leader, comforted some of Mr. Nixon's assistants when he told them about the public reaction to his statement on May 8 that the President should think about resigning if his situation continues to get worse. Nationwide, the wires and letters that poured in were 10 to one against resignation and critical of Rhodes. The reaction from his conservative constituency in Arizona ran three to one against Rhodes and in support of the President. Rhodes's press spokesman, Jay Smith, said the communications did not smack of organized and crank mail. They had the look and feel of valid, literate expressions from concerned citizens. They suggested that the public may not be quite as hell bent for impeachment or resignation as many polls indicate and many journalists assume.

June 15, 1974

XXI

Middle East Journey

Here is an account of some of the things, many of them too trivial for mention in the run of news reports, that interested and impressed me during a week of travel with the Nixon press party from Washington to Jerusalem by way of Salzburg in Austria and four cities in three Middle Eastern countries. After stops at Cairo and Alexandria in Egypt, Jeddah in Saudi Arabia and Damascus in Syria, I figured that I didn't have to watch that tried and generously rewarded friend of Richard Nixon and the United States, King Hussein of Jordan, greet the President at Amman in order to be convinced that Mr. Nixon and his Secretary of State, Henry Kissinger, had brought about at least the beginnings of an immense and probably beneficial change in the relationships between the US and the previously hostile Arab world without abandoning or importantly qualifying the American commitment to Israel. So I skipped Amman and flew from Tel Aviv to Washington to write this piece and prepare for the dubious pleasures of witnessing Mr. Nixon's next demonstrations, at a hastily arranged NATO summit meeting and in the Soviet Union, that there is nothing like foreign travel on foreign business to insulate a troubled President, however briefly and incompletely, from scandal at home.

From Cairo on I kept reaching for the word that would best describe the President's usual look and demeanor during his public appearances. The word wasn't "tired" or "preoccupied" or "bored," though the President seemed to be all of these at various times and on a few occasions to be all of them at once. Certainly the sought term was not "excited" or "stimulated." Never in my sight was Mr. Nixon moved to the spasms of jerky behavior and speech that huge crowds and thunderous acclaim have produced in the past. It was while watching him on Israeli television in a moment of pensive repose during the dinner given by the President and the new Prime Minister of Israel that the appropriate word jumped to mind. The word was "sad." Throughout the observed portion of a journey that was intended to symbolize and dramatize a major though as yet tentative achievement in foreign policy, a journey that afforded millions of people a chance to thank him with their presence and cheers for his presence and efforts, the look and air of sadness never left Mr. Nixon for long.

A likely cause of the sadness—a reporter can only guess, remember, at this isolated President's inner thoughts and motivations—was indicated by an incident in Jerusalem. Mr. Nixon remarked at the state dinner that "it is the prerogative of Presidents sometimes to break precedents" and said he was going to break one by proposing a toast to former Prime Minister Golda Meir before he offered the required toast to Israel's President Ephraim Katzir. After Mr. Nixon praised her courage, intelligence, stamina, determination and dedication to Israel, Mrs. Meir responded as follows in a flat and cold monotone: "As President Nixon says, Presidents can do almost anything and President Nixon has done many things that nobody would have thought of doing." The President flinched as if he had been slapped. In the pressroom where a pack of reporters watched and listened on a television monitor, shouts and laughter reflected the assumption that Mrs. Meir was referring to the President's known and alleged Watergate behavior. The shouts and laughter also drowned out the words that followed Mrs. Meir's supposed insult. My tape recorder didn't hear them through the clamor and I didn't know until I saw a transcript that Mrs. Meir concluded her response in this way: "All I can say, Mr. President, as friends and as an Israeli citizen to a great American President, thank you."

In Cairo, standing with Mrs. Nixon at his side and shaking hands

When the going gets tough, the tough get going

with 45 guests per minute at an outdoor reception and dinner, the President had the look and manner of a grieving robot. At what was billed as a display of Egyptian folklore after the dinner, a renowned belly dancer ended her act within inches of the seated President. Reporters who were there (I'd departed) said that Mr. Nixon came alive and appeared to be definitely interested. Along Mr. Nixon's way through the streets of Cairo and Alexandria and the route of a train trip from Cairo to Alexandria through the Nile delta, there were tumultuous displays of happiness. The displayed happiness was that of the millions of Egyptians who were commanded by their President, Anwar Sadat, to turn out for their visitor. Mr. Nixon said that he was happy, too, but very little happiness was to be seen in the grinning visage that he turned upon the enormous crowds. At the Great Pyramids on the day of his departure for Jeddah, there was a moment when Mrs. Nixon and President and Mrs. Sadat stepped away from Mr. Nixon and he was alone upon a terrace, his back to the pyramids and his face toward a group of reporters. We saw him but he didn't see us. His gaze and his thoughts were far away and sadness was all about him. In Jeddah walking along a marble pathway to meet King Faisal at one of the royal palaces, Mr. Nixon paused in the hot sun for an instant. Two Saudi dignitaries were with him, but for that instant it was as if he were alone again. His face went slack, his eyes were blank, and he seemed to me, standing perhaps 10 feet from him, to be engulfed once more in sadness. Then the President seemed to drag himself back to where we were from where he had been. King Faisal, magnificent in a black robe over a white robe and with the face of a sated hawk peering out between the folds of a white headdress, was walking toward the President. It was said and indicated later that the King and the President spent a couple of useful hours together in the Royal Office, discussing among other matters American arms for Saudi Arabia and oil at outrageous but not totally unmanageable prices for the US.

It was plain to guests at the state banquet for the President that Faisal thoroughly enjoyed his reaming of Mr. Nixon with the strongest reference that the President heard on his journey to the hideous problem of what to do with and for the hundreds of thousands of displaced Palestinian refugees who were driven from or left Israel in and after 1948. Faisal was seen to smile with a sort of wolfish glee when he intoned in Arabic: "We believe there will never be a real and lasting peace in the area unless Jerusalem is liberated and returned to Arab sovereignty, unless liberation of all the occupied Arab territories is achieved and unless Arab peoples of Palestine regain their rights to return to their homes and be given the right of self-determination." All of the President's other Arab hosts—Sadat in Egypt, President Hafez Al-Assad in Syria, King Hussein in Jordan—expressed approximately the same demands for the return of territories occupied by Israel in 1967 and for some form of Palestinian state. Only Faisal explicitly demanded the return of Jerusalem to Arab control and, in effect, the return of exiled Palestinians to Israel itself.

All of the Arab chieftains were expected by the President and his counsellors to take public positions on these matters for bargaining purposes, but there was one unpleasant surprise. Mr. Nixon and Henry Kissinger did not expect Kissinger's friend and collaborator in pacification, Anwar Sadat, to be as explicit and vehement in public as he was when he said at his welcoming dinner that "there is no other solution and no other road for a durable peace without a political solution to the Palestinian problem . . . its solution is indispensable." Sadat further jarred the President and Kissinger when he said of the vast Sinai desert expanse taken from Egypt in 1967 that "it is inevitable" that Egypt "regain its territory either by peaceful means or by might." Mr. Nixon indicated the course that he and Kissinger had expected Sadat to take when, in an informal press session during the train ride to Alexandria, the President said that Sadat is "a mature leader" who realizes that "what is needed is the step-by-step approach . . . in a quiet, confidential way." Sadat, the President said with gentle irony and hidden rebuke, knows better than to "put it all out on the table . . . in a huge public forum . . . and then have it blow up." Sadat said nothing more about the Palestinian problem at the Nixons' dinner for him and Mrs. Sadat in Alexandria that night. But he was back at the subject the next day in Cairo, saying at the climactic formal event of the visit that "the crux of the whole problem in the Middle East are [sic] the legitimate rights of the Palestinian people and unless this is implemented we feel that the prospects of peace . . . will be dwindling."

The event was the signing of a document entitled "Principles of Relations and Cooperation Between Egypt and the United States."

More than any other document signed and statements made on the Nixon trip, the joint Egyptian-US communique reflected and symbolized the historic turnabout in official US-Arab relationships that has occurred since Henry Kissinger addressed himself to the problems of the Middle East last year. This he did at the instance and with the authority of the President, and he and Mr. Nixon aren't faking when they say that Kissinger's success is also the President's. Yet you'd have thought from Mr. Nixon's demeanor at the Cairo ceremony that he was signing over every Watergate tape and document in the White House to the House committee inquiring into whether he should be impeached. He was pallid, languid, visibly indifferent to the people around him and what was going on. During Sadat's speech in Arabic and its horribly poor translation into English, the President had that vacant look of mental absence that I'd previously noticed and was to note again and again.

Two serious bobbles in the preparation and release of the document could have contributed to the President's evident unhappiness but probably didn't. Among the several promises of US material and technological aid to Egypt was a commitment "to sell nuclear reactors and fuel to Egypt" in order to enable the country to produce "substantial additional quantities of electric power" by the early 1980s. There were two references to supplying the fuel and reactors "under safeguard conditions" and "under agreed safe-guards." Any cautious and adequately responsible reporter would not have read into the sparse paragraph devoted to the nuclear arrangement an invitation to Egypt to join the nuclear arms club. A wire service reporter or editor did just this and there was hell to pay. Press Secretary Ronald Ziegler then did what he should have arranged to do before the document was released, explaining that the agreement was similar to many others and that—most importantly— an equivalent agreement to supply Israel with nuclear fuel and reactors was about to be announced in Jerusalem. In the light of India's recent explosion of a nuclear device, the wisdom of supplying nuclear facilities to countries that don't already have them remained open to question. The lackwit way in which this and one other item in the Cairo communiqué were handled was beyond question.

Given the importance that President Sadat attaches to the Palestinian issue, it was inconceivable that a document to be signed by him and Mr. Nixon should have appeared in advance with no reference whatever to the Palestinian people and their plight. The advance American version did precisely that. It said only that "a just and durable peace can be achieved only through a process of continuing negotiation . . . . within the framework of the Geneva Middle East Peace Conference" (a body that will be convened when and if the elements of an inclusive peace have been worked out). It developed before the signing that a crucial reference to "the legitimate interest of all the peoples in the Mid East, including the Palestinian people" had been omitted. Press Secretary Ziegler, acutely embarrassed, first said that "a communications error" in transmitting the final draft from Alexandria to Cairo caused the omission. He'd have done well to stick to that story, since the omitted language fitted perfectly into the place where it appeared in the corrected version and the original text read as if nothing had been omitted. Ziegler said instead that the reference was accidentally dropped during the matching of the final US and Egyptian drafts in Alexandria, early on the day of the signing, and that Kissinger and Egyptian Foreign Minister Ismail Fahmy caught the error when they reviewed the released version. This was believable to me but not to many of my colleagues. In the atmosphere that accompanied Mr. Nixon to the Middle East, the easy way was to believe that his spokesmen were lying again.

June 29, 1974

———

For a possible explanation of the President's sadness, see Chapter XXIII.

Identical language about the Palestinians was initially omitted and hastily inserted in the final communiqué following President Ford's meeting with Leonid Brezhnev at Vladivostok.

XXII

Kissinger's Threat

Brussels

President Nixon, Gen. Alexander Haig, Press Secretary Ronald Ziegler, Maj. Gen. Brent Scowcroft and Lawrence Eagleburger, the principal State Department assistant who accompanied Henry Kissinger on the Nixon trip to Salzburg and the Middle East, were told repeatedly by the Secretary of State during the weekend preceding his June 11 Salzburg press conference, and with bitter, unmistakable emphasis on the night and morning preceding it, that he was determined to resign if reports and commentaries that seemed to him to impugn what he called his "public honor" did not cease, and if the Senate Foreign Relations Committee did not reaffirm its previously stated confidence in him and in his integrity. Kissinger's display of hurt, anger and emotion in Salzburg, where he and the President had stopped on the way to Cairo, was widely described as "a tantrum." It was that in a narrow and literal sense, but it was not the tantrum of Kissinger alone. It reflected and it may have understated the frustration, fear, anger and emotion that at least two White House assistants, Haig and Ziegler, shared with Kissinger and encouraged him to vent in public.

The main purpose of this report is to tell that story rather than to rehash the record and merits of Kissinger's role in the wiretaps that were put upon four journalists and 13 officials, including several of his own National Security Council assistants, between 1969 and 1971, and his role in the broader surveillance operation conducted by the infamous White House "plumbers." Lest I be thought to evade those belabored issues, however, I'll state my reading of the record to date and be done with it.

My judgment is that Kissinger has been obscuring and unduly minimizing his role in the wiretaps and his knowledge of the plumbers operation ever since the rumors about his involvement began to plague him last year. He would have better served himself and the country if in the interest of candor he had overstated his wiretap role and admitted to more knowledge than he probably had of the shoddy activities of his sometime assistant, David Young, in the plumbers business. But nothing in the known record proves or, when appraised calmly and in the whole, substantially suggests that Henry Kissinger has perjured himself or disqualified himself. The very worst of the believable allegations are puny junk when measured against his achievements. The fact they have been taken as seriously as they have been is one of many indicators of the sickling times.

The story told here begins with Kissinger's press conference in Washington on June 6. The Secretary was tired after 33 continuous and wearing days in the Middle East. He was proud of what he had accomplished and he expected to be queried with intelligence and respect, in a context of implied though not necessarily explicit acclaim. Kissinger said in Salzburg that he expected and was prepared only for questions about Middle Eastern, European and Soviet diplomacy. If this statement was literally true, and I doubt that it was, it was a serious reflection upon his State Department press advisers, Robert McCloskey and Robert Anderson. Leaked, adverse reports about his wiretap and plumbers roles had been appearing during his absence and were getting sharper when he returned. If he was not told to expect questions on these subjects, he was poorly served. What he had some right to be surprised at was the sheer viciousness of one question and the brutality of a series of other questions.

Kissinger had the misfortune to encounter Peter Peckarsky, aged 27, who represents himself to be the Washington correspondent of

The Tech, a publication that according to Peckarsky appears twice a
week and has a circulation of about 8000, principally on and around
the Boston campus of the Massachusetts Institute of Technology.
Peckarsky has applied for congressional and White House press
credentials and holds temporary credentials, pending a determination that he is entitled to permanent accreditation. He turned up in
the White House press room in April and in my intensely biased
opinion has identified himself with some of his questions there as one
of those characters who mistake their press cards for licenses to
abuse, indict and malign public officials who do not enjoy their
approval. Peckarsky remarked in a recent question at the White
House that James St. Clair, the President's chief Watergate lawyer, is
handling the case as if he were defending "a common, ordinary
criminal." This is the sort of observation that any journalist has a
right to make in print or on the air, in his own name, but not on the
privileged but anonymous record of a briefing where the objective
should be, but all too often is not, to elicit usable information.

Although many of my colleagues will think me stuffy and
reactionary for saying so, I argue that such reporters as Peckarsky
and Clark Mollenhoff, the veteran and distinguished brutalitarian
who also shook Kissinger at the June 6 press conference, really ought
to go back to school for cram courses in journalism, courtesy and the
civil rights of other people. At the close of a long and complex
question—these journalistic prosecutors tend to long questions—
Peckarsky asked Kissinger "whether or not you have consulted and
retained counsel in preparation for a defense against a possible
perjury indictment?" It was a disgraceful question, not justified by the
nominally but not actually contradictory quotations that were cited
in the preliminaries to the question, or by anything else in the
Kissinger record.

Mollenhoff followed with four bellowed demands that Kissinger
acknowledge that he had recommended the wiretaps of his former
NSC assistants, a query that was remotely relevant only because
Kissinger in his defensive folly had obscured but not wholly denied
the fact that he did. Kissinger, audibly and visibly disturbed, said that
"I did not make a direct recommendation." Having been told by
Kissinger and having reported months ago in *The New Republic* that
the direct recommendations for wiretaps were made by Gen. Haig for
Kissinger, I was unable to regard this as a major journalistic triumph.

James Kilpatrick, a columnist, encountered Kissinger at a White House dinner that night and found him fuming and resentful at the treatment he had received at the press conference. At the State Department the next day he was still brooding about it but seemed to his associates to have calmed down. On Saturday morning, June 8, Kissinger taped a television interview with Howard K. Smith and Ted Koppel of ABC. Kissinger understood that about five minutes of the 30-minute interview were to be broadcast the following Friday while he was in the Middle East with the President. He and his press advisers correctly assumed that one passage in the interview was certain to be broadcast. In that passage Kissinger referred in public for the first time to the possibility that he might resign. In a clear though oblique reference to Watergate and its effect upon the conduct of foreign policy, Koppel asked Kissinger: "If you ever felt that foreign policy was being manipulated for the sake of domestic political reasons, what would you do?" Kissinger answered, "I would resign and I would say so publicly," meaning that he would publicly state his reason for resigning. The statement surprised and disturbed some people at the State Department, partly because it was the clearest indication to date that the Watergate situation troubled Kissinger more than he had previously acknowledged, and partly because what amounted to a threat of resignation and the expression of a fear that President Nixon was capable of misusing foreign affairs in a way that Kissinger would not tolerate was likely to make worldwide news and detract from the President's anticipated triumph in the Middle East. Kissinger himself seemed to his associates to be reasonably calm, however, and the impression at the department was that he had largely recovered from the shock of his press conference.

It was a short-lived impression. Anthony Lake and Richard Moose, two former Kissinger assistants who had been wiretapped, had filed civil suits that, if pursued, would help to keep the issue in the news for months or years. Bob Woodward, one of the *Washington Post* reporters who had made Watergate a national story, told State Department press officers that he and his partner, Carl Bernstein, were going to do the definitive Kissinger wiretap story and asked for the texts of everything that Kissinger had said on the subject. Kissinger heard that Philip Geyelin, a *Washington Post* editor, was saying around town that the *Post* was going to stay with and play up the Kissinger wiretap-plumbers affair and make it a second

Watergate sensation. The Sunday *Post* headed its lead editorial "What About Kissinger?" and said it was the duty of the Senate Foreign Relations Committee to recall Kissinger and "do its best to determine whether he spoke the truth." The Sunday *New York Times* reported in a front-page story that Gen. Haig, then Kissinger's deputy at the White House, ordered the FBI to end the wiretaps in question in February of 1971. If true this report and the information on which it was said to be based contradicted Kissinger's sworn testimony last September that he and his office had only indirect contact with the wiretap operation after May of 1970 and had no direct hand in terminating it.

The point that most interests me is that the impact of all this upon Kissinger did not differ greatly from the impact upon other White House officials, notably Gen. Haig and Ronald Ziegler. Kissinger said with mounting agitation, in discussion with them and others in Washington that these things could not be happening by coincidence. There had to be a "campaign" against him and there had to be somebody or somebodies directing the campaign. Haig and Ziegler agreed with him. Haig, who is generally considered to be one of the President's calmer and more thoughtful assistants, was especially insistent that a campaign against Kissinger and through him against the President was developing and that something had to be done about it. For a while before the departure for Salzburg, cooler types at State thought Kissinger had been persuaded either to settle for a statement setting forth his version of the disputed events or, preferably, to let the whole thing rest easy while he was in the Middle East with the President and see how matters stood when Mr. Nixon and he returned to Washington. As Kissinger related in Salzburg, he telephoned Sen. Fulbright, chairman of the Senate Foreign Relations Committee, on the Sunday before leaving Washington. Kissinger said that he was going to resign if the reports impugning his truthfulness and honor didn't cease and prepared Fulbright for a letter asking the committee to review the record and say publicly that Kissinger did or didn't have its full confidence. Fulbright perceived that Kissinger was very upset and thought it possible that he was saying things that he didn't really mean and might regret later. But the chairman agreed, rather sorrowfully, to initiate the inquiry and proceed to the public hearing that Kissinger said he wanted.

In news reports and commentaries that followed the Salzburg press conference, much was made of the indication that Kissinger had not told either the President or the assistants with whom he conferred that he was going to say at the press conference that he intended to resign if the critical stories did not cease and some appropriate body did not clear him of suspicion. It appears to be true that he didn't forewarn Haig, Ziegler and others that he was going to say this publicly. But he had said it in private to them, over and over. Whether Kissinger said it beforehand and explicitly to the President is unclear. The most that Kissinger would say about this at the press conference was that "I told the President that I should give you a public accounting and he agreed and we had no further discussion of the matter." It is certain that he had conveyed the message through others. Haig had told the President beforehand that Kissinger was saying that he would resign if the allegations continued and he wasn't cleared. It follows that the President knew what Kissinger had in mind when he authorized his Secretary of State to hold the press conference.

A theory developed afterward that Kissinger in his emotion went farther than he'd intended. According to this theory he had intended to content himself with saying no more than that he couldn't conduct foreign policy effectively if he remained under the sort of cloud that seemed to him to be gathering over him. The record does not support the theory. At the Salzburg conference, at a later one the same day across the border in Germany and at a still later one in Jerusalem, Kissinger was given repeated opportunities to say he had overspoken himself and to draw back from the threat to resign. In every instance he stuck by what he had said.

An impression that the President was surprised and displeased arose in part from a statement that Ziegler issued on Mr. Nixon's behalf. It said that "the President recognizes Secretary Kissinger's desire to defend his honor" and that "the Secretary's honor needs no defense." This could be read to mean that Kissinger had done something that he didn't need to do and had thereby annoyed the President. I deduce from what I've been told that a more interesting explanation lies behind the statement. The President is said to have received the news very calmly indeed when Haig and Ziegler told him that Kissinger had threatened to resign. Already aware that Kissinger had been saying in private what he had now said in public, the

President had made up his mind that he would never accept Kissinger's resignation in the current circumstances. Whether Kissinger knew this when he made the threat is something that I'd like to know and don't know. However that may be, a simple and straightforward endorsement of what Kissinger had said at the Salzburg press conference would have committed Mr. Nixon to accept the resignation when and if it was offered. In order to avoid this unlikely and unwanted prospect, the President resorted to cryptic ambiguity.

July 6 and 13, 1974

———

Peter Peckarsky protested that he had asked about but not "remarked" upon St.Clair's defense of the President and that I'd reversed the order of his adjectives "common" and "ordinary." Philip Geyelin protested that he had not been "saying around town" what Kissinger heard that he'd been saying. Henry Kissinger told me during an early morning walk around the Kremlin grounds in Moscow that he had talked of resigning in all seriousness and that he'd had no prior indication that the President would reject his resignation if it were offered. In any event, Kissinger said, he alone would decide whether to quit if it came to that. He got from the Senate Foreign Relations Committee the hearing and renewed avowal of confidence in him that he wanted. At the first presidential press conference that followed the publication of this piece—Gerald Ford's press conference, not Richard Nixon's—Clark Mollenhoff and another habitual bellower whom I disdain to name were noticeably restrained.

XXIII

One Way Out

Key Biscayne
Mr. Nixon's journey to his third Soviet-American summit began well for him, in rather surprising circumstances. He stopped in Brussels on his way to Moscow, ostensibly to join other heads of NATO governments in signing a new "Declaration on Atlantic Relations" that the North Atlantic council of foreign ministers had approved in Ottawa on June 19. The declaration was a feeble document, a meager accomplishment of the "Year of Europe" that Henry Kissinger proclaimed as the centerpiece of American policy in April 1973. It was little more than a restatement of principles and pieties that the original planners of the North Atlantic Treaty set forth in 1949. The crux of the declaration was supposed to be a passage in which the new President of France, Giscard d'Estaing, and his foreign minister tried to impose upon the United States a legally binding commitment to consult other members of the Atlantic alliance in any and all matters that might affect their interests. The passage was reduced in discussions with Secretary Kissinger in Ottawa to a vapid assertion that the welfare of the alliance "requires the maintenance of close consultations, cooperation and mutual trust."

Kissinger and Mr. Nixon were still in the Middle East, concluding the celebration of Israeli and Arab troop disengagement that took the President from Cairo to Amman by way of Jerusalem, when the accompanying White House staff announced that NATO Secretary General Joseph Luns had invited the heads of alliance governments to meet the President in Brussels on June 26. Reporters in the enormous Nixon press party took the announcement, in itself an arrogant action that should have been left to Secretary General Luns, to be final evidence (if any were needed) that the President was determined to use foreign policy and foreign travel to the very utmost in his struggle to distract the American public from Watergate and from the latest of the Watergate findings and disclosures that were about to cascade upon him. When Secretary Kissinger was subsequently reminded in Ottawa that the NATO allies had already been told of American plans for the Moscow summit and in view of that fact was asked what "the purpose and point" of the Brussels convocation was, the best answer that he could offer was that it would "give adequate solemnity" to the signing of the new declaration and give Mr. Nixon "an opportunity to exchange views with his colleagues before going to Moscow."

One might have expected, and this reporter did expect, an air of deprecation at best and of subdued resentment at worst from the officials who had been summoned in this fashion to greet Mr. Nixon in the NATO council hall on the outskirts of Brussels. The only (and perhaps deceptive) indication of such an attitude was the absence of Giscard d'Estaing. The observed attitude, discernibly and definitely not feigned by the chancellors, prime ministers, premiers and other officials who displayed it, was delight at meeting the President and a sense that their governments and the alliance were honored by his presence. The Belgian-European television network told viewers throughout the cool and cloudy morning that the transient appearance on the screen of the currently ascendant men of Europe, the smiling and preening dignitaries who preceded Mr. Nixon, was merely preliminary to the great event of the day, the arrival at NATO headquarters of the President of the United States. The announcers kept repeating without abbreviation, "the President of the United States." For an American reporter who was saturated with Watergate and imbued throughout the summit trip with a feeling that it could be this President's last journey of the kind, the Brussels reception was a valued reminder that there still are times and places when and where the presidency should be and is distinguished from the President. It must be added that I was not always sure that Chancellor Helmut Schmidt of Germany, Premier Mariano Rumor of Italy, Prime Minister Harold Wilson of Great Britain (whose jokey exchanges with Kissinger caused me to ask a colleague what a British prime minister could be laughing at just then) and the others in the greeting line were distinguishing all that completely between the presidency and the President. Some of them seemed with their show of cordiality to be saying to the cameras and to the world that they didn't understand how a chief of state who had tried to do so much for the American role in the world, whether they like the particular role or not, could have been brought to the verge of impeachment and ruin by such a thing as Watergate.

Reporters in the NATO hall noted with special interest and for a special reason that Mr. Nixon took his seat at the head of the horseshoe table before the others entered and remained seated while they stood greeting him. The reason for the special interest was that CBS correspondent Dan Rather had broken through 15 days of White House secrecy and reported on the evening before Mr. Nixon left Washington for Brussels that he had suffered from phlebitis throughout his Middle East trip and continued to suffer from it at the start of his trip to the Soviet Union. Phlebitis is a swelling of the leg veins that can be accompanied by blood clots and pain. It can be trivial and it can have grave consequences, ranging from disablement to abrupt death. The concealment of the President's phlebitis and subsequent handling of the matter by him, his physicians and his spokesmen tells so much about Richard Nixon, his mentality and the mentality around him that I turn from the summit journey as such and set down the gist of what has been observed and learned from Brussels through Moscow and Yalta and Minsk to Key Biscayne, about the phlebitis story.

At the village of Bad Axe, Michigan, in early April, Mr. Nixon was addressing a street rally when I noticed his chief physician, Maj. Gen. Walter Tkach, gazing at the President with a look of unmistakable and extreme concern. A few days later, in Key Biscayne, Tkach said that he was indeed concerned and presumably looked it, but only because he thought the President was unduly exposing himself to assault. That's for the Secret Service to worry about. I suspected that

Tkach was less than frank but there was nothing to go on, other than the weariness that Mr. Nixon frequently exhibits. During the President's flight to Brussels and at Brussels, Press Secretary Ronald Ziegler said it was true that Mr. Nixon briefly concealed his leg condition from Dr. Tkach, revealed it to him at Salzburg on the way to Cairo, and suffered some pain and wore an elastic bandage on his left leg during part of the time in the Middle East. As for the secrecy, Ziegler said the President didn't want to have everyone he met in the Middle East "asking him how is his phlebitis . . . and being concerned about his movements and so forth." When Ziegler was asked in Brussels whether the phlebitis had anything to do with the look of distraught sadness that I reported in my account of the Mideast trip, he first said the President didn't look distraught and sad. When he was asked whether the phlebitis had anything to do with the President's appearance, however it might be described, he answered that "maybe it did, a little bit." My view remains that Watergate had more than phlebitis to do with that look of sadness.

Now we jump ahead a bit, first to the Kremlin quarters where the President was staying on the morning of July 2 and then to the weekend following July 4 in Key Biscayne. A junior Nixon staffer told me at the Kremlin that Dr. Tkach and his assistant, Rear Adm. William Lukash, had begged the President in Salzburg to cancel the Mideast trip and had warned him in the most urgent terms that he risked death from a rush of blood clots to the lungs and arteries. The assistant said that the President rejected the advice and ordered his physicians, along with the few other assistants who knew of the problem, to keep absolutely quiet about it. After the President arrived at his home on Key Biscayne for rest and preparation for the Watergate ordeals to come in Washington, Dr. Tkach told Paul Healy of the New York *Daily News* essentially what the junior assistant had told me at the Kremlin. Ziegler confided to me that at times in the Middle East, particularly in Cairo and during a tiring train ride from Cairo to Alexandria, the President had been in "severe pain" and "terrible pain." Ziegler continued to say to the press party in Florida, as he'd been saying in Brussels and the Soviet Union, that the danger of a clot rush had passed but that the swelling and some mild pain persisted. Reporters learned for the first time of the scene in Salzburg when the President confessed that he'd been holding out.

Not only Tkach and Lukash but Haig and Ziegler insisted upon seeing for themselves the swollen, tender area of the left leg—they still were not saying just where it was—that signaled the phlebitis. Questions derived from all of this that I put in Key Biscayne to Ziegler and to Gen. Alexander Haig, the President's staff chief, elicited related but somewhat different answers. Understanding the questions and the answers requires a recapitulation of the President's behavior in the Middle East and in the Soviet Union.

Mr. Nixon didn't have to stand for hours in reception lines in Cairo and Alexandria, endure hours seated in punishing restriction in motorcade cars, and (as Ziegler later described it) suffer that agonizing train ride to Alexandria. But he did. He didn't have to clamber up rough slopes and stand on jagged rocks and otherwise exert himself in blistering heat at the Egyptian pyramids. But he did. He didn't have to walk under a blazing sun, in heat that damn near prostrated me and younger reporters, from one royal palace to another in Jeddah, Saudi Arabia. But he did. In Brussels after his heartening reception at NATO headquarters, he didn't have to walk three long blocks from the American ambassador's residence to the royal palace, part of the way over rough cobbles, shaking hands with delighted onlookers and, in front of the palace, retracing his steps to congratulate the commander of the royal horse guard upon his and his mounted men's handsome appearance. But he did. In Moscow he didn't have to repeat the ceremonial laying of a wreath to the war dead that he'd gone through in 1972, requiring a slow march to and up a flight of steps that would tax healthy legs. But he did.

At Yalta on the mountainous and lovely Crimean coast, to which he flew and motored from Moscow at the insistence of Leonid Brezhnev, the big and serious story was the shock—still not adequately explained—that the President and Henry Kissinger got when they were exposed to the full ferocity of Soviet refusal to accept any nuclear arms deal that would curtail Soviet freedom to achieve what its leaders consider to be a degree of parity that much of our officialdom would hold to be nuclear superiority over the US. The lesser story (if it *is* a lesser story) that interests me has still to do with Mr. Nixon's behavior. He didn't have to put up with a long drive, confining and harmful to phlebitic legs, from Simferopol airport to Yalta and back again. But he did. He could have taken a much shorter Soviet helicopter ride on one or both of these trips. But he didn't. He didn't have to take a longish walk with Brezhnev for the benefit of reporters but he did. He didn't have to follow his stay at Yalta with an empty and arduous stay at Minsk, the capital of the synthetic noncountry of Byelo-Russia, entailing among other activities a long walk over rough concrete slabs to and from the famous Khatyn memorial to millions of Soviet victims of Nazi atrocities. But he did and I saw him wince and stumble, slightly but visibly, at the end of the walk. Although Ziegler and Haig talked later as if it hadn't happened, the President suffered a substantial flare-up of his phlebitis in Minsk and his doctors were alarmed by it.

I had these and similar episodes in mind when I asked Gen. Haig in Key Biscayne whether he had reason to believe that Richard Nixon had wanted his phlebitis to free him from life and from Watergate. Gen. Haig might have been or pretended to be outraged by the question. He accepted it as a serious question. He said that so far as he knew the President had no such wish or thought. Ronald Ziegler reacted differently to a somewhat different question. When Ziegler was asked whether Dr. Tkach had discussed with others on the staff a possibility of disablement short of death, Ziegler misunderstood the question. He took it to be a revival of the notion, more popular in late 1972 and early 1973 than it's been lately, that Mr. Nixon was toying with the thought of pleading physical disability and resigning when and if impeachment and conviction became certain. Ziegler said that the President was not thinking of using his phlebitis in this way to escape judgment.

July 20, 1974

———

Soon after Mr. Nixon resigned and when clamor for his indictment was rising, one of the assistants whom he most valued and trusted recalled this piece and said very seriously that he wondered whether those who were hounding the former President realized that he might be driven to accomplish with a bullet what phlebitis might have accomplished.

XXIV

Awaiting Judgment

San Clemente

During the President's flight from Washington to California on July 12, several happenings aboard the magnificent aircraft that is provided for his travels around the country and the world typified his situation and his latest stay at what we of the accompanying press continue to call, somewhat inaccurately, "his" San Clemente estate. Press Secretary Ronald Ziegler confirmed a report that a mortgage payment of $226,400 on the estate had been postponed for six months because the inescapable payment of hitherto evaded federal income taxes had stripped Mr. Nixon of ready cash. Ziegler also told reporters on the plane that the President had conferred in Washington that morning with his chief Watergate attorney, James St. Clair, about the House Judiciary Committee's impeachment inquiry. Without attributing the view to Mr. Nixon, Ziegler indicated an expectation that the committee would recommend impeachment and that a majority of House members would vote against it. The chief of the White House staff, Gen. Alexander Haig, passed to the President the radioed news that a federal jury in Washington had found his sometime friend and senior assistant, John D. Ehrlichman, guilty of lying and of obstructing justice. Two of Mr. Nixon's economic advisers, Kenneth Rush and Roy Ash, spent two hours of the flight with the President in a discussion of inflation and the federal budget. They said afterward in San Clemente that he never once mentioned the Ehrlichman verdict or any other aspect of Watergate.

The first 10 days of the California visit were days of waiting for House committee action and for a Supreme Court decision that the President is or is not legally and constitutionally obligated to give Special Prosecutor Leon Jaworski tape recordings and all other existent records of 64 White House conversations that were presumed by Jaworski and federal Judge John Sirica to be related to Watergate episodes and prosecutions. Much that occurred in public in these days suggested that the President and his spokesmen had succumbed to fright and panic. I am persuaded by what White House acquaintances had told me in Washington and went on telling me in San Clemente that the true explanations were more complex and interesting. According to these accounts the President continued to believe that the massive publication of Judiciary Committee evidence and staff analyses of the evidence would not cause the required majority of House members to approve and send to the Senate for trial and final decision the articles of impeachment that a majority of the Judiciary Committee seemed to be determined to submit to the whole House. In these accounts the evidence of what I was initially inclined to consider fright and panic was said to be properly attributable to a White House cast of mind that has been ascendant there for many months and still persists.

One of the President's daughters, Tricia Cox, perfectly expressed this cast of mind when a group of reporters asked her about the House committee's inquiry and she replied: "If the committee votes to impeach, it will just be a political move by people who just want to get Richard Nixon out of office. And I can't believe that after they hear and see the evidence someone [*sic*] will really go ahead and vote for impeachment. Innocence is innocence and my father is innocent . . . People out of power just don't want to see my father in office. But they won't get away with it. This is a country of justice." The inclination in the White House press corps, including its female contingent, is to dismiss remarks of this kind by Mrs. Cox and by her more aggressive sister, Julie Eisenhower, as the vaporings of understandably committed advocates. It's a mistaken inclination. In essence, setting aside meaningless differences in wordage and nuance, fundamentally identical convictions were expressed during the San Clemente stay by the redoubtable Gen. Haig; by the previously mentioned economic advisers, Kenneth Rush and Roy Ash; by Kenneth Cole, John Ehrlichman's successor as assistant for domestic affairs and director of the Domestic Council; by Dean Burch, a White House counsellor and extremely tough cookie who is organizing an all-out White House campaign against impeachment in the House of Representatives; and by Raymond K. Price, Jr., a staff thinker and speechwriter who retains the respect of many journalists who have lost any respect that they may have had for Mr. Nixon. The neglected and weighty fact, weighty in the sense that it could importantly affect the outcome of the impeachment struggle, is that the President is surrounded and fortified by a corps of staff and familial devotees who are dedicated to belief in his basic innocence, and blessed or cursed, depending upon the observer's bias, with a seemingly unlimited capacity for rejecting the evidence that their man is in fact a shoddy and discredited caricature of the maligned leader that they suppose him to be.

The outrage that Mr. Nixon and the manifold betrayals of the public trust with which he stands charged arouse in many people is matched, to say the least, by the sense of outrage that the attacks upon him arouse among his immediate admirers and servitors. Much of the expression of this outrage in San Clemente, particularly by Press Secretary Ziegler and Counsellor Burch, was organized and orchestrated by the President's director of communications, Ken W. Clawson, Jr., a former newspaper reporter who is said to have impressed the President with his efforts to discredit evidence that cannot be convincingly disproved. The chief and current source of the evidence in question is the House Judiciary Committee, and Clawson's way of discrediting the evidence is to discredit the committee. Ziegler's suggestion at a White House briefing in San Clemente that the committee has let its chief counsel, John Doar, turn it into a "kangaroo court," and Burch's flat assertion at a press conference that Doar and his fellow attorneys on the committee staff have played the parts of "hired guns" were among Clawson's contributions to the impeachment debate. They do him and his master, the President, no credit and it may be doubted that in the end they will do Mr. Nixon and his cause as much good as they are thought at the Western White House to have done. But, taste and effectiveness apart, the outrage that such expressions reflect is profound, it is genuine and it goes far to explain the President's continuing determination to fight impeachment.

On the 11th day of the President's July stay in California, Clawson presented James St. Clair not only to the attendant Nixon press corps but to the nation over live television. Whether this turns out to be the public relations achievement that it was initially believed to be at the California White House is extremely doubtful at this writing. It is doubtful because, on the face of the St. Clair performance, it was based upon the faulty premise that the main interest of the questioners and the consequent thrust of the discussion would have to do with the concluding phase of the House Judiciary Committee inquiry. St. Clair justified his previous reluctance to appear at a comparable forum by saying that the committee proceedings had been in closed session, and justified his appearance now with the fact that the committee was about to go into public, televised sessions. Clawson first planned to precede the California press conference with release of excerpts from St. Clair's final summation of the President's case against impeachment at a closed committee session, then decided to release excerpts later. As it turned out, the reporters were more interested in the pending Supreme Court decision on whether the President had to obey a pending subpoena for crucial Nixon tapes than Clawson and St. Clair seemed to have expected. St. Clair was. asked five times whether the President would obey the decision regardless of whether it went for him or against him, and five times he refused to say whether the President would or wouldn't. Now the Supreme Court has unanimously decided that he must surrender the tapes, and the President's response may be known before this is read.

There's an interesting and untold bit of history to be recalled. On July 26, 1973, when Watergate issues involving the President were first moving into litigation, Deputy Press Secretary Gerald Warren said at a White House press briefing: "Of course the President, just as in any other matter, would abide by a definitive decision of the highest court." At a San Clemente press conference on August 22, the President paraphrased Warren's reference to what Mr. Nixon called "a definitive order of the Supreme Court" and said, "that statement stands." The President didn't want to say then that he'd obey any

Supreme Court decision or order, "definitive" or not. For reasons that I've never been able to get a White House lawyer to explain, beyond suggesting that Supreme Court decisions in cases involving a President might or might not be mandatory and compulsory, Mr. Nixon wanted to leave the matter open in July of 1973 just as he was leaving it open in July of 1974. He was told in 1973 that some of the lawyers in his service—I don't know which ones—would resign if he didn't make at least a qualified pledge to obey the Supreme Court. The qualifying use of "definitive" resulted. Even the qualified pledge was soon abandoned. I don't know of any lawyers who resigned because of that.

July 27 and August 3, 1974

———

This piece had gone to press when James St. Clair announced the President's intention to obey the Supreme Court. For crucial happenings on that day that I discovered and reported after Mr. Nixon resigned, see Chapters XXV and XXVI.

XXV

Judgment Days

San Clemente

The little that is known of how the President lived and comported himself through the days of judgment.that began to come upon him during his summer stay in California is summarized in this report.

We start with the morning of July 24. Eight of the nine members of the US Supreme Court unanimously rejected the substance of every argument that James St. Clair, the President's lawyer, had made in his behalf to the effect that this or any President is immune from judicial compulsion in matters that involve presidential communication with other people. The ninth member, Justice William Rehnquist, did not participate. The assumed reason was that he had been intimately associated with former Attorney General John Mitchell, one of the defendants in a criminal case that was involved in the infinitely larger issue before the Supreme Court. The fact, not necessarily determinative, was that the President had appointed Justice Rehnquist, praised him in public and cruelly derided him in private. The eight participating justices ruled in an opinion written by Chief Justice Burger, also a Nixon appointee, that the President had to surrender to federal Judge John Sirica the White House tape recordings and any other records of 64 White House conversations.

A distinction that press accounts tended to skip or elide was a vital part of the Supreme Court decision. It enjoined Judge Sirica, who had presided at previous Watergate trials, to take the greatest care to ensure that only those portions of the Nixon tapes and records that he found relevant to the criminal case involving Mitchell and other former Nixon associates be turned over to Special Prosecutor Leon Jaworski, who had originally subpoenaed the tapes and written records. It was not the order for total turnover to Jaworski that many accounts indicated it was. Chief Justice Burger noted in his opinion for the Court that "a presumptive privilege for presidential communications" is founded though not explicitly stated in the Constitution and that "the privilege is fundamental to the operation of government." But Burger and his fellows held with crushing breadth and finality that the President's "claim of absolute privilege" is constitutionally wrong and, in such a case as the one involved, must give way to the requirement that both prosecutors and defendants have for use in a criminal trial all of the evidence, including evidence in a President's possession, that may bear upon the guilt or innocence of defendants. It was the latest and perhaps the ultimate example of the ruin that the President had brought upon himself with what one of his White House lawyers called "those goddamn tapes."

A strange time ensued at San Clemente. St. Clair, who was there and at a press conference on the 23rd had said he had no reason to expect a decision on the 24th, had flatly assured Gen. Alexander Haig, the White House staff chief and communicator of most things to and from the isolated President, that the Court would not be deciding the case on the 24th. He based this on his understanding that the Court usually gave interested attorneys 24 hours' notice of important decisions and his office in Washington had had no such notice. At a party at his house on the evening of the 23rd Gen. Haig assured reporters that there would be no decision the next day in the Nixon case. How White House attorneys who are more familiar with Supreme Court practice than St. Clair is could have failed to tell him and Haig, and the President through them, that the Court in very sensitive cases often withholds notice to lawyers to "be at the counsel table" until as little as an hour before decision time is a mystery. Anyhow, that's what happened on the 24th. The President, Gen.

Haig, St. Clair, Press Secretary Ronald Ziegler and Communications Director Ken Clawson, the persons principally involved in subsequent discussion, were caught flatfooted and flatminded by the news at a little after 7 am Wednesday morning, San Clemente time, that the Court would be announcing its decision within an hour.

Now comes a part of the account that really mustn't be misunderstood or misinterpreted. A decision against the President and his claim of "absolute privilege" was expected. Charles Alan Wright, a distinguished constitutional lawyer who had endured a succession of incredibly stupid White House slights and remained loyal not so much to the President as to the proposition that he was entitled to the best available defense, had attended St. Clair's oral argument before the Court, listened to the Justices' questions, and predicted afterward that the best the President could hope for was a six-to-two decision against him. What wasn't so certain was a decision that would be totally mandatory and would leave no room for maneuver. A hope that it wouldn't be unanimous also lingered. Partly in the hope of something short of a totally mandatory decision and implementing order, the President's spokesmen including St. Clair had been refusing for months to commit him to obey any Supreme Court decision and had abandoned a short-lived pledge in July and August 1973 that he would obey "a definitive decision," whatever that meant. It didn't mean and wasn't supposed to mean anything. But the hangover from that interim of calculated and abysmally mistaken noncommitment affected the half hour or so of discussion in Gen. Haig's office at the Western White House that preceded facsimile transmission from Washington of the long decision text and the additional half hour or so that St. Clair and others required to absorb the (for them) shaking thrust and thoroughness of the decision. During that brief period, there was some discussion of whether the President *would have to obey* the Court order. I am told and, absent evidence to the contrary, elect to believe there was then and later in the day no discussion and debate over whether the President *should* obey the kind of order that this one turned out to be.

Another aspect of this interim discussion and of the hours that followed before St. Clair announced the President's disappointment with the decision and his intention "to comply with that decision in all respects" made it exceedingly (though not undeservedly) difficult for

White House spokesmen to dampen the persisting suspicion that Mr. Nixon spent the day trying to squirm out of compliance. It became known that the President called a few people and Haig called a good many more people in Washington and elsewhere, asking their advice, before the decision to comply was announced. What were they calling about, except to ask if there was any way for the President to escape compliance? About the President's calls, I have no firsthand knowledge. I'm told and in one instance *know* that Haig's calls dealt with how to do it and not with what to do. Haig was asked by a couple of people whom he called whether the President was going to obey. He is said to have replied, of course. Mostly he asked whether it should be done in a spoken or written statement, by the President or St. Clair or Press Secretary Ronald Ziegler, on TV or merely in a handout. St. Clair read a two-minute statement on TV. When Ziegler appeared later in the California press room, reporters gnawed at him with questions indicating the deepest doubt that Richard Nixon had decided without cavil or debate to obey the Court. It was all deserved. But, after the statement that he would comply, it was to this onlooker a painful reminder of the sad state of distrust to which Mr. Nixon has brought the country.

Worse was to come before the week and the California stay were ended, with the beginning of the House Judiciary votes to recommend the impeachment of the President and the acknowledged erosion of confidence among some of his most steadfast assistants, Haig included, that he would escape impeachment by a majority of the House of Representatives. So there will be rougher days in Mr. Nixon's presidency than the day of the Court decision. But it was a bitterly testing day for him. An assistant who was intermittently with the President before, during and after the hours that he spent in discussion of the Court decision with St. Clair and Haig said that Mr. Nixon was utterly cool, unflustered, amused by a chance opportunity to keep two visitors waiting half an hour beyond their appointed time of meeting. An assistant who worked with the President on an economic speech that he was to make the next day said that during two hours in the afternoon at this task he never mentioned the decision and concentrated totally upon the speech. A frequent companion of the President who is trained to note physical characteristics insisted that on this and other days Mr. Nixon really appeared, as his spokesmen kept saying, to have recovered from the phlebitis that pained him in the Middle East and caused me to wonder in print whether the President deliberately aggravated it for awhile.

Even about that kind of thing, with matters allegedly going well, his spokesmen either don't know or can't tell the whole and simple truth. Press Secretary Ziegler and Deputy Press Secretary Gerald Warren said within hours of each other that the President no longer bandaged his ailing left leg just above the ankle and that he was wearing an elastic support sock on it. These are what Nixon spokesmen call perfectly consistent statements.

August 10 and 17, 1974

———

It was my luck (good or bad? I don't know) that *The New Republic's* summer-fall publication schedule gave me an extra week to reflect upon and inquire into Mr. Nixon's resignation. I didn't expect it when the foregoing piece was written and went to press a week before he resigned.

XXVI

Demise

This is the story of the last 17 days of the Nixon presidency insofar as I have been able to learn the story. There have been many such accounts. Most of them, including some that pretended to be but in the main were not obtained at the White House, originated in Congress and in other peripheral quarters. The most to be said for this account, apart from views attributed to members of Congress, is that it reflects and is confined to what I was told at the White House by officials who were involved, some intimately and some at varying distances, in the agonies of discussion and maneuver that preceded and accompanied the first resignation of a President of the United States and the first accession to the office of a President who had not been elected to either it or the vice presidency.

We must start again, as I did in my account in *The New Republic's* August 10 & 17 issue of the President's final approach to judgment, with events in Washington and San Clemente on July 24. The US Supreme Court on that day announced its unanimous decision that President Nixon must surrender to federal Judge John Sirica, for passing after review and removal of irrelevant material to Special Prosecutor Leon Jaworski, the tapes and any other records of 64

White House conversations that might bear upon the guilt or innocence of defendants in a Watergate case. The President was at his Western White House and residence in San Clemente. Eight hours elapsed between the announcement of the decision and the announcement by Mr. Nixon's chief Watergate attorney, James D. St. Clair, that the President intended "to comply with that decision in all respects." It was explained then that it took time to absorb the nuances of so important and complex a decision and that the President and his chief assistant, Gen. Alexander Haig, needed and were taking time to solicit advice from people in Washington and elsewhere, not on whether to comply but on how best to announce the intention. Since then I've learned that the uses of the intervening eight hours were more murky and interesting than the previous account indicated and, in a way about to be noted, were fatefully indicative of what was soon to come.

One of the options suggested to the President, and rejected by him, was that he announce that he was defying the Supreme Court decision for the good and protection of the presidency and of future Presidents, publicly destroy all the remaining White House tapes, and then resign. This suggestion came from a longtime adviser to Republican Presidents, including Mr. Nixon and now President Ford—an adviser who is widely regarded by journalists as a moderate and a moderating influence. Mr. Nixon might have welcomed and paid serious attention to such a suggestion if a far more critical and immediate matter had not been on his mind that day in San Clemente. It was what to do about the ruinous passages that he knew and had known since at least early May to be on three of the taped recordings that Judge Sirica and now the Supreme Court had ordered him to surrender, through the judge, to Jaworski. They were portions, amounting to a total of some 18 minutes, in 129 minutes of three conversations with H. R. Haldeman on June 23, 1972. That was six days after the original break-in and arrests at the Democratic headquarters in the Watergate office building in Washington and nine months before March 21, 1973, when Mr. Nixon had said again and again that he first learned of efforts at the White House and at its election-year adjunct, the Committee for the Reelection of the President, to conceal or, in the tag phrase that has joined the national language, to "cover up" White House involvement in the Watergate crime. Because he had listened to the recordings on May 5 and 6, he knew that they proved that he not only knew about the attempt at cover-up but participated in and authorized a key part of it on June 23, 1972.

Here I combine fact with conjecture. The fact is that J. Fred Buzhardt, the President's staff counsel in Washington, called for the June 23 recordings as soon as the Supreme Court decision was announced and spent the rest of the decision day listening to them in his office in the Executive Office Building next door to the White House in Washington. Why did he go immediately to those particular tapes? "That is something I will never tell you," Buzhardt told an inquirer. My conjecture, supported to some extent by the impression of other White House assistants, is that Mr. Nixon ordered Buzhardt to review the June 23 tapes and tell him, the President, whether in Buzhardt's opinion they were as damaging as the President feared they were.

Buzhardt reported within hours to the San Clemente White House that he had listened to the tapes and that the Watergate passages would finish the President. In terms of strict and limited legalities, Buzhardt felt, they did not necessarily destroy the President's defense. In the political and human terms that concerned the country and the House Judiciary Committee, then moving toward its first impeachment votes, the taped passages were ruinous because they proved Richard Nixon to be a liar and an early participant in decisions that had led to the indictment of former Attorney General John Mitchell, H. R. Haldeman and five other Nixon men. The President, Haig and St. Clair knew that this was Buzhardt's opinion of the June 23 tapes when St. Clair announced Mr. Nixon's decision to comply with the Supreme Court decision. They knew it when, during the four remaining days of Mr. Nixon's last stay as President in California, Communications Director Ken Clawson and Press Secretary Ronald Ziegler raised the White House counterattack upon the House Judiciary Committee to a peak of irrational and, as it turned out, self-defeating frenzy. They knew it on July 27 when, after the committee had voted the first article of impeachment, Ziegler said in a written statement: "The President remains confident that the full House will recognize that there simply is not the evidence to support this or any other article of impeachment and will not vote to impeach. He is confident because he knows he has committed no impeachable offense." Did Ziegler know about the June 23 tapes and Buzhardt's estimate of them when he said this for the President? The available answer throws an explanatory light on the Nixon White House at its top and center in the final days. Ziegler and Haig, remember, were then and for many months had been the President's only regular and intimate official confidants. They were assumed to work in concert. On the 27th and later, until and after Mr. Nixon's resignation, Ziegler hid from reporters and refused to answer questions. It was said later and authoritatively that Haig didn't know whether Ziegler knew of the tapes and Buzhardt's report. Haig knew only that he hadn't told Ziegler. Haig didn't know whether Mr. Nixon had told Ziegler.

The Nixon party returned to Washington July 28. The peddled and generally reported story thereafter was that knowledge of the damaging passages came as a terrific shock to Haig and St. Clair when rough, partial transcripts were given them on July 31. Here again the fuller facts tell much about the Nixon White House in its death throes. St. Clair heard the key passages on July 30 and perceived that Buzhardt had, if anything, understated the damage. Buzhardt, who until then was Haig's only authority for what was on the tapes, stood low in Haig's judgment because of some fairly serious mistakes in the handling of subpoenas and tapes in the fall of 1973. Haig had laid down a rigid rule that transcripts be made only from copies of original tapes, in the sensible apprehension that the originals might be harmed during transcription. But Haig's opinion of Buzhardt and the time required for copying tapes did not entirely explain the slow dissemination of the bad news to and at the top of the Nixon staff. Only a realization by the President and Haig of the devastating effects that the Watergate passages were bound to have upon everyone who became aware of them could explain it. Henry Kissinger was told on the 31st that bad trouble was in the tapes, but he didn't know what the trouble was and how bad it was until the June 23 transcripts were released for publication late on August 5. Communications Director Clawson was vaguely alerted on August 2 but he, like Kissinger, didn't get the whole score until Haig imparted it to the White House staff just before the transcripts and an accompanying Nixon statement were issued.

Three "defense teams" of lawyers and White House staff writers had been put together after the return from California to deal with each of the three articles of impeachment voted by the Judiciary Committee. Raymond Price, the writer most esteemed by Mr. Nixon, headed one of these teams. Charles Lichstenstein, an assistant to counsellor Dean Burch, headed one. Patrick Buchanan, a conservative consultant to the President, and David Gergen, nominally the chief Nixon writer, each thought that he headed the third team. Price learned on Thursday night, August 1, and Buchanan on Friday, August 2, that they might as well forget the defense operation, and they did. Gergen sensed but was never told that he might as well forget it, too. Price was shown the Watergate portions of the June 23 transcripts that Thursday night and was told by Haig to begin thinking about a Nixon statement to accompany publication of the transcripts. Buchanan was shown the Watergate portions and given similar instructions Friday. Haig on Saturday, August 3, instructed Ziegler, Price, Buchanan and St. Clair to prepare to accompany him to Camp David, the presidential retreat in the Maryland mountains near Washington, on Sunday, for a conference with the President. Mr. Nixon was already there with his wife, his two daughters and their husbands, and Charles G. Rebozo, his Florida friend and companion in trouble.

Masses of tosh have been printed about the Camp David meeting. One of the few points worth making about it now is that the President didn't have to be persuaded at that stage to publish the June 23 transcripts and acknowledge, as he did the following day, that he'd been at fault in withholding vital information from his lawyers, his congressional defenders and his staff. The sole issue in substantial doubt and discussion was whether he should leave the way open for early resignation, which he resisted doing but finally did, or commit himself to see the impeachment process through to Senate trial and predictable conviction, which he preferred to do and, after waverings that continued well into the following Wednesday night, didn't do. I have talked with three of the five participants in the Camp David meeting. None of the three thought it odd, all thought it perfectly natural, that President Nixon conferred in person only with Haig and Ziegler and met them separately, never together.

Haig told Price on Tuesday night to begin drafting the resignation speech that the President delivered on Thursday night, August 8. The instruction to Price from the President through Haig never changed. The key instruction was to admit nothing more than a few "mistakes of judgment" and to avoid even the mild acknowledgment of guilt that had appeared in the Monday statement. Price discussed successive drafts with the President by telephone several times and once in person on the last Thursday morning. He never had the slightest intimation that the President might change his mind and refuse to resign. Mr. Nixon nearly changed several times and actually did once, in midafternoon of Wednesday before Haig had Senators Goldwater and Scott and Rep. Rhodes visit him and tell him how hopeless his situation in Congress was. Henry Kissinger, leaving Mr. Nixon at midnight Wednesday after assuring him for 2½ hours that he was right in believing that common sense and the international weal required resignation, but never demanding or explicitly recommending resignation, was not altogether certain on Thursday morning that the President would do what he did that night.

Thank God, he's gone. I'll miss him and I wish for him the mercy that he doesn't deserve and probably won't get.

August 24, 1974

XXVII

Nixon Postscript

Here are some afternotes on the final phase of Richard Nixon's presidency.

The disastrous potential of the June 23, 1972, tapes that completed the destruction of the Nixon presidency was sensed by though not known in precise detail to some of the President's attorneys last May and June. President Nixon listened in early May to the June 23 tapes and a few others that had been subpoenaed by Special Prosecutor Leon Jaworski. After hearing them, Mr. Nixon ordered special White House counsel James D. St. Clair to cancel an informal deal that he had made with Jaworski and federal Judge John Sirica for partial delivery of material on the subpoenaed tapes. Both the subsequent appeal of Judge Sirica's order that the tapes and related documents be surrendered to him for delivery in their relevant portions to Jaworski and the Supreme Court decision on July 24 that Sirica's order was valid and had to be obeyed flowed from the President's attempt to withhold the subpoenaed tapes. Mr. Nixon's special concern with the June 23, 1972, tapes was obvious to his attorneys, though so far as I have been able to determine they didn't know then that portions of three recorded conversations with H. R.

Haldeman proved that the President had connived in and authorized
an important part of the original Watergate cover-up—the effort to
restrict FBI investigation by claiming falsely that vital CIA
operations would be revealed. Chief among the 15 White House
attorneys who were handling the President's Watergate problems in
the summer of 1974 were St. Clair, staff counsel J. Fred Buzhardt and
Leonard Garment, a former Nixon law partner who hoped he'd got
himself free of Watergate matters after deep involvement in them
during part of 1973 but never had completely escaped them. In the
discussions about to be reported, I am certain only of Buzhardt's
participation and assume that St. Clair and Garment were also
involved to varying extents. The known circumstances suggest that
Garment was less involved than St. Clair and Buzhardt were.

Before the Sirica order to surrender the subpoenaed tapes and
documents, including the June 23, 1972, tapes, was appealed to the
Supreme Court, President Nixon was advised that there was a legal
way to "moot"—that is to kill—both the Jaworski subpoena and the
Watergate case that had brought on and justified the subpoena. This
was the case in which Haldeman, former Attorney General John N.
Mitchell, former senior adviser John D. Ehrlichman, former White
House lawyer and adviser Charles Colson and three other sometime
Nixon associates had been indicted. Jaworski justified his subpoena
entirely on the ground that information in the demanded tapes and
documents might bear upon the innocence or guilt of the indicted
defendants and that a fair trial would be impossible without access to
the tapes and documents. Buzhardt and (I believe but don't know)
other White House lawyers advised Mr. Nixon that he could vitiate
the subpoena that so obviously and deeply troubled him by
pardoning the defendants. As a lawyer Mr. Nixon presumably didn't
have to be reminded that the presidential pardoning power is not
limited to convicted persons. It can in theory extend even to persons
who have not been charged before the pardon setting forth the charge
is issued. The presumption that the President knew this is quite a
presumption, incidentally: Mr. Nixon's ignorance of elemental
criminal law was extraordinary even for an attorney who had
engaged principally in civil practice and it continually astounded his
White House attorneys after the Watergate cases began to develop.
The attorney (or attorneys) who advised the troubled President that
he could banish this particular trouble with pardons offered two

other pieces of advice. They were that the President had better
pardon himself, while he was about it, and resign. He was forewarned
that the storm that pardoning the Watergate defendants would
arouse, even if he didn't pardon himself, would be so fierce that he'd
have to resign eventually. In this context he was told that he might as
well prepare to resign immediately. Aware though he was of the
danger buried in the June 23 tapes, Mr. Nixon was in no mood to
resign and he rejected the advice. Here it must be noted that "advice"
may be an inaccurate term. It may be fairer to say that the course
outlined above was presented to the President as one of the options
open to him, but was not pressed upon him. It was one of the
alternatives to risking the adverse appellate decision and compulsory
order to surrender the tapes that he brought upon himself by rejecting
the suggested option.

Some serious discussion of Mr. Nixon's personal and prospective
Watergate problems, the Jaworski subpoena aside, occurred at the
White House in the months preceding his downfall. Whether these
discussions involved the President in person, and whether the
consensus developed during the discussions was reported to him are
unknown. Attorney General William B. Saxbe says that he wasn't
involved or consulted. Jaworski indicated on the night that Mr.
Nixon announced his intention to resign that the Special Prosecutor
and his office had not been involved. The interesting fact remains that
such discussions occurred at the White House. They indicated an
awareness of the President's possible if not likely involvement in
criminal charges at a time when he and his spokesmen, notably
including James St. Clair, were declaring his innocence of any
criminal action or involvement.

The discussions in question began with and rested upon the
proposition that a President may pardon a person before the person
has been formally charged with anything. The person principally
figuring in the discussions was President Nixon. The consensus
developed in the discussions was, roughly, that Mr. Nixon *could*
pardon himself. He *could* save himself from direct accusation by
pardoning certain of the Watergate defendants who had variously
been indicted, pleaded guilty or been convicted. Weaving through the
White House discussions was the thought that the Watergate pardons
might be made palatable to the public, or at least rendered tolerable,

if they were somehow linked with amnesty for Vietnam deserters and draft dodgers. This thought continued to permeate discussion, public and private, of the subject after Mr. Nixon resigned. The discussions reported here, however, preceded the resignation by weeks and months and foundered upon a quandary that nobody participating in them could resolve. The quandary was where to stop with the Watergate pardons. Should they include such as Jeb Magruder, John Dean, Charles Colson, Howard Hunt, Egil Krogh, Herbert Porter who had pleaded guilty and, in some instances, had served their bargained time? Most troublesome of all, should the pardons include former Nixon supporter, counsellor and Treasury Secretary John B. Connally, who had been indicted but not tried in a milk bribe case that was only remotely related to Watergate in its broadest meaning? The consensus was that there was no feasible way to foreclose Mr. Nixon's prospective court problems by use of the pardoning power. Not, anyhow, while the President was Mr. Nixon. So far as I know White House discussion of this subject lapsed after Gerald Ford became the President. The only evidence to the contrary—and it need not be connected with Mr. Nixon's problems—is that President Ford proposed a limited and vaguely defined degree of amnesty for Vietnam evaders on August 19.

In my August 24 report, I wrote that James St. Clair knew when he announced President Nixon's compliance with the Supreme Court's July 24 tapes decision that Fred Buzhardt had listened to the June 1972 tapes in Washington that day and had reported to the San Clemente White House, where St. Clair was, that the Watergate portions would finish the President when they became known. Did St. Clair fully believe what he been told, or did he have to be convinced and really shaken after he got back to Washington and listened to the tapes for himself? On Thursday night July 25, St. Clair flew to Washington on an Air Force Jetstar transport with his wife and Communications Director Ken Clawson. Clawson, the organizer and coordinator of Mr. Nixon's public relations defense, reminded St. Clair that he was to appear the following Sunday on ABC's television program "Issues and Answers." St. Clair told Clawson to cancel it . Clawson told St. Clair that the President had approved the commitment and wanted St. Clair to fulfill it. St. Clair said that if the President insisted on it, he'd have to get himself a new lawyer. The appearance was cancelled. This is the only authenticated instance I know of in which St. Clair made such a threat. I believe the White House story that on related issues—publishing the fatal transcripts, resignation itself—the President had to be persuaded but not pressured in explicit and threatening terms.

Clawson was one of four people in positions of influence at the White House who opposed resignation to the very last and argued that Mr. Nixon should fight impeachment through to the Senate trial and what by then was recognized to be certain conviction and removal. According to Clawson and assistants who verify his story, the other three diehards were Julie Nixon Eisenhower; Rose Mary Woods, Mr. Nixon's confidential secretary and executive assistant; and Bruce Herschensohn, a staff publicist who coordinated and sought the support of unofficial groups.

For readers who are interested in how this strangest of presidencies worked at the end, here are some additional and previously unreported details of the Sunday staff meeting at Camp David that preceded the publication of the June 1972 transcripts on Monday, August 5. As was indicated but not stated as clearly as it should have been in my August 24 report, there was no "Camp David meeting" with the President in a meaningful sense. Gen. Alexander Haig, Mr. Nixon's (and President Ford's) staff chief, brought four people to Camp David with him on that Sunday: St. Clair, staff writer Raymond K. Price, Jr., staff consultant Patrick Buchanan and Press Secretary Ronald Ziegler. Only two of these five, Haig and Ziegler, met and talked with the President and he saw them separately. Mr. Nixon having already decided to publish the transcripts before Judge Sirica, Jaworski or the House Judiciary Committee could, the only issue in effective discussion was whether and when to commit the President to resignation. Buchanan on Friday told the President, through an intermediary, that after reading the Watergate references in the transcripts he, Buchanan, believed that Mr. Nixon had to resign. Buchanan asked Haig on Saturday whether the President had received and noted this advice, and Haig said he had. St. Clair briefly offered and quickly dropped a suggestion at Camp David that the President announce his intention to resign in a statement to be drafted by Price and issued the next day with the June 23 transcripts. Haig told St. Clair, Price and Buchanan that he told the President that the four believed resignation was inevitable and advised Mr.

Nixon to reconcile himself to it. But, Haig said he said to the President on the four's behalf, don't act upon our advice; await the impact of the transcripts to be published on Monday afternoon. Then, Haig said he told the President, he could no longer doubt that Haig, St. Clair, Price and Buchanan were right. Mr. Nixon couldn't and didn't for long. Some of the others at Camp David said that Ziegler in his discussions with them neither opposed nor advocated resignation. He desperately sought alternatives to it and got none from his four companions. What Ziegler said to Mr. Nixon at Camp David is unknown. A senior White House assistant who participated importantly in later discussions and does not admire Ziegler said that Ziegler came down for resignation and helped to divert Mr. Nixon from the crazy impulse to fight on, to an end that could have been disastrous for the country.

Mr. Nixon came near to doing that. His erratic behavior in the final days and hours coupled with some aspects of his behavior during his presidency, convinced an assistant involved in the final discussions that the President was mentally ill and had been for many years. This opinion was impressive because it came from a man whose friendship with and loyalty to Mr. Nixon predate the Nixon presidency. About nine hours before Mr. Nixon announced his decision to resign, after having made and revoked and resumed it during the previous 24 hours, I showed this assistant a letter that I had received from Mrs. A. Perry Phillips of Columbia, Missouri. She urged me to consult the late Dr. Karen Horney's *Neurosis and Human Growth,* a famous study of neuroses short of what is commonly considered to be insanity, and said that I would find in it explanations of "the ambiguities, contradictions, and irrationalities" that seemed to her to have marked President Nixon's career. The assistant glanced at the letter, remarked that he was familiar with Dr. Horney's book and said in a voice torn with pain, "Of course, that is exactly it." Others were less explicit. Seven days before Nixon announced his resignation, Patrick Buchanan—who was to see the decisive transcripts within 12 hours—said that he could imagine the President resigning only in one of his "moody moments" when, Buchanan implied, Mr. Nixon could act irrationally. A Nixon lawyer who probably has seen more evidence of Mr. Nixon's odd attitudes and actions in the past two years than anyone else in his service would in the recent past have thrown anybody who questioned President Nixon's basic stability out of his office. When this lawyer was asked after Mr. Nixon quit and departed for California whether he'd noted anything recently and during his time at the White House that led him to worry about his President's mental condition, he answered: "Mr. Nixon is a very complex man. Who among us would measure up completely to anybody's particular definition of sanity?"

Defense Secretary James R. Schlesinger confirmed reports that he had taken care that no improper orders from the White House were conveyed to or carried out by US military forces during the last days of Richard Nixon's agony. Let this be said. Richard Nixon in his presidency never misused the authority of the Commander-in-Chief in the fashion implied in these reports. The reports were interesting indicators of anxieties that did prevail in the final fortnight. The fact is that, in contradiction of these anxieties, Mr. Nixon had the guts and sense to resign when he did and as he did.

September 7, 1974

———

The reaction to the last paragraph of this piece provided a lesson in the dangers of ambiguity. Readers, including some at the White House, thought I was implying that Mr. Nixon might have misused his authority to order nuclear bombing. Of whom, for God's sake? I and, I am quite sure, Secretary Schlesinger had in mind only a remote possibility that Mr. Nixon or others in his service might ask the military to interfere with his displacement. Mr. Nixon did not and I am persuaded that he never thought of doing so.

XXVIII

The Pardon

Let the first of my reports on the Ford White House—what a dull ring the phrase has, incidentally—begin with a confession. I'm glad that President Ford pardoned former President Nixon. I hoped that Mr. Ford would do it before he did it and I'm sorry only that he did it in the worst possible way.

I hoped for, welcomed and still applaud the Nixon pardon for a reason that will seem to many and perhaps most readers of *The New Republic* to be empty, illogical and outrageous. It is a reason (or nonreason, some may say) that has nothing to do with the prerogatives of Presidents and respect for the presidency as such, although a tendency to respect Presidents and the presidency must have been apparent to readers of these reports in the Nixon time. I simply had and have a gut feeling that the prolonged spectacle of indictment, prosecution and trial of *this* former President, Richard Nixon, would have been bad for the country. It would be better, I thought and still think, to settle for the acknowledgment and plea of guilt that were implicit first in Mr. Nixon's resignation and then in his acceptance of the pardon. Some of the extreme demands that he explicitly acknowledge his guilt and the more strident denunciations of Mr. Ford for not requiring Mr. Nixon to do so seem to me to have in them a quality of savagery that is close to sadism. What more should we require from the broken man who showed himself to the nation on television when he said good-bye to his staff on the morning of August 9? No more, I say. As for the complaint that the pardon jeopardized the prosecution and pending trial of H. R. Haldeman, John Mitchell, John Ehrlichman and three other Watergate defendants, and that it clouded the previous indictments, guilty pleas and convictions of numerous other Nixonites, I refer the screamers to Special Prosecutor Leon Jaworski. He knew without being told during the week before the pardon was announced that it was coming and he did not object. On the contrary he let his staff's report that Mr. Nixon was under investigation in 11 areas of possible criminal involvement and his estimate that nine months to a year and possibly longer would have to elapse between indictment of Mr. Nixon and even the beginning of a trial be cited in support of the pardon.

So much for my opinion. Now to the little that I know and the much else that I heard but don't know to be true about the origins and aftermath of the Nixon pardon. It's a story that is notable for its gaps, anomalies and contradictions. It suggests that Mr. Ford and his people aren't telling a lot that needs to be told.

A fact that Mr. Ford at this writing has not confided to his closest and most senior associates is that he briefly but seriously considered announcing his intention to grant the pardon at his first press conference on August 28. Probably because he had not had time to have his own lawyers satisfy him that he had the power to pardon Mr. Nixon prior to indictment or conviction, he postponed the decision and announcement. At the senior staff meeting at which the press conference was "game planned," with assistants trying anticipated questions out on the President and suggesting answers, one of the anticipated questions was whether he agreed with former Governor and Vice President-designate Nelson Rockefeller, who had just agreed with Senator Hugh Scott that the departed Mr. Nixon had been "hung" and should not be "drawn and quartered" by indictment, prosecution and trial. The answer discussed at the preparatory meeting stopped with Mr. Ford saying merely that he agreed with Rockefeller and leaving the impression that he leaned toward leniency for the former President when and if it became necessary.

The expected question proved to be the first question asked at his press conference and Mr. Ford began his answer as his assistants had understood he would. But in the rest of his first answer and in his answers to the second and third of four questions he got on the subject, he went on to say: "There have been no charges made, there has been no action by the courts, there has been no action by any jury. And until any legal process has been undertaken, I think it is unwise and untimely for me to make any commitment . . . . Of course, I make the final decision. And until it gets to me, I make no commitment one way or the other . . . . I am not ruling it [a pardon] out. It is an option and a proper option for any president."

These answers were generally reported to mean that Mr. Ford had committed himself to await the indictment and possibly the conviction of Mr. Nixon before a pardon would be considered or granted. Did he mean to convey this impression and, if he did, what happened in the next 48 hours to cause him to indicate at a meeting with four senior associates that he was inclined to pardon Mr. Nixon as soon as possible? These remain essentially unanswered questions. They were poorly asked and feebly answered at his second press conference on September 16. Private inquiries got better answers than the September 16 performance did, but those answers as reflected here are far from satisfactory. One of the President's assistants understood him to say soon after the August 28 press conference that he hadn't meant to convey the reported impression. Another assistant understood him to indicate with regret that he had misunderstood the law of pardon and the extent of his power to pardon when he answered as he did. Nobody in his private councils appears to have asked him explicitly whether he intended to convey the reported impression and, after he had decided to pardon Mr. Nixon immediately, whether he considered this a basic change of position. When Robert Hartmann, one of the few assistants that Mr. Ford brought with him into the presidency from the vice presidency, tried to warn him that an immediate pardon would surely be thought to be in total contradiction of his August 28 position, Mr. Ford showed a singular lack of interest. This suggested to me, though apparently not to Hartmann, that the President didn't think there was a substantial contradiction. At any rate the only development between the press conference on August 28 and a crucial meeting with four senior assistants on the morning of August 30 that is known to or acknowledged by some of these assistants is that the reaction to his statements at the press conference made Mr. Ford uneasy and caused him to call for two things. They were thorough research of the law of pardon and his power to pardon and the best indication that could be obtained from Special Prosecutor Jaworski of the extent and imminence of Mr. Nixon's legal peril. In particular the President wanted to know how long the judicial process would take if it were allowed to proceed from indictment to trial.

The four assistants at the August 30 meeting were Hartmann; another counsellor, John Marsh, a former Virginia congressman and assistant to Ford during his brief vice presidency; the new President's staff counsel, Philip Buchen, a longtime friend and former law partner from Mr. Ford's hometown of Grand Rapids; and Gen. Alexander Haig, the staff chief inherited from Mr. Nixon who was about to return to active army duty and take over the American and NATO military commands in Europe. They and one other, a young lawyer named Benton Becker who was a friend of Mr. Ford's and a temporary assistant to Buchen, were the only White House people who knew about the approach to an early pardon until it was disclosed to a very few others on Saturday, September 7. Haig didn't know before the preceding Thursday night and Hartmann learned on Friday the 6th that Mr. Ford had definitely decided to issue an immediate pardon. At the August 30 meeting he indicated his wish but not a firm decision to do so.

According to the assistants whose accounts are reflected here, including Philip Buchen and his statements at two on-record press conferences, four occurrences during the week following August 30 principally accounted for Mr. Ford's final decision to act as he did when he did on Sunday, September 8. Buchen assured the President that he did have the power to pardon before indictment. Considering that President Nixon's lawyers had established this fact months before and had exhaustively discussed every implication of it, the asserted fact (I still find it hard to credit) that Mr. Ford didn't know this before and on August 30 indicates that the gulf between President Nixon's people and Vice President Ford's people before the resignation was even wider than it was known to be. The second major factor was Leon Jaworski's advice that nine months to a year and maybe longer would have to elapse after indictment and before trial could begin. The strong impression around Mr. Ford is that this estimate bothered him more than any other factor. The third element was the information, also from Jaworski, that no less than 11 areas of criminal misbehavior that could involve Mr. Nixon were under investigation. The fourth factor was the belated conclusion of an agreement between President Ford and former President Nixon, negotiated by Becker at San Clemente and signed by Mr. Nixon on Friday the 6th, committing the tapes and documents accumulated during the Nixon presidency to his custody in California under his and the federal government's joint control. Jaworski's staff and a congressional committee raised hell about this agreement later and Philip Buchen, acting for Mr. Ford, agreed to postpone transfer of the tapes and other materials to California. But the President was satisfied with it when it was signed. Although he had his spokesmen insist that a satisfactory agreement was not a condition to the pardon, Mr. Ford was equally insistent that he would not announce the pardon before an agreement was concluded. It appears, in short, that the agreement was a condition to the announcement but not to the pardon as such. The terms of the tapes agreements seem to have mattered much more to the President than did the wording of Mr. Nixon's grudging admission of error but not of guilt.

Benton Becker, the aforementioned lawyer and temporary assistant to Buchen, returned from San Clemente to Washington with the tapes agreement and reported to the President on Saturday, September 7. Haig, Hartmann, Marsh and Buchen were present when Becker reported to Mr. Ford. Accounts of that meeting are the most persuasive evidence known to me that Mr. Nixon's physical and mental health was not the decisive factor in Mr. Ford's calculations and decision to grant the pardon that it has been widely reported and believed to be and that he and his assistants say it wasn't. Mr. Ford spent far more time at the meeting on the tapes agreement and showed far more interest in it than he displayed in what Becker, who had conferred in person with Mr. Nixon, had to say about the former President's health. Becker said nothing about Mr. Nixon's spreading phlebitis and apparently didn't notice the enhanced swelling in the left leg that others reported. Becker said that Mr. Nixon appeared to have aged and shrunken—*shrunken* was a frequent term. His shirt collar flapped around his neck. His jowls hung pathetically loose and flabby. His whole upper torso, hitherto massive for so slight a figure, appeared to have diminished. His attention span seemed to be short, he tended to leave remarks unfinished in midsentence and he rambled. These last observations, which could have been taken to be indirect comments upon Mr. Nixon's mental state, did not particularly impress or interest Mr. Ford and the others present. Physical shrinkage apart, Mr. Nixon had been disjointed, rambling, prone to drift off into some far yonder for months before he resigned. Vice President Ford was talking about that last March, to my knowledge.

After Becker finished his report he left the Oval Office with Haig and Marsh. Hartmann and Buchen remained with the President. Mr. Ford leaned back in his chair, clasped his hands behind his head, and proceeded to tick off, for the benefit of Hartmann who would draft the pardon announcement, the reasons that should be stated for granting the padon. Mr. Ford never once mentioned Mr. Nixon's health during this soliloquy. The reasons he mentioned were the reasons that Hartmann wrote into the delivered statement: mercy; an end to the passions and divisions that a trial would prolong; "Richard Nixon and his loved ones have suffered enough." When Hartmann gave his draft to the President on Sunday morning, Mr. Ford made two changes. Where Hartmann had written that the Nixon tragedy "could go on and on," the President wrote "on and on and on." He also inserted the subsequently famous reference to serious allegations and accusations "threatening the former President's health as he tries to reshape his life." These additions neither surprised nor specially impressed Hartmann and Mr. Ford didn't make any great thing of them. What did impress Hartmann and Buchen during the final preliminary session with the President on Saturday, after Becker had reported and gone, was Mr. Ford's adamant insistence that the pardon be announced immediately. He would have done it that Saturday night if he hadn't been persuaded with considerable difficulty that it would take time to complete the necessary paper work and duplication, line up television and assemble the national press. He was urged to put the announcement over into the following week. Mr. Ford said Sunday at the absolute latest. He was asked why the rush? His only answer was that somebody might ask him about it and he didn't want to have to lie about it. Why not simply say, he hadn't decided? "Because I *have* decided," the President answered. The answer didn't satisfy the few assistants who heard it or learned

"I am not a crook . . . anymore"

about it. They suspected that the President was holding something back. A natural suspicion was that it had something to do with concern for and about Mr. Nixon. If Mr. Ford was holding something back and we knew what it was, we'd have the solution of any mystery there may be about the Nixon pardon.

Mr. Ford's press secretary and friend of 25 years, Jerry terHorst, resigned in protest. A matter of principle, he said. He was suspected at the White House of wanting out anyhow and of using the pardon as a pretext. Mr. Ford believed it was indeed an act of principle. "You just don't understand these evangelical Michigan Dutchmen," he told an outraged loyalist.

September 28, 1974

———

Mr. Ford told a House subcommittee on October 17 that General Haig, in the course of informing him on August 1 that White House tapes about to be given to the House Judiciary Committee so deeply and clearly implicated President Nixon in the Watergate cover-up that he probably would have to resign, mentioned a pardon for Mr. Nixon by his successor as one of the options being discussed by Nixon assistants. Mr. Ford also said: "I assure you that there never was at any time any agreement whatsoever concerning a pardon for Mr. Nixon if he were to resign and I were to become President." Longtime friends of Gerald Ford make sense to me when they argue that there didn't have to be an explicit agreement; nobody who knew Mr. Ford as well as they and Richard Nixon did could have doubted that the new President would at some point pardon the former President. Mr. Ford's account to the subcommittee of how he came to grant the pardon when he did coincided in all substantive respects with what I was told and wrote in the preceding piece a fortnight after the pardon was announced. The prediction that my approval of the pardon would outrage readers of *The New Republic* proved to be correct.

XXIX

Ghosts

Within an hour after Vice President Gerald Ford became President Ford on August 9, he gathered some 20 of his predecessor's principal assistants in a conference room across a corridor from the Oval Office that had suddenly become his office and told them to relax. He said that he didn't want the automatic resignations that are customarily submitted to a new President. He said that he needed their help, he wanted them to stay with him "through the transition," and he wanted them to assure their subordinates that there were to be no abrupt changes and dismissals. There would be changes in due time, of course. But those who chose or were asked to leave the White House staff would have plenty of time to find other jobs and those who wished to work elsewhere in government would be helped to find jobs. Mr. Ford used a rather odd figure of speech to make his central point. Nobody, he said, was going to be thrown off the airplane without a parachute.

It was a kindly and generous gesture, in sharp and instantly noted contrast with Richard Nixon's cold and witless demand on the day after his reelection in 1972 for the resignations of most of his assistants. It also was in recognition of the obvious fact that the

Nixon staff had to be kept pretty much intact for awhile if the business of the presidency was to be done. Some of the effects, however, were unintended and unfortunate for all concerned. Two months after Mr. Ford took over, many veterans of the Nixon time still didn't know whether they were expected to remain or quit. Many who knew that they were expected to leave didn't know when they had to be out. Very few had been given firm termination dates. A few assistants in the upper ranks had come to vague understandings with Gen. Alexander Haig, the staff chief who was replaced on September 30 by Donald Rumsfeld, that they'd have until dates ranging from October 15 to December 1 to find other jobs.

In the meantime the term "Nixon holdover" had become an epithet in the White House press room and in much of the media. Reporters and commentators reproached the President for not adopting and enforcing a policy of arbitrary dismissal that media union contracts generally forbid and a company management would be criticized for applying to its executives. Some of Mr. Ford's own people, under strict orders though they were to be considerate and patient, were getting impatient for a practical reason. They wanted to put their own choices into the budget slots still occupied by Nixon people and were beginning to let the Nixon people know it in ways varying from subtle to savage. Although I applaud Mr. Ford's policy of patience and deplore the vengeful attitude toward anything and anybody associated with Richard Nixon that accounts for much of the pressure upon the President to make a quick and total sweep, the Ford White House at times seems even to me to be populated with ghosts from the Nixon past.

Eight of the 13 assistants who attended the first senior staff meeting that Donald Rumsfeld, himself a former Nixon counsellor, presided over were Nixon appointees. No changes that can be attributed to Mr. Ford's advent have occurred on the staffs of two of the principal White House entities, the Domestic Council and the National Security Council. Kenneth Cole, executive director of the Domestic Council, says he's had enough of government after five years and intends to quit early next year. Tod Hullin and Joyanna Hruska, who were respectively confidential assistant and secretary to Cole's indicted predecessor, John Ehrlichman, remain on the council staff and are said to be doing good work. Lawrence Higby, a former assistant to the departed and indicted H.R. Haldeman, is at the Office of Management and Budget and hopes to stay. Rose Mary Woods, Mr. Nixon's $36,000-a-year executive assistant, and her $23,000 "staff assistant," Marjorie Acker, work on Nixon files in the former President's hideaway suite in the Executive Office Building.

One of the more interesting survivors is J. Fred Buzhardt, who was staff counsel to Mr. Nixon and briefly to Mr. Ford. Buzhardt and James St. Clair, the former President's chief Watergate lawyer, displeased President Ford by ruling rather arbitrarily that the tapes and documents accumulated by Mr. Nixon during his presidency are his personal property. A resultant and prevalent impression is that Buzhardt is an unwanted hanger-on at the Ford White House. Nothing could be farther from the truth. He remains, he hopes not very much longer, at the urgent request of his successor as counsel to the President, Philip Buchen. Buchen wants Buzhardt around for a fascinating reason. The written records of Mr. Nixon's Watergate maneuvers and defense are sequestered with other Nixon papers and are not available to the Ford staff. The chief and in some instances the only source of information that Buchen needs in dealing with the Watergate aftermath is Fred Buzhardt's memory of what went on. Michael Sterlacci, one of 15 lawyers who worked under St. Clair, is also helping Buchen and other Ford lawyers with Watergate problems. Sterlacci is among 22 government employees who were listed the other day as on detail to Mr. Nixon. Sterlacci was in San Clemente for a few days, working on legal problems connected with the transition, but at this writing is back at work for Buchen and the President. Jean Staub, another St. Clair lawyer, was retained until recently at the insistence of federal Judge John Sirica, who wanted a White House attorney available on demand to help him when he was screening subpoenaed Nixon tapes. She has joined a Washington law firm and Sterlacci is the only St. Clair attorney who remains on the Ford staff.

Five assistants who were among the most aggressive in Mr. Nixon's defense and among the most bitterly hurt when he resigned provide a cross-view of what's happening. Bruce Herschensohn, who coordinated private support for Mr. Nixon, resigned four days after Mr. Ford became President and is executive director of a new conservative organization that professes to be dedicated to support of the presidency as an institution. Father John McLaughlin, a Jesuit priest who joined the Nixon staff as a speech writer and wound up making speeches to conservative audiences in Mr. Nixon's behalf, resigned on October 2 after ignoring for many weeks repeated indications that his early departure from the Ford staff would be welcomed. Richard Moore, a lawyer and sometime broadcast executive who was a public relations adviser first to John Mitchell and then to Mr. Nixon, resigned on September 30 and probably will have departed when this is read. Patrick Buchanan, a conservative consultant to Mr. Nixon and an outspoken critic of what he considers to be the dangerously liberal and biased national media, hoped for awhile to stay in government and would have liked to be ambassador to the Republic of South Africa. He's changed his mind or had it changed for him and in early October he was planning to quit and write a syndicated newspaper column.

The fifth example is Ken W. Clawson, who as Mr. Nixon's second and last director of communications managed the final propaganda campaign in his behalf. Clawson is one of the assistants who had or thought they had an understanding with Gen. Haig. It was that Clawson could count on remaining on the federal payroll until November 15 or December 1. Nobody pretended that he would do or would be expected to do any work for President Ford. Although he is not among the officials and employees listed on detail to Mr. Nixon, Clawson went to San Clemente in mid-September and was still there on October 1. He said in the previous week that "I'm simply doing for The Old Man what he's been asking me to do, which is just transition-type stuff." Mr. Nixon had entered a Long Beach hospital for treatment of his phlebitis. Clawson cited as an example of what he was doing a statement that he had drafted for Mr. Nixon, thanking the thousands of people who had wired, written and telephoned their hopes for his recovery and their general good wishes. At this writing, no trace of the statement has been noted in print or on the air. Clawson, who was one of the best national reporters in Washington when he let Charles Colson talk him into leaving *The Washington Post* for the Nixon White House in early 1972, is in the market for a job and hasn't been offered one that suits him. It's no fun and no asset, being known as a loyal assistant to and apologist for Richard Nixon.

October 12, 1974

I was writing the foregoing reference to uncertainty prevailing at the White House as a result of Mr. Ford's intended kindness when Donald Rumsfeld, a friendly acquaintance since he joined the Nixon staff in 1969, telephoned and asked me what I thought most needed doing. All I could think to say was that a lot of Nixon people needed to be told where they stood with the new regime. Rumsfeld proceeded to tell them or have them told, as he presumably would have done anyway, with consequences that are noted in Chapter XXXI.

XXX

Troubles

A White House assistant who was on duty with Richard Nixon in San Clemente for awhile noticed quite a change in the former President when he came home from his first visit to the Long Beach hospital where his phlebitis was treated. The assistant wondered before Mr. Nixon entered the hospital whether he'd be found some morning on the bottom of his swimming pool. Afterward at home he was still as tired and wasted as he appeared to be in the television pictures of his departure from the hospital. But he seemed to the assistant to have snapped out of the apathy and depression that often engulfed him during the early weeks of his enforced retirement. He was talkative, feisty and angry, still cursing the Long Beach photographer whom he'd called a son-of-a-bitch and god-damning the restrictions that his ailment imposed upon him.

This report was among the few cheerful items that reached Washington from San Clemente and a lot more cheerful than what was happening to Mr. Nixon in Congress and at the Ford White House. At the risk of seeming to invite a degree of sympathy for Mr. Nixon that he does not deserve and that I do not feel for him, I summarize in this account the essence of what I've heard from his people about his situation and about the scene at what used to be the Western White House.

Any such account must begin with the atmosphere aboard Air Force One when it took Mr. Nixon, his wife, his daughter Tricia, her husband Eddie Cox, and 10 or so assistants and other staff associates from Washington to California on August 9. Mr. Nixon and his family were in his forward compartment. The assistants were in a midship staff compartment. Their recollections vary on some points but not on the point that they shared a sense, so deeply felt that it didn't have to be spoken, that they were a gallant band enlisted in a gallant cause, the service of Richard Nixon. One of them remembers silence throughout the trip, as on a funeral train. Another of them recalls that they were variously numbed, in trauma, near hysteria, and talkative. They knew that Mr. Nixon's formal resignation was to be handed to Secretary of State Henry Kissinger at precisely 11:35 am, Washington time. Some of them kept saying to each other until that moment, "He is still the President of the United States. *He is still the President.*" Mostly, though, they remember and still talk of the sense of togetherness that bound them and would do much to see them through the first weeks of decompression and what seemed to them to be deprivation in San Clemente. At about 11 am Mr. Nixon walked aft and joined them for a few minutes. Some of them remember that they were amazed at his recovery, whether real or pretended, from the condition of incoherence and near collapse that the nation observed on television during his farewell to the White House staff. He joked. He had words of recognition and thanks for each of them. He told them to cheer up and they were cheered, a little.

Their sustaining sense of gallantry and togetherness has begun to fade. The attacks in the media and in Congress upon what they collectively are costing the public and the impact of those attacks upon Mr. Nixon's prospects for staff support in the future have had a depressing effect. The public listing of former press secretary Ronald Ziegler at $42,500 a year, former special assistants Frank Gannon at $35,500 and Stephen Bull at $34,000, press assistant Dianne Sawyer at $21,000, staff writer Raymond K. Price, Jr., (who wasn't on the plane) at $40,000 make the support accorded Mr. Nixon at San Clemente appear to be far more lavish than it seems to be to those providing the assistance. The annual salaries of 18 people whom the Ford staff considers to be on chargeable detail to Mr. Nixon until the six months of transition support authorized for him end next February 9 total $375,800. With either per diem expense allowances that can but in most cases don't run up to $40 per day per person, or the "justifiable expense" arrangements that Ziegler prefers and has demanded from the General Services Administration, the scale of support provided in San Clemente and Washington can be made to seem extravagant and seems so at this writing to most congressmen, Republican and Democratic. President Ford's original request on behalf of Mr. Nixon for $850,000 for the period ending next June has been cut by the House of Representatives and a Senate subcommittee to $200,000 and the Senate subcommittee has recommended a ceiling of $220,000 upon the salaries of White House and other employees detailed to Mr. Nixon during the statutory transition period of six months. If that ceiling holds and even if Congress finally prorates against it only the 18 salaries that the Ford White House considers chargeable, Mr. Nixon will have little or no money left from the initial transition period for staff support during the remainder of the fiscal year. The $100,000 so far appropriated and recommended for the period between February 9 and June 30 will allow only $45,000 for staff and other assistance after $55,000 in pension to be paid from it is deducted. The $45,000 seems to many people to be too much. But I do think the San Clemente scene as his people see it is of interest, considering the all but universal impression that he is being munificently supported in his disgrace.

Imagine that you are a Nixon assistant who knew how it was at the Western White House before August 9 and are revisiting the Coast Guard base where the Nixon office compound is situated, next to the Nixon estate. At the gate where Coast Guardsmen control entry both to the base and to the office compound, uniformed sentries in white gloves go through their familiar minuet. Beyond the gate all is unbelievably changed. On the helipad where a gleaming green and white helicopter, sometimes two helicopters, always stood in waiting for the President, a tennis net and a volleyball net are stretched for the use of Coast Guard families. On the lots where 20 to 30 official cars used to be parked, three or four cars and maybe a couple of golf carts are seen. The Executive Protective Service policemen and the Secret Service agents who were always around when the President was there are no longer in sight. Agents are assigned, but not in the obtrusive numbers they used to be. Inside the lesser of two office buildings, one-story affairs that never were impressive and seem forlornly modest now, most of the cubicles are bare of occupants and furniture. Ziegler, Gannon, Dianne Sawyer, Ray Price on the latest of several visits and Lt. Col. Jack Brennan, a military aide, are in their offices with a couple of secretaries, but the place seems weirdly quiet. You walk to the rear. The dining patio that once was the delight of the Western White House is bare of furniture, excepting one table and four chairs. In the adjoining kitchen crates of chinaware and utensils are packed for removal. The remaining supply has been reduced to one cup, one plate, etc., per person. A few cheese sticks and a nearly empty jelly jar indicate that somebody has been using the kitchen. The navy stewards and cooks are long gone. Anne Grier, a White House secretary, cooked hotdogs and prepared tuna lunches for the group for awhile but has stopped. They fend for themselves.

A cubicle in this wing is piled with some 40,000 pieces of unopened mail addressed to Ziegler for Mr. Nixon. Some 400,000 pieces are scattered about the place. Across an open walkway in the senior staff and presidential wing, scores of thousands of telegrams and letters are stacked in the office that used to be Henry Kissinger's. It's Mrs. Nixon's now. She seldom uses it. Mr. Nixon uses his front office occasionally, riding over from his home in a golf cart. He shares a secretary, Nora Vandersommen, with Stephen Bull and they occupy small offices near his. The office that was H.R. Haldeman's and then Gen. Alexander Haig's is stripped and usually locked. It's to be a library for Mr. Nixon's immediate use, if and when his presidential files are released from preventive custody and shipped to California. Whether he gets them is problematical, the concern about Watergate evidence and the hatred of him being as fierce as they are in Congress and the country. The remaining Nixon tapes aside, convenient access to the sequestered documents is essential if Mr. Nixon is to fulfill the book contracts to which he must be looking for money to bail him out of debt, pay lawyers' fees and generally support him in the style that he likes. Reports to the contrary notwithstanding, the public that he betrayed is not supporting him in that style now.

October 19, 1974

———

This piece was being read in *The New Republic* when Mr. Nixon returned to the hospital and nearly died. Bull and Anne Grier left the shrinking San Clemente staff and the faithful Ziegler let it be known that he, too, would be leaving as soon as he felt that Mr. Nixon could make do without him.

XXXI

Shakeout

White House happenings in the ninth and tenth weeks of Gerald Ford's presidency told something of how it was shaking out and shaping up.

When the President introduced General Alexander Haig's successor, Donald Rumsfeld, to the senior staff on September 30 and said that Rumsfeld was to be called and thought of as a coordinator rather than a chief of staff, Mr. Ford emphasized two other things. One of them was that he expected Rumsfeld to devise and administer an "orderly" decision process. The President bore down heavily on "orderly," implying a recognition that the presidential process since he took over from Richard Nixon on August 9 had been somewhat disorderly. The second thing he emphasized, with great force, was that he expected and wanted no news leaks from his White House and looked to Rumsfeld to see that they did not occur. Just what Mr. Ford meant by "leaks" was not made clear. The sensible judgment among his hearers was that he meant advance, unauthorized reports of unannounced decisions that had been recommended to him or he was about to take. A plethora of such leaks, in advance of his economic speech to Congress, occurred forthwith and were followed by a series of errors and "clarifications" that reflected a bobbly staff process. My own experience, not necessarily typical, suggested that some of the President's assistants took him to mean that he wanted contact with the allegedly "open" Ford White House to be confined to his press spokesmen. Rumsfeld himself indicated as much in a brief appearance in the White House press room after his introductory session with the senior staff. He soon was the subject of a leak to the effect that Mr. Ford expected to replace Defense Secretary James R. Schlesinger with Rumsfeld in about six months. A supplementary rumor had it that Rumsfeld had told some reporters that he looked upon the White House assignment as a six-months job. Rumsfeld, who was about to leave for Brussels where he had to make his formal farewells as ambassador to the NATO Council, sent word to me that the six-months rumor was false. The extraordinarily weak denial that Press Secretary Ron Nessen accorded the Rumsfeld-for-Schlesinger story, followed by a spate of contradictory reports that the President was expecting and preparing to clean out the Nixon cabinet after the November 5 elections, with no two accounts agreeing on whom he plans to keep and discard, reminded me of a conversation that Mr. Ford has acknowledged having with me last March 30 when he was still Vice President Ford. Then he was of a mind, among other matters, to fire Schlesinger and keep Labor Secretary Peter Brennan. The other day I read that he's firing Brennan and keeping Schlesinger. My policy is to await further word and action from Gerald Ford.

Rumsfeld moved fast to form his own temporary staff, lay the basis for a permanent central staff, and establish his primacy over the White House staff at large, including the very few chums and long-time associates whom Mr. Ford brought with him from the vice presidency into the presidency. Four lawyers and a political scientist who were associated with Rumsfeld after he quit Congress in early 1969 to become director of the Office of Economic Opportunity and to be simultaneously a White House assistant to President Nixon, comprise his temporary staff. The political scientist and, more recently, adviser to institutional investors, is Richard Cheney, Rumsfeld's executive assistant at OEO and now at the White House. Three of the lawyers—John Robson, Don Lowitz and Don Murdoch—are friends and associates who have come aboard as temporary consultants and are fighting off suggestions from

Rumsfeld that they take permanent staff jobs. The fourth lawyer, William Walker, is Rumsfeld's appointee to the powerful post of White House personnel chief, meaning chief recruiter both for the White House staff and for political spots in departments and agencies. One of the first assignments given Lowitz and Murdoch was to draft a code of ethical conduct for White House assistants, with provisions for monitoring and enforcing it in such a way as to prevent any more Watergates. The draft had been on Cheney's desk less than an hour when Cheney got telephone calls from two journalists. They said a tipster outside the White House had a copy of the draft and was trying to sell it to them.

A lively question was whether and to what extent Robert Hartmann, a longtime and valued associate of the President and his principal speechwriter, would subordinate himself to Rumsfeld. Hartmann made no secret of his dislike of General Haig and of his efforts, by means of news leaks and internal prods, to get Haig out. Along with other devices, Hartmann made a point of his refusal to attend Haig's senior staff conferences and boasted of his instant access to the President without Haig's or anybody else's permission. Hartmann turned up at a few of Rumsfeld's morning staff meetings, so that nobody could say he refused to attend, and not often enough to acknowledge that he had to be there. Hartmann's appointments with the President suddenly began to be scheduled in advance through Rumsfeld, like those of other senior assistants. Other events on the schedule permitting, Hartmann's regular appointment is at 9 or 9:15 am.

Initial organization and status apart, one of Rumsfeld's first moves was to resolve the problem posed by Nixon assistants and by Mr. Ford's overly vague and generous indication that they could stay until they had other jobs. Rumsfeld ruled that it was each division head's responsibility to indicate clearly who was to stay and who was to leave, and when. Where no division heads were available, Rumsfeld did it himself. He told Helen Smith and Lucy Winchester, respectively Mrs. Ford's and previously Mrs. Nixon's press secretary and social secretary, that he wanted their resignations effective November 1. They understood that they were welcome to stay until around January 1. Mrs. Winchester quit immediately. Hurt but forbearing, Mrs. Smith agreed to stay until November 1 to break in her successor, a TV newsperson named Sheila Weidenfeld. Nancy

Lammerding, a capable and delightful veteran of the early Nixon press staff who lately had been in the State Department's protocol office, succeeded Mrs. Winchester. A typically injured and embittered victim of the new precision was Ken Clawson, the Nixon regime's last director of communications. He had understood from Gen. Haig that he might be detailed to Mr. Nixon until February 9 or, failing that, retained on the federal payroll until December 1. He was not detailed to the former President and, while trying to negotiate a new job from the strength of his White House position, was reminded by Press Secretary Nessen that Gen. Haig had gone. Nessen told Clawson to submit his resignation effective as of November 7. David Gergen, the chief of the White House writing staff, and three of his writers were told by his successor, Paul Theis, to be out by and as of November 15. Raymond K. Price, Jr., Mr. Nixon's favorite writer, was luckier than most. He had his own deal for a Nixon book lined up and told the firers before they told him that he'd be out and away in early November. The Rumsfeld, media and political heat on Nixon holdovers caused Philip Buchen, the senior among President Ford's three lawyers with the title of counsel, to forgo his wish to keep former counsel J. Fred Buzhardt around awhile for his knowledge of the Nixon tapes and the Nixon time. Buzhardt left on October 5, well before he had expected to.

Rumsfeld kept strictly out of a more important area of Buchen's business. This was the attempt to renegotiate with Mr. Nixon's chief Washington attorney, Herbert J. Miller, the agreement on custody of the Nixon tapes and documents that preceded President Ford's announcement of the Nixon pardon on September 8. The negotiation was mainly between Special Prosecutor Leon Jaworski, who had complained that the original agreement gave Mr. Nixon too much control and the prosecutor too little access to Watergate-related tapes and documents in the presidential files. Buchen delegated to Phillip Areeda, a distinguished newcomer to the counsel staff from Harvard law school, and William Casselman II, the third counsel, the job of following the Miller-Jaworski negotiations. Before Jaworski resigned he, Miller and the Ford lawyers were close to a mutually satisfactory revision, leaving the tapes in White House custody and permitting shipment of most of the Nixon documents to California as originally intended. Congressional opposition to any surrender to Nixon's control of either tapes or documents wrecked the prospect.

Miller was said at the White House to have argued, and Buchen to have agreed, that there would be no point in a new agreement that Congress seemed certain to abrogate. It was a serious matter. Mr. Ford, already committed to defend his unpopular pardon of Richard Nixon before a House subcommittee, faced the distinct possibility of having to accept or veto a bill that would require publication of the content of all the Nixon tapes. The President is said to believe that such a bill would constitute a gross violation of many people's privacy. He knows that he will be accused of protecting Mr. Nixon if he vetoes such a bill.

October 26, 1974

The pother about "Nixon holdovers" seemed silly to me. The foremost Nixon holdover was, of course, Gerald Ford.

President Ford first agreed, and Congress voted with his approval, that the Nixon tapes and documents must remain public property in federal custody in Washington. Right in principle. Tough on Mr. Nixon. A weak and indicative retreat from Mr. Ford's and Philip Buchen's original view that Mr. Nixon had the same ownership of his documents that Presidents since George Washington had enjoyed.

Appendixes

Statement by the President
on the Release of Additional Transcripts
of Presidential Conversations

August 5, 1974

I have today instructed my attorneys to make available to the House Judiciary Committee, and I am making public, the transcripts of three conversations with H. R. Haldeman on June 23, 1972. I have also turned over the tapes of these conversations to Judge Sirica, as part of the process of my compliance with the Supreme Court ruling.

On April 29, in announcing my decision to make public the original set of White House transcripts, I stated that "as far as what the President personally knew and did with regard to Watergate and the coverup is concerned, these materials—together with those already made available—will tell it all."

Shortly after that, in May, I made a preliminary review of some of the 64 taped conversations subpoenaed by the Special Prosecutor.

Among the conversations I listened to at that time were two of those of June 23. Although I recognized that these presented potential problems, I did not inform my staff or my Counsel of it, or those arguing my case, nor did I amend my submission to the Judiciary Committee in order to include and reflect it. At the time, I did not realize the extent of the implications which these conversations might now appear to have. As a result, those arguing my case, as well as those passing judgment on the case, did so with information that was incomplete and in some respects erroneous. This was a serious act of omission for which I take full responsibility and which I deeply regret.

Since the Supreme Court's decision 12 days ago, I have ordered my Counsel to analyze the 64 tapes, and I have listened to a number of them myself. This process has made it clear that portions of the tapes of these June 23 conversations are at variance with certain of my previous statements. Therefore, I have ordered the transcripts made available immediately to the Judiciary Committee so that they can be reflected in the Committee's report and included in the record to be considered by the House and Senate.

In a formal written statement on May 22 of last year, I said that shortly after the Watergate break-in I became concerned about the possibility that the FBI investigation might lead to the exposure either of unrelated covert activities of the CIA or of sensitive national security matters that the so-called "plumbers" unit at the White House had been working on, because of the CIA and plumbers connections of some of those involved. I said that I therefore gave instructions that the FBI should be alerted to coordinate with the CIA and to ensure that the investigation not expose these sensitive national security matters.

That statement was based on my recollection at the time—some 11 months later—plus documentary materials and relevant public testimony of those involved.

The June 23 tapes clearly show, however, that at the time I gave those instructions I also discussed the political aspects of the situation, and that I was aware of the advantages this course of action would have with respect to limiting possible public exposure of involvement by persons connected with the re-election committee.

My review of the additional tapes has, so far, shown no other major inconsistencies with what I have previously submitted. While I have no way at this stage of being certain that there will not be others, I have no reason to believe that there will be. In any case, the tapes in their entirety are now in the process of being furnished to Judge Sirica. He has begun what may be a rather lengthy process of reviewing the tapes, passing on specific claims of executive privilege on portions of them, and forwarding to the Special Prosecutor those tapes or those portions that are relevant to the Watergate investigation.

It is highly unlikely that this review will be completed in time for the House debate. It appears at this stage, however, that a House vote of impeachment is, as a practical matter, virtually a foregone conclusion, and that the issue will therefore go to trial in the Senate. In order to ensure that no other significant relevant materials are withheld, I shall voluntarily furnish to the Senate everything from these tapes that Judge Sirica rules should go to the Special Prosecutor.

I recognize that this additional material I am now furnishing may further damage my case, especially because attention will be drawn separately to it rather than to the evidence in its entirety. In considering its implications, therefore, I urge that two points be borne in mind.

The first of these points is to remember what actually happened as a result of the instructions I gave on June 23. Acting Director Gray of the FBI did coordinate with Director Helms and Deputy Director Walters of the CIA. the CIA did undertake an extensive check to see whether any of its covert activities would be compromised by a full FBI investigation of Watergate. Deputy Director Walters then reported back to Mr. Gray that they would not be compromised. On July 6, when I called Mr. Gray, and when he expressed concern about improper attempts to limit his investigation, as the record shows, I told him to press ahead vigorously with his investigation—which he did.

The second point I would urge is that the evidence be looked at in its entirety and the events be looked at in perspective. Whatever mistakes I made in the handling of Watergate, the basic truth remains that when all the facts were brought to my attention I insisted on a full investigation and prosecution of those guilty. I am firmly convinced that the record, in its entirety, does not justify the extreme step of impeachment and removal of a President. I trust that as the constitutional process goes forward, this perspective will prevail.

Transcripts of Presidential Conversations

Oval Office, June 23, 1972
10:04 — 11:39 A.M.

(President, Haldeman)

(Unintelligible)

P (Unintelligible) . . . . they've got a magnificent place—

H No, they don't. See, that was all hand-held camera without lighting - lousy place. It's good in content, it's terrible in film quality.

P (Unintelligible) Rose, she ought to be in here.

H No, well let her in if you want to, sure—

P That's right. Got so goddamned much (scratching noises)

H Goddamned.

P I understand, I just thought (unintelligible).
If I do, I just buzz.

H Yeah. Ah—

P Good, that's a very good paper at least (unintelligible). The one thing they haven't got in there is the thing we mentioned with regard to the Armed Services.

H   I covered that with Ehrlichman who says that can be done and he's moving. Not only Armed Services, but the whole government.

P   GSA? All government?

H   All government procurement, yeah. And, I talked to John about that and he thought that was a good idea. So, Henry gets back at 3:45.

P   I told Haig today that I'd see Rogers at 4:30.

H   Oh, good, O.K.

P   Well, if he gets back at 3:45, he won't be here until 4:00 or 4:30.

H   It'll be a little after 4:00 (unintelligible) 5:00.

P   Well, I have to, I'm supposed to go to Camp David. Rogers doesn't need a lot of time, does he?

H   No sir.

P   Just a picture?

H   That's all. He called me about it yesterday afternoon and said I don't want to be in the meeting with Henry, I understand that but there may be a couple of points Henry wants me to be aware of.

P   Sure.

P   (Unintelligible) call him and tell him we'll call him as soon as Henry gets here, between 4:30 and 5:00 (unintelligible) Good.

H   O.K., that's fine.

H   Now, on the investigation, you know the Democratic break-in thing, we're back in the problem area because the FBI is not under control, because Gray doesn't exactly know how to control it and they have - their investigation is now leading into some productive areas - because they've been able to trace the money - not through the money itself - but through the bank sources - the banker. And, and it goes in some directions we don't want it to go. Ah, also there have been some things - like an informant came in off the street to the FBI in Miami who was a photographer or has a friend who is a photographer who developed some films through this guy Barker and the films had pictures of Democratic National Committee letterhead documents and things. So it's things like that that are filtering in. Mitchell came up with yesterday, and John Dean analyzed very carefully last night and concludes, concurs now with Mitchell's recommendation that the only way to solve this, and we're set up beautifully to do it, ah, in that and that—the only network that paid any attention to it last night was NBC - they did a massive story on the Cuban thing.

P   That's right.

H   That the way to handle this now is for us to have Walters call Pat Gray and just say, "Stay to hell out of this - this is ah, business here we don't want you to go any further on it." That's not an unusual development, and ah, that would take care of it.

P   What about Pat Gray—you mean Pat Gray doesn't want to?

H   Pat does want to. He doesn't know how to, and he doesn't have, he doesn't have any basis for doing it. Given this, he will then have the basis. He'll call Mark Felt in, and the two of them—and Mark Felt wants to cooperate because he's ambitious—

P   Yeah.

H   He'll call him in and say, "We've got the signal from across the river to put the hold on this." And that will fit rather well because the FBI agents who are working the case, at this point, feel that's what it is.

P   This is CIA? They've traced the money? Who'd they trace it to?

H   Well they've traced it to a name, but they haven't gotten to the guy yet.

P   Would it be somebody here?

H   Ken Dahlberg.

P   Who the hell is Ken Dahlberg?

H   He gave $25,000 in Minnesota and, ah, the check went directly to this guy Barker.

P   It isn't from the Committee though, from Stans?

H   Yeah. It is. It's directly traceable and there's some more through some Texas people that went to the Mexican bank which can also be traced to the Mexican bank - they'll get their names today.

H   —And (pause)

P   Well, I mean, there's no way—I'm just thinking if they don't cooperate, what do they say? That they were approached by the Cubans. That's what Dahlberg has to say, the Texans too, that they—

H   Well, if they will. But then we're relying on more and more people all the time. That's the problem and they'll stop if we could take this other route.

P   All right.

H   And you seem to think the thing to do is get them to stop?

P   Right, fine.

H   They say the only way to do that is from White House instructions. And it's got to be to Helms and to - ah, what's his name . . ? Walters.

P   Walters.

H   And the proposal would be that Ehrlichman and I call them in, and say, ah—

P   All right, fine. How do you call him in—I mean you just—well, we protected Helms from one hell of a lot of things.

H   That's what Ehrlichman says.

P   Of course, this Hunt, that will uncover a lot of things. You open that scab there's a hell of a lot of things and we just feel that it would be very detrimental to have this thing go any further. This involves these Cubans, Hunt, and a lot of hanky-panky that we have nothing to do with ourselves. Well what the hell, did Mitchell know about this?

H   I think so. I don't think he knew the details, but I think he knew.

P He didn't know how it was going to be handled though - with Dahlberg and the Texans and so forth? Well who was the asshole that did? Is it Liddy? Is that the fellow? He must be a little nuts!

H He is.

P I mean he just isn't well screwed on is he? Is that the problem?

H No, but he was under pressure, apparently, to get more information, and as he got more pressure, he pushed the people harder to move harder—

P Pressure from Mitchell?

H Apparently.

P Oh, Mitchell. Mitchell was at the point (unintelligible).

H Yeah.

P All right, fine, I understand it all. We won't second-guess Mitchell and the rest. Thank God it wasn't Colson.

H The FBI interviewed Colson yesterday. They determined that would be a good thing to do. To have him take an interrogation, which he did, and that - the FBI guys working the case concluded that there were one or two possibilities - one, that this was a White House - they don't think that there is anything at the Election Committee - they think it was either a White House operation and they had some obscure reasons for it - non-political, or it was a - Cuban and the CIA. And after their interrogation of Colson yesterday, they concluded it was not the White House, but are now convinced it is a CIA thing, so the CIA turnoff would—

P Well, not sure of their analysis, I'm not going to get that involved. I'm (unintelligible).

H No, sir, we don't want you to.

P You call them in.

H Good deal.

P Play it tough. That's the way they play it and that's the way we are going to play it.

H O.K.

P When I saw that news summary, I questioned whether it's a bunch of crap, but I thought, er, well it's good to have them off us awhile, because when they start bugging us, which they have, our little boys will not know how to handle it. I hope they will though.

H You never know.

P Good.

H Mosbacher has resigned.

P Oh yeah?

H As we expected he would.

P Yeah.

H   He's going back to private life (unintelligible).
     Do you want to sign this or should I send it to Rose?

P   (scratching noise)

H   Do you want to release it?

P   O.K. Great. Good job, Bob.

H   Kissinger?

P   Huh? That's a joke.

H   Is it?

P   Whenever Mosbacher came for dinners, you see he'd have to be out
     escorting the person in and when they came through the receiving line,
     Henry was always with Mrs. Mosbacher and she'd turn and they would
     say this is Mrs. Kissinger. He made a little joke.

H   I see. Very good. O.K.

P   Well, good.

H   (unintelligible) Congressional guidance to get into the Mills thing at all.
     It was reported that somebody - Church met with Mills.

P   Big deal (unintelligible).

H   Well, what happened there is - that's true - Church went . . . Um?

P   Is it pay as you go or not?

H   Well, Church says it is, our people don't believe it is. Church told Mills
     that he had Long's support on adding social security and Wilbur
     equivocated on the question, when Johnny Burns talked to him about
     whether he would support the Long/Church Amendment, but Long
     and Church telling him that it is fully funded - and our people are afraid
     Mills is going to go along if they put the heat on him as a partisan
     Democrat to say that this would be damned helpful just before our
     Convention to stick this to the White House. Ah, Johnny Byrnes, he
     talked to Wilbur about it afterwards and this has been changed, so
     don't be concerned about it - you should call Mansfield and you should
     tell Mansfield that Burns is going to fight this in conference and that he
     will demand that it go to rules and he will demand a three-day lay-over,
     which means he will carry the conference over until July 7, which would
     be - and then before they even start the action, so it will mean they have
     to stay in - they can't—

P   All right.

H   (Unintelligible).

P   Go ahead.

H   Clark made the point that he should handle this, not you, and is doing
     this through Scott to Byrd, who is acting (unintelligible) still in the
     hospital. And ah, Clark's effort is going to be to kill the Church/Long
     Amendment. They got another tactic which is playing a dangerous
     game, but they are thinking about, which is, if they put Social Security
     on (unintelligible) that they will put Revenue Sharing and H. R. 1 in it

and really screw it up.

P   I would. Not dangerous at all. Buck up.

H   They're playing with it - they understand. Clark is going off with the mission to kill it.

P   Revenue Sharing won't kill it, but H. R. 1 would.

H   So, that's what he is off to.

P   But, boy if the Debt Ceiling isn't passed start firing (expletive deleted) government workers, I really mean it - cut them off. They can't do this - they've got to give us that Debt Ceiling. Mills has said that he didn't (unintelligible) on the Debt Ceiling earlier. Well, it's O.K. - it's O.K.

H   Well, Byrnes says that he is justifying it on the basis that they have told him that it's finance. Ehrlichman met with them - the Republicans on Senate Finance yesterday and explained the whole thing to them. They hadn't understood the first six-months financing and they are with it now and all ready to go and hanging on that defense. He feels, and they very much want, a meeting with you before the recess, finance Republicans.

P   All right. Certainly.

H   So, we'll do that next week. Did you get the report that the British floated the pound?

P   No, I don't think so.

H   They did.

P   That's devaluation?

H   Yeah. Flanigan's got a report on it here.

P   I don't care about it. Nothing we can do about it.

H   You want a run-down?

P   No, I don't.

H   He argues it shows the wisdom of our refusal to consider convertability until we get a new monetary system.

P   Good. I think he's right. It's too complicated for me to get into. (unintelligible) I understand.

H   Burns expects a 5-day percent devaluation against the dollar.

P   Yeah. O.K. Fine.

H   Burns is concerned about speculation about the lira.

P   Well, I don't give a (expletive deleted) about the lira. (Unintelligible)

H   That's the substance of that.

P   How are the House guys (unintelligible) Boggs (unintelligible)

H   All our people are, they think it's a great - a great ah—

P   There ain't a vote in it. Only George Shultz and people like that that think it's great (unintelligible) There's no votes in it, Bob.

P   Or do you think there is?

H   No, (unintelligible) I think it's - it looks like a Nixon victory (shuffling) major piece of legislation (unintelligible)

P   (unintelligible)

H   Not til July. I mean, our guys analysis is that it will - not going to get screwed up. The Senate will tack a little bit of amendment on it, but not enough to matter and it can be easily resolved in Conference.

P   Well, what the hell, why not accomplish one thing while we're here.

H   Maybe we will.

P   Yep. Not bad.

H   In spite of ourselves.

P   O.K. What else have you got that's amusing today?

H   That's it.

P   How's your (unintelligible) (Voices fade) coverage?

H   Good newspaper play - lousy television - and they covered all the items, but didn't (unintelligible) you gotta (unintelligible) but maximum few minutes (unintelligible)

P   (unintelligible)

H   Sure. One thing, if you decide to do more in-office ones—

P   Remember, I, I - when I came in I asked Alex, but apparently we don't have people in charge. I said I understood, that you had told me that the scheme was to let them come in and take a picture—an Ollie picture—but (expletive deleted), what good does an Ollie picture do?

H   Doesn't do any good.

P   Don't know what it was but apparently he didn't get the word.

H   Well, I think we ought to try that next time. If you want to see if it does us any good, and it might, let them.

P   Well, why wasn't it done this time?

H   I don't know.

P   It wasn't raised?

H   I don't know. You said it—

P   Because I know you said - and Ollie sat back there and (unintelligible) and I said (unintelligible) But, (expletive deleted) Ollie's pictures hang there and nobody sees them except us.

H   Now what you've got to - it's really not the stills that do us any good on that. We've got to let them come in with the lights.

P   Well in the future, will you make a note. Alex, Ron or whoever it is - no Steve. I have no objection to them coming in, and taking a picture with stills, I mean with the camera. I couldn't agree more. I don't give a (expletive deleted) about the newspapers.

H   You're going to get newspaper coverage anyway.

P   What (unintelligible) good objective play—

H   Oh, yeah.

P   In terms of the way it was—

H   Or in the news.

P   Needless to say, they sunk the bussing thing, but there was very, very little on that (unintelligible) Detroit (unintelligible)

H   Two networks covered it.

P   We'll see what Detroit does. We hope to Christ the question (unintelligible) SOB, if necessary. Hit it again. Somebody (unintelligible) bussing thing back up again.

H   What's happened on the bussing thing. We going to get one or not? Well, no we're out of time. No. After.

P   I guess it is sort of impossible to get the word to the research people that when you say 100 words, you mean 100 words.

H   Well, I'm surprised because this is Buchanan, and I didn't say time on this one, I said 100 words and Pat usually takes that seriously, but that one - I have a feeling maybe what happened is that he may have started short and he may have gotten into the editing - you know the people - the clearance process - who say you have to say such and such, although I know what's happened.

P   I don't know - maybe it isn't worth going out and (unintelligible) Maybe it is.

H   Well, it's a close call. Ah, Ehrlichman thought you probably—

P   What?

H   Well, he said you probably didn't need it. He didn't think you should, not at all. He said he felt fine doing it.

P   He did? The question, the point, is does he think everybody is going to understand the bussing?

H   That's right.

P   And, ah, well (unintelligible) says no.

H   Well, the fact is somewhere in between, I think, because I think that (unintelligible) is missing some—

P   Well, if the fact is somewhere in between, we better do it.

H   Yeah, I think Mitchell says, "Hell yes. Anything we can hit on at anytime we get the chance—and we've got a reason for doing it—do it."

P   When you get in—when you get in (unintelligible) people, say, "Look the problem is that this will open the whole, the whole Bay of Pigs thing, and the President just feels that ah, without going into the details—don't, don't lie to them to the extent to say there is no involvement, but just say this is a comedy of errors, without getting into it, the President believes that it is going to open the whole Bay of Pigs thing up again. And, ah, because these people are plugging for (unintelligible) and that they should call the FBI in and (unintelligible) don't go any further into this case period! (inaudible) our cause—

H   Get more done for our cause by the opposition than by us.

P   Well, can you get it done?

H   I think so.

P   (unintelligible) moves (unintelligible) election (unintelligible)

H   They're all—that's the whole thing. The *Washington Post* said it in it's lead editorial today. Another "McGovern's got to change his position." That that would be a good thing, that's constructive. Ah, the white wash for change.

P   (unintelligible) urging him to do so - say that is perfectly all right?

H   Cause then they are saying—on the other hand—that he were not so smart. We have to admire the progress he's made on the basis of the position he's taken and maybe he's right and we're wrong.

P   (Inaudible) I just, ha ha

H   Sitting in Miami (unintelligible) our hand a little bit. They eliminated their law prohibiting male (unintelligible) from wearing female clothes - now the boys can all put on their dresses - so the gay lib is going to turn out 6,000 (unintelligible).

P   (unintelligible)

H   I think

P   They sure test the effect of the writing press. I think, I think it was still good to have it in the papers, but, but let's—perfectly—from another standpoint, let's just say look, "Because (unintelligible) people trying and any other damned reason, I just don't want to go out there (unintelligible) what better way to spend my time than to take off two afternoons or whatever it was to prepare for an in-office press conference." Don't you agree?

H   That's, that's—

P   (unintelligible) I spend an hour—whatever it was—45 minutes or so with television executives (unintelligible) all in and outs (unintelligible). "Look, we have no right to ask the President anything (unintelligible) biased." (unintelligible) says I'm going to raise hell with the networks. And look, you've just not got to let Klein ever set up a meeting again. He just doesn't have his head screwed on. You know what I mean. He just opens it up and sits there with eggs on his face. He's just not our guy at all is he?

H   No.

P   Absolutely, totally, unorganized.

H   He's a very nice guy.

P   People love him, but damn is he unorganized.

H   That's right, he's not.

P   But don't you agree that (unintelligible) worth doing and that it's kind of satisfying.

H   Sure. And as you point out there's some fringe benefits with—going through the things is a good exercise for you—

P   That's right.

H   In the sense of getting caught up on certain items—

P   Right.

H   It's a good exercise for the troops in having to figure out what the problems are and what the answers are to them.

P   Three or four things. Ah - Pat raised the point last night that probably she and the girls ought to stay in a hotel on Miami Beach. First she says the moment they get the helicopter and get off and so forth, it destroys their hair and so forth. And of course, that is true—even though you turn them off and turn them on so on. The second point is—

H   Could drive over—

P   Well, the point is, I want to check with Dean to be sure what the driving time is. If the driving time with traffic is going to be up to an hour—

H   Oh no.

P   With the traffic—

H   But they have an escort.

P   How long would it take?

H   Half an hour. Less than half an hour. You can make it easy in a half hour without an escort, and they would - they should have an escort. They should arrive with - and they may not like it - it may bother them a little, but that's what people expect - and you know at the Conventions—every county—

P   She has another point though which I think will please everybody concerned. She says, "Now, look. You go there - she says as far as she was concerned she would be delighted - the girls would be delighted to every reception - everything that they have there." They want to be busy. They want to do things and they want to be useful. Of course, as you know, our primary aim is to see that they are on television (unintelligible) coming into the hall (unintelligible) shooting the hall (unintelligible) plan on television. My point is, I think it would be really great if they did the delegations of the bit states. Just to stop in you know. Each girl and so forth can do—

H   Sure.

P   The second thing is—just go by and say hello, and they'll do the handshakers (unintelligible) you know (unintelligible).

H   Well, the big point is, there's several major functions that they may want to tie that into.

P   Yeah. Yeah.

H   There's - a strong view on the part of some of our strategists that we should be damned careful not to over use them and cheapen them. That they should—there is a celebrity value you can lose by rubbing on them too much—

P   I couldn't agree more.

H   and so we have to—their eagerness to participate should not go—

P   California delegation (unintelligible) think I'm here. I mean we're going to have (unintelligible)

P   You understand—they're willing. Have them do things—do the important things, and so forth, and so on.

H   There's the question. Like Sunday night they have the (unintelligible) whether they should go to that—now at least the girls should go. I think I ought to go too!

P   Yep.

H   You know, whether Pat—one thought that was raised was that the girls and their husbands go down on Sunday and Pat wait and come down with you on Tuesday. I think Pat should go down and should be there cause they'll have the Salute—

P   (Inaudible)

H   She should arrive separately. I think she should arrive with the girls. Another thought was to have the girls arrive Sunday, Pat arrive Monday and you arrive Tuesday. I think you're overdoing your arrivals.

P   No, no, no. She arrives with the girls and they—they should go. I agree.

H   But, I don't think you have to be there until Tuesday.

P   I don't want to go near the damned place until Tuesday. I don't want to be near it. I've got the arrival planned (unintelligible) my arrival of, ah—

H   Now we're going to do, unless you have some objection, we should do your arrival at Miami International not at Homestead.

P   Yes, I agree

H   Ah, we can crank up a hell of an arrival thing.

P   Alright

P   (unintelligible) is for you, ah, and perhaps Colson probably (inaudible).

P   I was thumbing through the, ah, last chapters of (unintelligible) last night, and I also read the (unintelligible) chapters (unintelligible). Warm up to it, and it makes, ah, fascinating reading. Also reminds you of a hell of a lot of things that happened in the campaign—press you know, election coverage, the (unintelligible) etc., etc.

H   Yeah

P   So on and so on. I want you to reread it, and I want Colson to read it, and anybody else.

H   O.K.

P   And anybody else in the campaign. Get copies of the book and give it to each of them. Say I want them to read it and have it in mind. Give it to whoever you can, O.K.?

H   Sure will.

P   Actually, the book reads awfully well—have to look at history I want to talk to you more about that later in terms of what it tells us about how our campaign should be run, O.K.?

H   O.K. In other words, (unintelligible) the media and so forth

P   to a great extent, is responsible to what happened to Humphrey both in '68. If that's true, it did not apply in 1960. The media was just as bad (unintelligible) two weeks. In 1960 we ran—

H   It was a dead heat.

P   all the way through the campaign and it never changed, clearly. It may be—it may be that our—as you read this on how (unintelligible) our campaign was—how much television, you know. We didn't have (unintelligible) at all. It may be that our '60 campaign (unintelligible) was extremely much more effective and it may be too, that we misjudged the (unintelligible). You read it through and (unintelligible) see what I mean. I mean, it's it's—even realize that '68 was much better organized. It may be we did a better job in '60. It just may be. It may tell us something. Anyway would you check it over?

H   Yep.

P   (unintelligible) check another thing—gets back? Convention?

H   He was, I'm not sure if he still is.

P   Could find out from him what chapters of the book he worked on. Ah, I don't want coverage of the heart attack thing. I did most of the dictating on the last two but I've been curious (unintelligible). But could you find out which chapters he worked on. Also find out where Moscow is—what's become of him—what's he's doing ten years. Say hello to him (unintelligible) might find it useful (unintelligible) future, despite the (unintelligible). You'll find this extremely interesting, read (unintelligible).

H   Read that a number of times (unintelligible) different context—

P   Ah, I would say another thing—Bud Brown (unintelligible) did you read it? (unintelligible) candidates. I don't know who all you discussed that with. Maybe it's not been handled at a high enough level. Who did you discuss that with? (Unintelligible)

H   MacGregor and Mitchell. MacGregor and Mitchell, that's all.

P   Yep. (Unintelligible) I don't mind the time—the problem that I have with it is that I do not want to have pictures with candidates that are running with Democrats—or against Democrats that may either be (unintelligible) or might be for us. On the other hand, all sophisticated Democratic candidates you understand—the damned candidates (unintelligible) they gotta get a picture with the President. The way to have the pictures with the candidate—this would be a very clever thing, is to call both Democrats—the good Southern Democrats and those few like (unintelligible), who did have a picture with me, see, and then call them up and say look (unintelligible) came on and they took a picture and maybe (unintelligible) President. Wants you to know that if you would like a picture, if you would like to come down to the office, you know, you can have a picture taken that you are welcome to use. How does that sound to you as a (unintelligible)? Let me say this. I'm not—I'm not—I think that getting to the candidates out there that are very busy and so forth may help us a bit. If the candidates run too far behind you, it drags you too much.

H   Yeah. That's right

P   On the, on the other side, I don't think it's going to hurt you particularly if you always (unintelligible) there's some quality—

H   O yeah, but they aren't going to (inaudible)

P   (Unintelligible) quite candid with you—I think when I ran in '46, remember, I would have gotten on my hands and knees for a picture with Harold Stassen and (unintelligible) whole story. We (unintelligible) to do what we can (unintelligible) in the House and the Senate—as well as we can.

H   (unintelligible) have our loyalists feel that we're—

P   That's right. (Unintelligible) and I'll be glad to do it next week, and I think on that basis we can handle the Democrats. Say, "Look they had a picture," and then call each one. I mean they'll have to check this list. Check each one (unintelligible) and say, look (unintelligible) if you'd like a picture with him—not on a basis of support—See?

H   Yeah.

P   (Unintelligible) not going to make any statement—not going to make any statement. (Unintelligible) have a picture, he'd be glad to have a picture (unintelligible).

H   Picture of the—

P   That's right. Be glad to if you like, but it's up to you and so forth.

H   You did the Democrats in here. Would you do a, would you do the Republicans? Do a different picture (unintelligible) full shot.

P   Yeah. Another point I was going to mention to you, Bob, is the situation with regard to the girls. I was talking to Pat last night. Tricia and I were talking, and she mentioned—Tricia said that apparently when she was in Allentown there were 20 or 30 thugs—labor thugs out booing.

H   Hmmm.

P   And when she went to Boston to present some art—her Chinese things to the art gallery there—two the (unintelligible) from the press were pretty vicious. What I mean is they came through the line and one refused to shake. One was not with the press. Refused to shake hands, so forth and so on. Tricia (unintelligible) very personal point, (unintelligible) good brain in that head. She said first she couldn't believe that the event that they do locally (unintelligible) understand. You know she does the Boys' Club, the Art Gallery (unintelligible). She says the important thing is to find this type of (unintelligible) to go into the damn town (unintelligible) do television, which of course, they do. (Unintelligible) she says why (unintelligible) control the place. She says in other words, go in and do the Republican group. Now, sure isn't (unintelligible) to say you did the Republican group, as it is the Allentown Bullies Club? But, that's the paper story. The point is, I think Parker has to get a little more thinking in depth, or is it Codus now who will do this?

H   They are both working on it.

P   What's your off-hand reaction on that, Bob? I do not want them, though, to go in and get the hell kicked (unintelligible).

H   There's no question, and we've really got to work at that.

P   Yep. (unintelligible)

H   Ya, but I think - I'm not sure - if you can't get the controlled non-political event, then I think it is better to do a political event (unintelligible).

P   For example - now the worse thing (unintelligible) is to go to anything that has to do with the Arts.

H   Ya, see that - it was (unintelligible) Julie giving that time to the Museum in Jacksonville.

P   The Arts you know - they're Jews, they're left wing - in other words, stay away.

P   Make a point.

H   Sure.

P   Middle America - put that word out - Middle America-type of people (unintelligible), auxiliary, (unintelligible). Why the hell doesn't Parker get that kind of thing going? Most of his things are elite groups except, I mean, do the cancer thing - maybe nice for Tricia to go up - ride a bus for 2 hours - do some of that park in Oklahoma - but my view is, Bob, relate it to Middle America and not the elitist (unintelligible). Do you agree?

H   Yep. Sure do.

P   I'm not complaining. I think they are doing a hell of a job. The kids are willing—

H   They really are, but she can improve.

P   There again, Tricia had a very good thought on this, but let's do Middle America.

H   Yep.

P   (Unintelligible).

P   I don't know whether Alex told you or not, but I want a Secret Service reception some time next week. I just gotta know who these guys are. (Unintelligible). Don't you think so? I really feel that they're there - that ah, I see new guys around - and Jesus Christ they look so young.

H   Well, they change them - that's one (unintelligible) any reception now would be totally different (unintelligible).

P   Get 100 then - so it's 200 and I shake their hands and thank them and you look (unintelligible) too - (unintelligible). They have a hell of a lot of fellas, let's face it, (unintelligible) friends (unintelligible), but I just think it's a nice -

H   They all - you have such - that's why it's a good thing to do, cause they are friends - and they have such overriding respect for you and your family - that a

P   I wouldn't want the whole group - something like (unintelligible). Third point - I would like a good telephone call list for California, but not a huge book, and the kind is - This would be a good time where (unintelligible) and just give thanks to people for their support. For example, Colson had me call (unintelligible) the other day - (unintelligible) thing to do, but, here you could take the key guys that work - I wouldn't mind calling a very few key contributors - maybe, but we're talking about magnitude of ten - very key ten.

H   Ten - you mean ten people?

P   Ya.

H   Oh, I thought you meant $10,000.

P   No, ten. Ten. I was thinking of very key (unintelligible), people like - that worked their ass off collecting money, just to say that - people that - the people that are doing the work - very key political (unintelligible) just to pat them on the back. I mean that means a helluva lot - very key political VIPs, you know, by political VIPs - ah (unintelligible) just get the South - get a better (unintelligible). Our problem is that there are only two men in this place that really give us names - that's Rose - the other is Colson, and we just aren't getting them. But I mean ah, and then editors - by editors and television people - like a (unintelligible) call, but a few key editors who are just busting their ass for us where there's something to do. But give me a good telephone list, and Rose should give me a few personal things - like I do a lot of things, but I called (unintelligible) here today some (unintelligible) and things of that sort. But I think this would be a very good use of my time while I'm in California. I never mind doing it you know when I've got an hour to put my feet up and make a few calls - don't you agree?

H   Yep.

P   I think of the campaign - that's going to be a hell of a (unintelligible). I think sometimes when we're here in Washington, you know, supposedly doing the business of the government, that I can call people around the country - people that will come out for us - and so forth - like (unintelligible) for example, Democrats come out for us. They're (unintelligible) right across the board - Democrat or labor union. (unintelligible)

H   Ya.

P   Religious leaders (unintelligible) say something. You gotta be careful some ass over in (unintelligible) checked on (unintelligible) that's why you can't have Klein (unintelligible). He just doesn't really have his head screwed on Bob. I could see it in that meeting yesterday. He does not.

H   That's right.

P   He just doesn't know. He just sort of blubbers around. I don't know how he does TV so well.

H   Well, he's a sensation on that - that goes to the (unintelligible) meaning of the thing, you know. What's his drawback, is really an ass.

P   Ya. If you would do this. Pat, and tell Codus, (unintelligible), but I will go to Camp David (unintelligible) half hour. Key Biscayne - might want to stay there if she can go in less than a half hour with an escort. Do you think you can? Frankly, Miami Beach (unintelligible) but we can arrange it either way? Leave it to her choice.

H   It wouldn't take as long.

P   Leave it to her choice - she'd - it's

H   She'd—it's so miserable. If she's at Miami Beach she'll be a prisoner in that hotel.

P   Yeah. Tell her, tell her that's fine. But it's up to her.

H   Fair enough!

P   I'll be anxious to (unintelligible) sign that stuff (unintelligible). I suppose most of our staff (unintelligible) but that *Six Crises* is a damned good book, and the (unintelligible) story reads like a novel— the Hiss case—Caracas was fascinating. The campaign of course for anybody in politics should be a must because it had a lot in there of how politicians are like. (unintelligible) elections, and how you do things. (unintelligible) as of that time. I think part of the problem as an example, for example, I'm just thinking—research people something they really missed (unintelligible) Byrnes. Pat and I, she said (unintelligible) no, she had remembered. She remembered (unintelligible) that was pretty far back (unintelligible). (unintelligible) and Jimmy Byrnes said well (unintelligible) hard for me to come, but I just want you to know (unintelligible) but because (unintelligible) want you to know you are still my friend (unintelligible). Wonderful item to put in.

H   Is that in the book?

P   It's in the book! Hell yes. It's in the book.

H   Is it?

P   (Unintelligible) Why don't you reread it?

Enter Ziegler

Z   We're delaying our briefing until noon for the higher education (unintelligible) and so forth. But I thought, if you agree, that I would not for press purposes, but just sit on the side for this economic thing.

P   Sure. How many of them are there?

Z   Well there's the entire cabinet of economic advisers, I mean Council of Economic Advisers, plus Shultz—fairly big group.

P   Shultz

Z   Well.

H   (Unintelligible)

P   See what I mean?

H   Sure.

P   It's the kind of thing that I get in toasts and that sort of thing, but, but you see, I don't think our guys do that kind of - that should be must reading - that book is crammed full - crammed full - see. It would be helpful for those to get it. O.K. Oh, can we take another second? I mean, on that thing on the All Time Baseball greats—I would like to do that and, if you could, if you could get it.

Unidentified Voice
    There's already a story at random—

P   I saw it.

UV   Indicating that you were going to

P   If you would get that—if you would get the three or four. I don't want the—I'm only speaking of the All Times Greats.

UV   Right.

P   And then, and then get me a couple of other people (unintelligible) very badly (unintelligible) and I'll go down through the - quietly (unintelligible)

UV   So do you want names from me or just a list of others you have picked?

H   No, just the names that have been picked (unintelligible) various people.

UV   Right.

P   (Unintelligible)

UV   Right, I got it.

P   O.K.

UV   Yes Sir. (Unintelligible)

H   You did, huh.

Z   Yeah. Incidentally, in the news summary (unintelligible) preferred television. Did you see that? (unintelligible) I talked to

H   We may (unintelligible) we may not.

Z   No, the point I'm making -

P   I know Ron, but let me say - but I think - apparently, the TODAY Show this morning (unintelligible) two minutes of television.

Z   I thought he got good play. Particularly in light of the fact that ah, helluva a lot of other (unintelligible) would take place in the nation.

P   Right

H   We have an overriding—
P   What, weren't, how about the guys that were there? They were pleased
    with the—
Z   (unintelligible) and then (unintelligible)
P   Huh?
P   Cause I didn't think they would—
Z   But they always are—
P   Helluva a lot of news and—
H   Well that snaps all our own machinery into motion too.
Z   (Unintelligible) damn. Feel it?
P   (Unintelligible) that's good, warm—
Z   Right. They came to me and then said (unintelligible)
P   (Unintelligible) should have some more
Z   And, they liked the color. They made the point about—you know.
    How relaxed you were, and at the end, sitting down and talking about
    the baseball thing after the whole thing—after it was over. You know,
    you just chipped those things off with such ease and so forth. It was so
    good.

———

Oval Office, June 23, 1972
1:04-1:13 P.M.

(President, Haldeman)

P   O.K., just postpone (scratching noises) (unintelligible) Just say
    (unintelligible) very bad to have this fellow Hunt, ah, he knows too
    damned much, if he was involved - you happen to know that? If it gets
    out that this is all involved, the Cuba thing it would be a fiasco. I would
    make the CIA look bad, it's going to make Hunt look bad, and it is
    likely to blow the whole Bay of Pigs thing which we think would be very
    unfortunate - both for CIA, and for the country, at this time, and for
    American foreign policy. Just tell him to lay off. Don't you?
H   Yep. That's the basis to do it on. Just leave it at that.
P   I don't know if he'll get any ideas for doing it because our concern
    political (unintelligible). Helms is not one to (unintelligible)- I would
    just say, lookit, because of the Hunt involvement, whole cover basically
    this
H   Yep. Good move.

P   Well, they've got some pretty good ideas on this Meany thing. Shultz did a good paper. I read it all (voices fade).

————

Executive Office Building Office
June 23, 1972, 2:20-2:45 P.M.

(President, Haldeman, Ziegler)

H   No Problem

P   (Unintelligible)

H   Well, it was kind of interest. Walters made the point and I didn't mention Hunt, I just said that the thing was leading into directions that were going to create potential problems because they were exploring leads that led back into areas that would be harmful to the CIA and harmful to the government (unintelligible) didn't have anything to do (unintelligible).
(Telephone)

P   Chuck? I wonder if you would give John Connally a call he's on his trip - I don't want him to read it in the paper before Monday about this quota thing and say - look, we're going to do this, but that I checked, I asked you about the situation (unintelligible) had an understanding it was only temporary and ah (unintelligible) O.K.? I just don't want him to read it in the papers. Good. Fine.

H   (unintelligible) I think Helms did to (unintelligible) said, I've had no -

P   God (unintelligible).

H   Gray called and said, yesterday, and said that he thought—

P   Who did? Gray?

H   Gray called Helms and said I think we've run right into the middle of a CIA covert operation.

P   Gray said that?

H   Yeah. And (unintelligible) said nothing we've done at this point and ah (unintelligible) says well it sure looks to me like it is (unintelligible) and ah, that was the end of that conversation (unintelligible) the problem is it tracks back to the Bay of Pigs and it tracks back to some other the leads run out to people who had no involvement in this, except by contacts and connection, but it gets to areas that are liable to be raised? The whole problem (unintelligible) Hunt. So at that point he kind of got the picture. He said, he said we'll be very happy to be helpful (unintelligible) handle anything you want. I would like to know the reason for being helpful, and I made it clear to him he wasn't going to get explicit (unintelligible) generality, and he said fine. And Walters (unintelligible). Walters is going to make a call to Gray. That's the way we put it and that's the way it was left.

P   How does that work though, how, they've got to (unintelligible) somebody from the Miami bank.

H   (unintelligible). The point John makes - the Bureau is going on on this because they don't know what they are uncovering (unintelligible) continue to pursue it. They don't need to because they already have their case as far as the charges against these men (unintelligible) and ah, as they pursue it (unintelligible) exactly, but we didn't in any way say we (unintelligible). One thing Helms did raise. He said, Gray - he asked Gray why they thought they had run into a CIA thing and Gray said because of the characters involved and the amount of money involved, a lot of dough (unintelligible) and ah, (unintelligible)

P   (Unintelligible)

H   Well, I think they will.

P   If it runs (unintelligible) what the hell who knows (unintelligible) contributed CIA.

H   Ya, it's money CIA gets money (unintelligible) I mean their money moves in a lot of different ways, too.

P   Ya. How are (unintelligible) - a lot of good—

H   (Unintelligible)

P   Well you remember what the SOB did on my book? When I brought out the fact, you know—

H   Ya.

P   that he knew all about Dulles? (Expletive Deleted) Dulles knew. Dulles told me. I know, I mean (unintelligible) had the telephone call. Remember, I had a call put in—Dulles just blandly said and knew why.

H   Ya

P   Now, what the hell! Who told him to do it? The President? (Unintelligible)

H   Dulles was no more Kennedy's man than (unintelligible) was your man (unintelligible)

P   (unintelligible) covert operation - do anything else (unintelligible)

H   The Democratic nominee, we're going to have to brief him.

P   Yes sir. Brief him (unintelligible). We don't (unintelligible).

H   Oh no. Tell him what we want him to know. I don't think you ought to brief him.

P   Me? Oh, hell no!

H   (unintelligible) you would have been if Johnson called you in—

P   Johnson was out of office.

H   That's the point - he was

P   Eisenhower, Eisenhower did not brief Kennedy.

H   and wouldn't be proper anyway (unintelligible) because you're too (unintelligible)

P   (unintelligible) same thing that Eisenhower did. Course Eisenhower (unintelligible)
     Phone rings

P   Ya. Ah, I'll call him tomorrow.

H   (Unintelligible) sure, that you want to

P   No. I just simply think that we provide for (unintelligible) from the appropriate authorities (unintelligible) of course not, and I don't think we ought to let Kissinger brief - I'd just have Helms (unintelligible) (unidentifiable)

P   What did you say that poll, Gallup (unintelligible) wonder why he got it out so quickly. Usually lead time is two weeks.

H   Well, actually, this is where lead time usually was and until the last few months (unintelligible). This time he's putting it out fast.

P   (Unintelligible) want to get it out before the Convention.

H   Well, because he's got a trial heat, and he wants to put this out before - set the stage for the trial heats.

P   (Unintelligible) before the Convention. (Unintelligible) God damn (unintelligible) well what do you

H   Sure.

P   You know we sat here and talked about (unintelligible) year and a half ago. But we had no idea - we thought they do it on the TODAY Show (unintelligible) and all that (expletive deleted). And at that time (unintelligible) took events didn't we?

H   (Unintelligible) always known was the case, but—

P   China, May 8, and Russia. That's all.

H   If you don't have the events you gotta make (unintelligible) everything (unintelligible) better off putting three months or three year's effort against one event than you are putting the same amount, tenth of that effort, non-event type thing.

P   I'm really impressed with Shultz and all those guys—

H   I told him.

P   Fine.

H   I talked to Shultz about calling Connally and I said that you had mentioned how impressed you were with the paper he had done (unintelligible).

P   Eisenhower - (unintelligible) sure elections (inaudible) and then in November, before the election, he dropped a 57 (unintelligible) The reason for that was nothing he did, Congressional election (unintelligible)

H   Ya.

P   I'm saying to you, McGovern candidate (unintelligible) problem got to take on (unintelligible) In 1958 (unintelligible) March, (unintelligible) 52

H   Eisenhower?

P   Eisenhower.

H   (Unintelligible)

P   Yes sir (unintelligible) May 54-31, June 53-32, July 52-32, August (unintelligible) September (unintelligible) October (unintelligible) 26, November election 52- (unintelligible) January. For example, here's early July 1961, July 57. August 61. September - September 58, October 58, November 58. That's when we were running. We were running lower (unintelligible) A little lower (unintelligible) Kennedy, you really can't tell about that. At the eve, his lowest was 62 (unintelligible) elections. But in 63 at the end he was 57. Johnson then, of course, he was up in the 80s. We've never been very high -

H   That's incredible. I don't think you ever will get up in the 80s.

P   No. Well Johnson, of course 66 46, 56 September October 44, November 44, December 48, that's all. Except his negatives were higher 42, 44, 41 our negatives have never been that high. He run around 49 (Unintelligible).

H   Ya.

P   Then it goes on 46, 48, 45, 41, 39, 39, 38, 51, 46, 58, 48, 39. 40, 41 (unintelligible) then back up to 49, 46, 42. The point that I'm trying to make (unintelligible) cause you're under attack

H   Sure.

P   (Unintelligible)

H   Before the public eye - the focus of attention is on the negatives of the Administration. It's an interesting point. Buchanan, in response to the response to his attack—

P   Ya

H   argues quite strongly that the point that the attacks should always turn to the positive side. He argues that that is wrong, and the attacks should stay on the negative side. Do not try to weave in also positive points. That there should be an attack program that is purely attack

P   Except on foreign policy.

H   That's what he is talking about primarily. You hammer your strong point.

P   I just think you've got to hit that over and over again. We gotta win—

H   You don't argue against our hammering our strong point. His argument is when you are attacking - we should do some of our advertising - should be an attack on McGovern advertising - and that attack should not (unintelligible) Nixon strongpoints. It should only (unintelligible) McGovern negative points.

P   Ya.

H   argument being that it is impossible in this election for you to get less than 40% of the vote, equally impossible for you to get more than 60. (unintelligible) that up over there. We should go over early if we could get this (unintelligible) on the networks. Wait until 3:00 - we got a problem because of - what is it (Unintelligible) because they are shooting with one camera (siren) (unintelligible) we're better off

P   Clear over there on the other side? You get the word to them.

Z   Yes sir. But I don't want to take your time to do it.

P   I'll go across - I just wanted to (unintelligible)

Z   Yes sir. Absolutely.

E   And, based from the thing this morning, do you feel it worthwhile to (unintelligible) till Monday?

Z   Yes, sir.

H   Well, let's do it earlier in the day, because we are (unintelligible) jeopardizing

Z   At 2:00.

P   Are you set up? You want me to come right this minute?

Z   Well, I don't - anytime you feel comfortable.

P   (Unintelligible)

Z   As soon as possible.

H   His argument is to start with, you got 40% of the people who will vote for you no matter what happens,

P   I agree

H   and you got 40% of the people that will vote against you no matter what happens, so you got 20% of the vote left in the middle who may vote for you or may not - and that 20% is what you gotta work on. His argument is that you're so well known, your pluses are as clear as your minuses; that getting one of those 20, who is an undecided type, to vote for you on the basis of your positive points is much less likely than getting him to vote against McGovern by scaring him to death about McGovern; and that that's the area that we ought to be playing.

P   Well.

H   (Unintelligible)

P   Well, I am not going to do it. I really want you to bring in Flanigan and all these others (unintelligible) and lay it to them (unintelligible)

H   Yep.

P   Don't you think he'll agree? Oh, you don't?

H   No, I think they will. They'll agree for awhile (unintelligible) agree— they'll say well why not do it anyway.

P   No, No, Nope, No - Never! I can't take it for granted. Listen, he could think I'm setting him up (unintelligible) reasonable man. God damn it, (unintelligible) I have him be against Muskie. We don't give a (expletive deleted). Or, Nixon! Muskie - screw him otherwise - fine. I don't know if our people would be scared (unintelligible) about Muskie.

H   (Unintelligible) they are. They aren't, but I think you got to build that up. His point is that so little is known, better chance of (voices fade)

Resignation of President Nixon

August 9, 1974

Dear Mr. Secretary:
I hereby resign the Office of President of the United States.
Sincerely,

RICHARD NIXON

[The Honorable Henry A. Kissinger, The Secretary of State, Washington, D.C. 20520]

NOTE: The White House announced that the letter was delivered by Alexander M. Haig, Jr., to the Secretary of State in his White House office at 11:35 a.m. on Friday, August 9, 1974.

Index

Index